A Student's Guide to Studying Psychology

3rd edition

Thomas M. Heffernan

Psychology Press
Taylor & Francis Group

HOVE AND NEW YORK

First published 2005 by Psychology Press, a part of *T&F Informa Plc*
27 Church Road, Hove, East Sussex, BN3 2FA

Simultaneously published in the USA and Canada by Psychology Press
270 Madison Avenue, New York NY 10016

Reprinted 2005

Psychology Press is a part of the Taylor & Francis Group

© 2005 Thomas M Heffernan

Typeset in Palatino by Garfield Morgan, Rhayader, Powys
Printed and bound in Great Britain by TJ International Ltd, Padstow, Cornwall
Paperback cover design Sandra Heath

British Library Cataloguing in Publication Data
A catalogue record for this book is available from the British Library

Library of Congress Cataloging in Publication Data
Heffernan, Thomas M.
    A student's guide to studying psychology / Thomas M. Heffernan.– 3rd
ed.
        p. cm.
    Includes bibliographical references and indexes.
    ISBN 1-84169-393-6 (hardcover) – ISBN 1-84169-394-4 (pbk.)
    1. Psychology–Study and teaching (Higher) 2. Psychology–Vocational
guidance. I. Title.

    BF77.H44 2005
    150'.71'1–dc22
                                                                2004020152

    ISBN 1-84169-393-6 (hbk)
    ISBN 1-84169-394-4 (pbk)

2006003538

Contents

Preface   ix

Acknowledgements   x

Preface to third edition   x

1   **Introduction to psychology**   1
What is psychology?   1
Perspectives and methods in psychology   3
The psychoanalytic perspective   3
The biological perspective   6
Developmental psychology   8
Humanistic psychology   10
Behaviourism   13
The cognitive perspective   16
Social psychology   18
Twenty-first century psychology   20
Finally   22

2   **A study guide to lectures, seminars and tutorials**   23
Skills developed on a psychology course   23
Practical classes   25
Contact time   26
Lectures   29
Seminars   31
Tutorials   35
Effective note taking   37
Reference materials   41
Summarising a piece of work   43

3   **A guide to essay writing and referencing**   45
Stages in essay writing   45
Example: A completed coursework essay   55
Important points about coursework essays   61

A guide to writing style
   Neil McLaughlin Cook   62
A guide to referencing
   Sue Thomas and Keith Morgan   66

4 A guide to research methods   79
The quantitative/qualitative distinction   79
Sampling procedures   80
The experimental method   82
The quasi-experimental method   86
The non-experimental method   88
Data, statistical analysis and causal inference   97
Qualitative approaches   104

5 Ethics in research   107
Ethical considerations when testing humans   108
Ethical considerations when testing animals   110

6 Empirical research report writing   113
Structure of the report   114
Title page   114
Abstract   115
Introduction   116
Method   118
Results   121
Discussion   123
References   124
Appendices   125
Summary   125
Example: A practical write-up   126
Additional guidelines for second-year practicals   135
Additional guidelines for the third-year practical   136
When using an observational method   138
Writing a qualitative report   139
Presenting research at a conference   142
Example: A research article   143

7 A guide to preparing for examinations   153
Examinations   154
Revising for the examination   155
Taking the examination   164
Example: A first-year examination essay   167
Critical assessment   169
Example: A second-year examination essay   170

Critical assessment   172
After the examination   174
Failing an examination   174
How essays are marked   175

**8   After the degree: Opportunities for a psychology
    graduate   179**
Graduate status   181
Postgraduate training and research   181
British Psychological Society   184
Applied psychology   185
Clinical psychology   186
Educational psychology   188
Occupational/organisational psychology   190
Criminological/forensic psychology   191
Health psychology   194
Counselling psychology   196
Research and teaching   196
Other areas (non-accredited)   198
Other specialisms   201
Preparing your curriculum vitae (CV)   201
Some important points about the CV   204

References   209

Author index   221

Subject index   225

Preface

The impetus for writing this book comes from years of teaching on undergraduate courses in psychology and from listening to students themselves. Throughout those years, consistent weaknesses in student work have been evident in those aspects of studying that are crucial skills in getting a student through a degree course, and for achieving the best possible degree classification at the end of that course. As competition increases for places on postgraduate courses, and in the general "careers market", achieving the best possible grades (and subsequent degree classification) can be crucial.

This text represents a practical guide to studying psychology at an undergraduate level, as well as at pre-degree level (e.g., on an Access course). The text will also be of use to those who are seriously thinking about studying psychology, but have not yet applied. Undergraduate students often complain of not knowing what is expected of them in terms of the reports or essays they write, how to study during lectures, for seminars, etc., and how to prepare effectively for examinations. It is expected that this guide will be of practical use to students of psychology by providing a concise set of guides in a easy to follow format.

Chapter 1 is an introduction to psychology, explaining how psychology as an academic subject differs from the layperson's view of it, and provides an overview of the major perspectives within psychology, demonstrating the multidisciplinary nature of the subject. Chapter 2 focuses on what different modes of presentation there are on a psychology course – lectures, seminars, tutorials – and provides concise, practical guidelines on how best to approach these. Chapter 3 comprises a study guide on essay writing and referencing skills. Chapter 4 is a guide to research methods and statistics in psychology. Chapter 5 provides guidelines on ethics in research using humans and animals. Chapter 6 provides guidelines and examples on empirical research report writing. Together, essay writing and report writing will make up the bulk of a student's work on a psychology course. Chapter 7 contains good advice on how best to revise for examinations and useful tips on taking an exam. Chapter 8 provides advice on what to do on completion of an undergraduate psychology degree. This final chapter considers what it means to have graduate status; it covers postgraduate study and applied areas of psychology, as well as other applications. It also provides advice on writing a curriculum vitae (CV).

The main emphasis of this text is on providing good practical advice on major aspects related to studying on a psychology course, as well as what to do after the degree. It is expected that existing students of psychology, as well as those who are considering studying psychology as an academic subject, will benefit from this book.

Acknowledgements

I am very grateful to the following people for their contributions to the book: Faye Harvey, Neil McLaughlin Cook, Keith Morgan, and Sue Thomas. I would like to thank all those students who have offered their kind remarks and positive feedback on the first and second editions of the book.

Preface to the third edition

The format of the book has remained the same as in the second edition. The third edition is fully updated in terms of its reference sources. This new edition incorporates additional material relevant to studying, searching and writing about psychology. The major additions include the following. Chapter 1 has been expanded to include examples of current areas of study in psychology in the twenty-first century. Three current areas are considered – *cognitive neuroscience, evolutionary psychology*, and *positive psychology*. Chapter 3 has been expanded to include guidelines on web-based literature searching and how to reference sources of information obtained from the internet, such as documents from websites and online images. Chapters 2, 4, 5, 6, and 7 have remained essentially the same, with some expansion on the contents and updating of reference sources. Chapter 8 has been extended to include additional postgraduate specialisms in psychology, such as neuropsychology, psychotherapy and sports psychology, as well as the provision of useful websites associated with postgraduate areas of study and general careers advice.

Finally, I should like to express my thanks to my wife, Anne, for all her support throughout the completion of the first, second and third editions of this book.

Thomas M. Heffernan
Newcastle, 2004

Introduction to psychology 1

This chapter defines psychology, considers the study of psychology as a scientific discipline, and introduces the reader to the major perspectives within psychology.

What is psychology?

To the layperson, the term "psychology" might mean something like "the study of people" or "the study of the mind", both of which are correct but a little vague. A more formal definition of psychology would be the *scientific study of human mental processes, motivations, and behaviour*. Animal research is also conducted so that comparisons can be made between animal and human behaviour – from which many models of behaviour have been developed (Pinel, 2003). The origins of psychology has been much debated over the years. One school of thought is that psychology really only began when the first experimental study in psychology was carried out (for example, Hermann Ebbinghaus's experimental investigations into human memory in the late nineteenth century), whereas there are good arguments in support of the roots of psychological thought and inquiry dating back much further (see e.g., Eysenck, 1998, chap. 1).

Early influences include those of the Greek philosophers such as Plato and Aristotle during the fourth and fifth centuries BC, as well as experiments into psychophysics (the study of the relationship between mental and physical processes) carried out in Germany in the early to mid-nineteenth century. Hermann von Helmholtz's physiological research on colour vision in the nineteenth century has contributed much to physiological psychology. Charles Darwin's work on the origin of species and the work by Francis Galton on the study of individual differences and intelligence (both developed in the nineteenth century) firmly established the importance of biology to the study of humankind. Sigmund Freud's work on the psychoanalytic approach to the study of human thought and behaviour (particularly in the current realms of abnormal psychology) in the late nineteenth to early twentieth century, and the growth in behaviourism during the early to mid part of the twentieth century, have all contributed to the development of psychology.

All of these influences, it could be argued, have made invaluable contributions to the scientific study of human mental processes, motivations, and behaviour – psychology. Amongst the other major influences of the twentieth century are Gestalt psychology and humanism. Gestalt psychology has as its focus the direct description of human conscious experience, and was pioneered in the early part of the twentieth century by Max Wertheimer, Kurt Koffka, and Wolfgang Kohler. Humanism focuses particularly on personal growth (self-actualisation), and was pioneered in the mid part of the twentieth century by Carl Rogers and Abraham Maslow. Very recent influences include social constructionism, cross-cultural psychology, and feminist psychology (see Eysenck, 1998).

During its development, psychology has undergone a number of changes. One of these changes is a greater reliance on the *scientific method*. This means the use of scientific techniques, approaches, designs, and analyses, all of which allow the psychologist to study and interpret a range of human behaviour systematically, and predict or control it with some precision (Solso & Maclin, 2002). The use of systematic study allows us to test long-held, often erroneous, beliefs about the nature of human beings. For example, during the latter half of the Middle Ages, abnormal behaviour was predominantly thought to be the result of possession by devils or evil spirits. Often, "treatments" involved torturous, exorcistic procedures such as flogging, starving, immersion in hot water, etc. (Sue, Sue, & Sue, 2002, chap. 1). In current times, however, the recognition of psychological disturbances (and biological dysfunction) has led to more humane treatment of the mentally ill within society (see also Seligman, Walker, & Rosenhan, 2001).

Most psychologists might agree that all aspects of functioning should be considered in order to gain a fuller understanding of the human being. However, they will differ on what aspects they believe are of greatest importance. These differences reflect the variety of perspectives and methods adopted in psychology and the different lines of research being carried out by psychologists. The influences mentioned previously (e.g., philosophy, biology, physiology, the scientific method), are all evident in the modern-day perspectives within psychology. These major perspectives and methods include: *psychoanalytic, biological, developmental, humanistic, behaviourist, cognitive,* and *social approaches* to the study of human functioning. In practice, many psychologists do not adhere to just one perspective, but will take a somewhat eclectic approach.

Before considering some of the major perspectives and methods in psychology, it should be noted that, historically speaking, psychology stems from a variety of strands. The two major influences come from philosophy and the biological sciences, which has led to different "schools" of psychology being developed. In this sense a "school" refers to a group of individuals who hold common notions about the nature of human beings. These influences are still with us today in psychology and are represented on any undergraduate degree in psychology, as well as having a significant influence on specialisms in psychology.

Further reading: For some good reviews on the history of psychology see, for example, Herganhan (1992), Hothersall (1995), Malim, Birch, and Wadeley (1996), and Watson and Evans (1991).

Perspectives and methods in psychology

Psychology is ultimately the study of the person. Since there are many factors that work to "shape" each of us (e.g., genetics, learning processes, social influences, etc.), it is no surprise that psychology is a multi-perspective subject. Thus, when studying psychology at pre-degree and degree level, a number of perspectives or approaches are considered. For example, psychology can be looked at from a biological perspective, or from a combined approach (e.g., the study of psychological and social factors – a psychosocial approach). On the first year of a psychology course there is a wide coverage of the different perspectives, theories, and methods that have evolved within the discipline of psychology. The purpose of the rest of this chapter is to introduce you to the major topics encountered when studying psychology.

The psychoanalytic perspective

The psychoanalytic (also referred to as psychodynamic) approach is one of the oldest of the psychological perspectives. The onset of this approach can be traced as far back as 100 years ago when Sigmund Freud began his work. Indeed, Freud (1856–1939) is often referred to as the "father" of the psychoanalytic approach. According to this view, human behaviour is governed by impulses that lie buried in the unconscious part of the psyche (a Greek word meaning "soul", currently used to refer to the "mind"). Freud believed that each of us experienced a series of psychosexual stages that would shape our adult personality. The behaviour we show to the world is like the tip of an iceberg, beneath which are the vast realms of the unconscious. Freud developed a number of techniques for studying the patients who came to him for treatment for a range of disorders (Herganhan, 1992; Smith, Nolen-Hoeksema, Fredrickson, & Loftus, 2003).

Freud maintained that one's personality is made up of three parts – the *id*, the *ego*, and the *superego*. The *id* is thought to be the seat of all our basic, innate, drives and impulses such as sexual and aggressive drives. The *id*, for Freud, was the most inaccessible and primitive part of the personality, from which emanated such strong impulses that they could govern our overt behaviour. The second part of one's personality is the ego. According to Freud, this part of the personality acts to regulate the impulses emanating from the *id* and transforms them into a more socially acceptable form. The ego, therefore, acts to mediate between the drives of the *id* and the constraints of the outside world. The *id* operates on a "pleasure principle" because it seeks immediate gratification of the drives and impulses emanating from it. The *ego* operates on a "reality principle" because it transforms the basic drives of the *id* into a socially acceptable form. The final part of the personality is the *superego*. The superego develops within the first 5 years of life and, according to Freud, is the result of the child's incorporation of parental and social moral standards. The superego is seen as a "conscience mechanism", which works with the ego in order to mediate between the strong impulses of the id and to conform to what the external world expects of us. In this way, the personality is thought to be in a constant state of struggle as these individual components interact to deal with basic innate drives and outside forces. The system is said to be a dynamic one (see Freud, 1927/1974).

In addition to the notion of a three-part personality, Freud believed that child development was a strong indicator of the type of personality characteristics a person would show as an adult. According to this aspect of Freudian theory, a person progresses through five basic stages in their psychosexual development, each of which brings with it a potentially significant change in the person's psychological make-up. (Psychosexual relates to psychological development that is strongly linked with sexual experiences.) The first three stages are experienced within the first 6 years of life; the final two occur between the age of 6 years and adulthood. A summary of these stages are: the *oral stage* (from birth to about 1 year); the *anal stage* (from 1 to 3 years of age); the *phallic stage* (with a major development between 5 and 6 years); the *latency stage* (from about 6 to 12 years of age); and the *genital stage* (from 12 years to adulthood).

Further reading: For further consideration of these development stages see Alloy, Acocella, and Bootzin (1998), Gleitman, Fridlund, and Reisberg (2003), and Sternberg (1998).

Freud further maintained that if an individual progressed through these stages successfully then he or she would develop an adult personality that was, relatively speaking, problem-free (i.e., a person would not demonstrate maladaptive thought and behaviour patterns). However, if a particular stage was not "negotiated" successfully, then that person would develop what Freud referred to as a *fixation*. A fixation has been likened to having personality characteristics that are "frozen" in time, resulting in the manifestation of immature thinking and behaviour dependent on where the fixation lies. In some cases fixations can lead to various forms of neuroses (Alloy et al., 1998). So think carefully, if you are the type of person who is a chain-smoker, who likes chattering constantly, and/or who eats excessively, because, according to Freudian theory, you might well be the victim of a fixation at the oral stage of your psychosexual development. (See also Eysenck, 1994; Smith et al., 2003.)

Freud's writings have undoubtedly had a significant influence on theory and application in the field of psychology, as well as on other fields such as psychiatry. A number of post-Freudian theories and techniques have emerged, many of which owe a great debt to Freud's work (see Gleitman et al., 2003; Hayes, 1994; Mischel, 1999; Smith et al., 2003). Freudian theory is, like all theories, open to criticism (Fisher & Greenberg, 1977). For example, the theory has proved difficult to test under experimental conditions. Indeed, Freud's own writings offer little in the way of "hard data" that can be subjected to rigorous statistical analysis. There is little doubt that, in a time when discussion about sexuality was regarded as something of a taboo, Freud was unreserved in his explorations of the subject. Since Freud expounded his theory, many "post-Freudians" have written about the development of human personality, building on Freud's ideas and developing theories of their own. These include Carl Jung, Alfred Adler, and Karen Horney, to name but a few (see Brown, 1977; Fransella, 1981). In addition, a whole branch of psychoanalytic treatment has sprung up as a direct result of Freud's work. Freudian theory has also had an influence on the contemporary psychotherapies presently used in the clinical field (see Davison, Neale & Kring, 2003).

The biological perspective

Charles Darwin's *The Origin of Species* (1859) has been heralded as one of the most significant influences on the way in which we viewed human nature. Prior to Darwin, thought was guided by the principle that human beings were unique in the sense that they were the only species that possessed a "soul". Therefore, humans were seen as being fundamentally different from other species. Darwin was a biologist who spent many years making comparisons between different species of animals (including humans). He suggested that humans had evolved out of other species, and should therefore be seen as part of the wider animal kingdom.

Darwin's work had a number of implications for the development of a biological perspective in psychology. Eysenck (1994) outlines four such implications. Each of these implications is briefly indicated here, along with an example of a current research focus that has directly influenced contemporary theory, research, and application:

1. The notion that we should look at the interface between biological factors and psychological factors. An example of what influence this has had comes from the work currently being undertaken to discover the biological foundations of psychopathological disorders, for example, current research into the potential causes of schizophrenia, as well as treatments that have been developed (see Seligman et al., 2001; Sue et al., 2002).
2. The realisation that the study of animals can further our understanding of human functioning. For example, research into basic animal nervous systems, such as that of the Aplysia (a simple marine organism), has contributed to the development of a "model" of basic memory systems in humans (Pinel, 2003).
3. Darwin reinforced the view that heredity played an important role in the development of a particular species. Again, the genetic foundations of "normal" functions in humans, as well as in psychopathological conditions, are all too evident in contemporary psychology (see, e.g., Gleitman et al., 2003).
4. Darwin's observations on the variation between individual members of a given species and evolutionary selectivity has influenced our thinking on personality, intelligence, and individual differences in psychology (see, e.g., Smith et al., 2003; Sternberg, 1998).

Currently, the biological perspective is an attempt to understand emotions, thoughts, and behaviour in terms of the physical processes taking place in the body (Smith, 1993). Biological psychologists have developed a good understanding of how our nervous system operates; the development of the brain and how its various sites govern different functions; and how artificial stimulants can impact on our physiology and, in turn, on our behaviour. Indeed, they have even begun to unravel the mysteries of the very building blocks of humankind – genetics. (See Carlson, 2004; Eysenck, 1994; Kimble & Colman, 1994; Pinel, 2003; Smith, 1993; Smith et al., 2003.)

One example of the impact that a biological approach has had on the study of humans comes from work on a *biomedical model* of abnormality. Abnormality is where a person is judged to be psychologically disturbed in terms of her or his personality and/or behaviour (Seligman et al., 2001, chap. 1). Normally, a clinical diagnosis of abnormality would only be made using a set of selected criteria and a range of diagnostic tools. The *biomedical approach* assumes that abnormality is an illness that exists within the body, as opposed, for example, to the idea that society is the cause of abnormality. This approach is founded on three basic assumptions:

- that the various manifestations of the abnormality – the symptoms – can be grouped together to form a syndrome;
- that once the syndrome has been identified the physical aetiology or cause can be identified and located within the individual's body;
- that a treatment, biological in nature, can be administered to alleviate the abnormality (see, e.g., Seligman et al., 2001; Sue et al., 2002).

The biomedical approach has had a significant influence on theory and application with regard to conditions such as anxiety neurosis, depression, and schizophrenia (Davison et al., 2003; Sue et al., 2002).

Another example, that has emerged from this Darwinian approach (more specifically from Darwin's theory of evolution), is that of *evolutionary psychology* – a branch of psychology that views social behaviour (such as interpersonal relationships, work, and so on) as being determined, at least in part, by biological factors and the goal of gene survival (Eysenck, 1998). This area is given further consideration towards the end of this chapter under the section "twenty-first century psychology".

Although the biomedical model has proved a useful framework from which many aspects of human functioning are studied, including certain cases of abnormal behaviour (such as the chemical imbalance implicated in schizophrenia), it does have its weaknesses. For example, behavioural and cognitive factors (such as direct negative experience and irrational thoughts) can lead to psychopathology, without any clear biological determinant (Davison et al., 2003; Marks, 1969). Other approaches, such as the psychophysiological approach (the interface between psychology and physiological states) have proved useful as an explanation for a range of conditions, including everyday complaints such as migraine headaches (Sue et al., 2002).

Developmental psychology

Developmental psychology is defined as the scientific study of change in humans. Thus, within developmental psychology, a student will study how humans develop and why these changes occur. This approach encompasses changes that occur at the prenatal stage, right through to old age – with specific focus points. These focus points come at babyhood (from birth to age 3 years); early childhood (from 3 to 6 years of age); adolescence (from 6 to 12 years of age); young adulthood (from 12 to 18 years of age); middle adulthood (from about 18 to 40 years of age); mature adulthood (from age 40 to 65 years of age); and finally, the ageing adult (age 65 years onwards). Development through these stages is a gradual and continuous process, which means that a change from one stage to another may not be dramatic or even obvious (Kaplan, 1999). In current literature this area is sometimes referred to as "lifespan psychology", reflecting the focus on development across the human lifespan (from birth to old age).

Therefore, the focus of developmental psychology is change and this change can be quantitative or qualitative. So, what is the difference? A *quantitative change* in developmental psychology refers to an increase or decrease in some phenomenon, such as the average memory span of a child, changes in height, brain size, etc. An example of this is demonstrated when one looks at the amount of words an individual can hold in their auditory-verbal working memory (known as their working memory span), which has a clear developmental trend. For example, the average span for words increases from 3 to 4 words at age 5 years, through to 4 to 5 words at age 8 years, and through to 5 to 6 words at age 11 years. There is also progression from here into their early adulthood (see e.g., Hitch, Halliday, Schaafstal, & Heffernan, 1991). The span will depend upon what type of memory material one is looking at, for example, whether it is auditory-verbal or visuo-spatial materials. Such an observation is useful if one were devising an experiment to test what factors affect memory span development, but might not tell us why this change takes place. For that, perhaps, we would need to look for qualitative change.

A *qualitative change* in developmental psychology, therefore, refers not merely to a change that is measuring a quantity (increase or decrease), but to a change in the structure or process of some phenomenon. An example of a qualitative change comes from the literature on the developmental aspects of cognition. For example, research supports the view that, as they develop, children begin to use more strategies to aid remembering. When 5-year-olds are compared with, say, 12-year-olds or adults, the youngest age group do not appear to utilise memory strategies, whereas the two older age groups do use strategies (see Kail, 1990). There are a number of explanations for this observation: For example, as the child develops she or he comes to learn the benefits of using memory strategies – a qualitative change. It is clear, therefore, that quantitative and qualitative observations can be used to understand the occurrences that take place at each of the stages in development outlined earlier. (It should be noted that the quantitative/qualitative distinction is one that exists in other areas of psychology, and is not restricted to developmental psychology.)

The developmental perspective/approach represents a major area of theory and research in psychology and is usually well represented on any psychology degree course (as well as on pre-degree psychology courses). The topics covered in developmental psychology include: genetics; prenatal development and birth; the physical, cognitive, personality and social development at all the subsequent childhood stages (outlined earlier), as well as during adulthood.

Further reading: Gardner (1982), Gleitman et al. (2003), Hughes and Noppe (1990), Kail (1990), Kaplan (1999), Schroeder (1992), and Smith et al. (2003).

One example of an area studied from a developmental perspective is that of the cognitive system and how it develops. Cognition refers to all those processes that allow us to encode and interpret sensory inputs from our world, and includes sensation, perception, imagery, memory, and thinking. One developmental theorist and researcher who has made perhaps the most significant contribution in this area is Jean Piaget (1896–1980). Piaget's theory is based on a lifetime's work in which he investigated a number of issues concerning cognitive development. Piagetian theory is a *stage* theory, one that envisages the cognitive system as developing through a series of stages, each representing a qualitative change in the cognitive structures of the child. The four basic stages are: the *sensorimotor stage* (from birth to 2 years); the *preoperational stage* (from 2 to 6 or 7 years); the *concrete operational stage* (from about 7 to 12 years); and the *formal operational stage* (from 12 years to adulthood). These stages can themselves be further divided into substages (see, for example, Gardner, 1982; Hughes & Noppe, 1990; Kaplan, 1999 for details of stages and substages). By the time the child reaches the formal operational stage, she or he is able to think through problems in their mind, before making a decision – indicating an advanced level of thinking.

Although Piaget's contributions continue to provide the impetus for much research in developmental psychology (see Best, 1995; Hughes & Noppe, 1990; Kaplan, 1999; Schroeder, 1992), his theory has been heavily criticised over the years. For example, Piaget's failure to consider cultural differences in the development of strategies such as conservation (the principle that a quantity of material (e.g., liquid) does not change merely because its presentation has changed), and his failure to identify important contextual cues that affect children's cognitive development and performance (see Donaldson, 1980 and McShane, 1991 for critical reviews of these areas).

As well as looking at normal growth and development, some developmental psychologists specialise in particular phenomena, such as those that are subsumed under the area known as developmental psychopathology. Developmental psychopathology refers to a branch of study that focuses on developmental disorders that manifest themselves at different stages of development. These disorders include childhood schizophrenia, autism, conduct disorders, and attentional deficit hyperactivity disorder; childhood anxiety; eating disorders; and mental retardation.

Further reading: Sue et al. (2002, chap. 17), Van Hasselt and Hersen (2000, Pt. IV), and Wenar (2000).

Humanistic psychology

This approach or perspective began during the 1950s with the work of Carl Rogers and Abraham Maslow. The main tenet of this approach to studying humans is the idea that the person is constantly growing, changing, and attempting to reach their full potential. Humanistic psychologists focus upon self-direction, free will, and the ability of the person to make choices independently, as being the most important characteristics of the person. Humanistic psychologists believe, therefore, that we each have the potential to become a better human being and attain a higher level of functioning.

Abraham Maslow (1908–1970) is seen as the founder of humanistic psychology; that is, he developed it into a formal branch of psychology (Herganhan, 1992). Maslow is most widely cited for his theory of a "hierarchy of needs" – intrinsically linked with Maslow's belief that an individual strives to reach what he referred to as a state of *self-actualisation*. Self-actualisation basically refers to the idea that people attempt to fulfil themselves to their highest possible level of achievement in their personal life, work life, etc. However, Maslow believed few individuals ever reach self-actualisation. Maslow maintained that there were five basic classes of needs and that an individual strives to achieve the more basic class of needs before gradually ascending the hierarchy to reach her or his state of self-actualisation. The basic needs are similar to those striven for in the animal kingdom, whereas the higher classes of needs are thought to be distinct to humans (Smith et al., 2003).

Figure 1.1.
Maslow's hierarchy of needs.

Maslow's hierarchy of needs is represented in diagrammatic form in Figure 1.1. At the lowest level, an individual strives to achieve her or his basic *physiological needs* such as food, water, oxygen, activity, and sleep. Once these needs have been satisfied, she or he can strive to achieve their next class of needs. The second class of needs relate to *safety*, which basically refers to having a secure and safe childhood, as well as security and safety as an adult. The third set of needs relate to the feeling that one *belongs* somewhere and is *loved* by others. Thus, having a good social life and good, stable relationships with others (sexual and non-sexual) would be primary aims at this stage of one's progression.

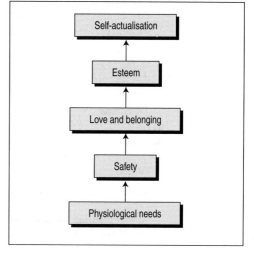

The penultimate stage is *esteem*. This refers to the need to be respected by others, to be seen as honourable and as someone who makes a positive contribution to the well-being of others. If the individual reaches this level and fulfils her or his needs at this level, then she or he becomes *self-actualised*. Maslow's major contribution to psychology was the impetus he provided for the development of humanistic psychology itself (see Fransella, 1981; Gleitman et al., 2003).

Carl Rogers (1902–1987) focused on the uniqueness of each person and how they viewed the world. Rogers believed that the role of an individual's self-perception and how they viewed the world would have a profound effect on their personality. For these reasons, Rogerian theory has become known as a "self" theory (Sternberg, 1998). Rogers believed that each of us has a self-concept and an ideal self. Self-concept refers to all those perceptions we have about ourselves, such as the way we look, or how good we are. The ideal self refers to those self-attributes each of us would like to possess. Rogerian theory further asserts that each of us struggles to match our actual self with our ideal self (a process very similar to Maslow's self-actualisation) and that by doing so we each have the potential to improve, grow, and change (Rogers, 1995).

One of the main contributions made by Rogers has been in his therapeutic technique called "person or client-centred" counselling. The basic aim of this form of therapy is for the individual to identify, with the help of the therapist, the differences between the actual self and the ideal self. This would involve the person's current status and some form of retrospective analysis, since the "self" develops from an early age and is affected by early experience. Where there is incongruous information (say, for example, the person overemphasises her or his negative points and underplays her or his positive points) then the therapist works to facilitate an acceptance of the negative points, as well as increasing the emphasis on the person's positive aspects. This form of therapy can be quite intensive, but is effective in improving the person's feelings of self-worth, self-esteem, and putting them on the path to "self-actualisation".

Further reading: Davison et al. (2003), Fransella (1981), Hayes (1994), and Smith et al. (2003).

Humanistic psychology is not without its critics. For example, it cannot be tested through the rigours of the scientific method, which must leave open the question of the validity of the approach. Also, if one looks throughout history, there are examples of people attempting to fulfil a higher class of needs without first securing a lower class of needs (as suggested by Maslow); for example, those who would starve themselves in order that others may be afforded their human rights, or those who would forfeit their own life for the good of society as a whole. In addition, as pointed out by a number of authors, Rogerian therapy (or other forms of so-called "insight" therapy) may not be appropriate for severe forms of psychological disorder (Davison et al., 2003). Since the pioneering work of Maslow and Rogers, humanistic psychology has continued to flourish; see, for example, the work of George Kelly (Herganhan, 1992).

Behaviourism

The behaviourist approach, or behaviourism, became popular in the West about 80 years ago with the work of John B. Watson. However, as Herganhan (1992) points out, the study of objective psychology (the psychological study of only those things that are directly measurable) was well developed in Russia before 1910. Before considering what contribution Watson, and others who came after him, made to the development of behaviourism, it is first necessary to consider the work of the Russian scientist, Ivan Petrovitch Pavlov (1849–1936).

Pavlov developed a theory that has become known as Pavlovian or classical conditioning. During the 1890s, whilst carrying out research into the digestive systems of dogs. Pavlov observed that, after a number of occasions, the dogs began to salivate as he entered the room prior to feeding them. Thus, the dogs appeared to have learned that his (Pavlov's) appearance signalled a subsequent event – the administration of food. Pavlov called this type of learning a conditional reflex because the reflex (e.g., salivation) is conditional upon learning from past events: in this case, that the presence of the experimenter signals the delivery of food. This response occurred when a contiguous association was formed between the presentation of food and some other event, such as Pavlov entering the laboratory and opening the food cupboard. Through a series of experiments, Pavlov gathered information and developed a theory now referred to as classical conditioning theory.

The basic principles of the theory are as follows: The subject is given an unconditioned stimulus (US) such as food; the reflexive response is known as the unconditioned response (UR), such as salivation. A conditioned stimulus (CS) is introduced that would not normally elicit the UR, such as the sound of a bell, immediately followed by the presentation of the US (food). After several pairings of the bell and the food, Pavlov discovered that the mere sound of the bell alone was enough to elicit salivation. The result of this pairing is called the conditioned response (CR), since the bell had gained the power to elicit the response of salivation. The association of the bell with the food to produce the salivation is conditioning. The whole procedure is the basis of classical conditioning theory. Pavlov spent years expanding upon the various aspects of classical conditioning, such as extinction, generalisation, and discrimination (see Costello & Costello, 1992; Gleitman et al., 2003; Gray, 1979; Smith et al., 2003).

Intuitively, we are all familiar with the idea of classical conditioning: a hungry child, the ringing of a dinner bell, the child salivating at the thought of what comes next – dinner. Classical conditioning principles have been applied to a number of areas of research and application in the field of psychology; for example, to the study of conditioned fears and phobias; as a partial basis for interventions with offenders within the field of forensic psychology; as well as providing an explanation for a number of everyday occurrences.

Further reading: Blackburn (2001), Quinn (1995), and Seligman et al. (2001).

J.B. Watson (1878–1958) believed that one could understand human functioning by adopting methods of enquiry that involved the observation of a person's behaviour and that this observation could be carried out by impartial, objective researchers. He also maintained that researchers could compare the results of their individual observations with a view to explaining the interaction between an external stimulus and a person's behaviour. Watson also believed that by understanding the conditions under which a particular behaviour, or set of behaviours, are performed, one could learn how to control behaviour (Eysenck, 1994, 1998). A strict behaviourist approach places little emphasis on mental processes being important in trying to understand humans and how they function within their world. Watson believed that all human behaviour could be broken down into basic components, and that these could be found in terms of learned stimulus–response (S–R) associations which were built up over time by the two events (stimulus–response) being repeated (Hayes, 1994). So for Watson, the aim of the psychologist was to develop a full understanding of how learning via S–R associations took place, and how this could be applied; e.g., how behaviour could be changed. He further asserted that it was sufficient to explain behaviour as the result of S–R associations repeatedly occurring in the environment, a limitation that has led some theorists to extend this further – most notably B.F. Skinner.

B.F. Skinner (1904–1990) is often credited with taking Watson's ideas further. Like Watson, Skinner emphasised the role of stimulus–response associations as a way of explaining human function and placed little emphasis on mental processes within the individual's mind. Skinner's major contribution was the introduction of the concept of *operant conditioning*. Based on the work of E.L. Thorndike (1874–1949), operant conditioning extended the S–R theory and emphasised the importance of reward following a particular behaviour. Skinner proposed that *reinforcers*, some *operant*, and a *discriminative stimulus*, were crucial to understanding the interaction between an environmental stimulus and response behaviour. A reinforcer is some event that impacts upon the probability of some behaviour occurring. If the reinforcer is positive then its presence increases the probability of repetition of a behaviour or event that preceded it. A simple example of this is where a person engages in some activity (e.g., work) to receive some reward (e.g., monetary gain). The payment at the end of the week's work increases the probability of the person repeating that behaviour (i.e., work) the following week. If the reinforcer is negative (say a shock was administered to a person who refused to work), its removal increases the probability of a recurrence of an event that preceded it. Punishment is different because its presence decreases the probability of recurrence of a behaviour or event that preceded the punishing stimulus. An *operant* refers to the event itself that is affected by the positive or negative reinforcement, or punishment. The *discriminative stimulus* refers to a "signal" that signifies that a particular reinforcement is likely to occur if the operant reveals itself (e.g., a particular behaviour).

The major difference between classical and operant conditioning lies in the nature of the response to a given stimulus. Whereas classical conditioning offers a good explanation of behaviour that is simple, reflexive, and automatic in nature (such as the knee-jerk response, the eye-blink response, and autonomic responses), operant conditioning, by contrast, focuses on behaviour that is voluntary in nature – such as behaviour that is carried out for a reward (see Herganhan, 1992; Smith et al., 2003). As with classical conditioning, S–R theory has acted as a good framework from which a number of specialisms in psychology explain maladaptive human functioning, as well as offering an explanation for everyday phenomena. Some examples include the study of psychopathological disorders (such as learned fears and phobias); a partial basis for interventions in the field of forensic psychology and forensic psychiatry; and contributions to more contemporary theories such as social learning theory – which itself offers good insights into many social phenomena, such as the study of aggression, prejudice, and so on.

Further reading: Aronson (2003), Baron and Byrne (2004), Blackburn (2001), Faulk (1994), and Seligman et al. (2001).

In addition to these applications, operant conditioning theory has led to a whole field of study in relation to behaviour shaping – which basically refers to the gradual changing of an organism's behaviour through the process of applying the principles of operant conditioning theory. Behaviour shaping (also known as behaviour modification or successive approximation) has been successfully applied in a number of fields, not least within a clinical context (see the work on behaviour therapy in Alloy et al., 1998, chap. 19; Davison et al., 2003, chap. 19).

One drawback with a traditional behaviourist approach to the study of humans is that it does not place enough emphasis on the role of other factors in determining a person's actions, such as the cognitive processes that can lead to a given behaviour. Another reason why people sometimes resist behaviourist explanations is that behaviourism is seen as reducing human functioning to merely animal responses, likening the human species to other animals – which possibly reduces the human qualities each of us like to feel we have. Having said that, current behaviourists accept that cognition does play some role in mediating behaviour, although they would argue that its role is of minimal importance. (See e.g., Eysenck, 1998, chap. 3.)

The cognitive perspective

The cognitive perspective has grown enormously since the pioneering work of Donald Broadbent during the 1950s, and emphasises the role of processes associated with the mind in human functioning. Cognitive psychology focuses on the way in which information is processed by the brain. Hypothetical constructs (e.g., the idea of a "short-term memory system") or models are used to develop knowledge and test predictions about psychological phenomena. Thus, a cognitive psychologist might develop and test hypotheses about a range of phenomena, such as: the ways in which a person's memory is organised and operates; how an individual acquires language skills; problem-solving abilities; how a person forms images about the world; how belief systems are formed; and what impact such factors have on behaviour; as well as artificial intelligence.

Further reading: Baddeley (1997), Eysenck and Keane (2000), Groome, Dewart, Esgate, Gurney, Kemp, and Towell (1999), and Smith et al. (2003).

In addition to this, some cognitive psychologists attempt to gain an understanding of the cognitive system by observing and testing people who have suffered brain damage that has led to specific cognitive deficits, an approach referred to as cognitive neuropsychology (see Ellis & Young, 1996; McCarthy & Warrington, 1990).

Two key aspects provided the impetus for establishing a cognitive psychological approach as a mainstream psychological perspective. First, behaviourism was on the decline during the 1950s as more emphasis was placed on the role of a person's thought processes in determining behaviour. Second, scientists were developing computers which, it was believed, could simulate the way in which humans think. It was within such an era that Donald Broadbent conducted research into how, under particular circumstances, humans were able to actively gather information from their environment and interact with that information to solve particular problems (Broadbent, 1958). In short, Broadbent believed that each human being was an active information processor. This concept has developed into a keystone of cognitive psychology and the contributions made by Broadbent have given rise to a mass of theoretical thinking and empirical research (see, for example, Baddeley, 1997; Best, 1995; Eysenck & Keane, 2000). Cognitive psychology currently represents one of the biggest areas of theory, research, and application within the field of psychology, and accounts for a sizeable portion of the psychology section of most university libraries.

Further reading: See Eysenck (1994), French and Colman (1995), Groome et al. (1999), Parkin (2000), Payne and Wenger (1998), and Robinson-Riegler and Robinson-Riegler (2004) for good coverage of cognitive psychology.

As with other approaches, cognitive psychology has also proved fruitful in combination with other perspectives, with some current psychologists adopting a combined approach – particularly in the applied field. One example of this is the *cognitive-behavioural approach*, which has been applied to the study of a number of aspects of human functioning. This approach basically focuses on the interface between cognitive factors and behaviour, and has led to the development of a number of cognitive-behavioural therapies for a range of conditions. For example, cognitive-behavioural therapy for mood disorders such as depression focuses on "faulty" cognitions or thoughts and how such cognitions can contribute to psychological and behavioural symptoms associated with a given mood disorder (Sue et al., 2002). The process here is to identify negative cognitions, such as "I am a bad person, the problems I face are insurmountable"; compare these thoughts with the reality, such as "you are not really a bad person, the problems faced can be overcome"; and change or restructure the overall cognitive pattern with more adaptive thinking. An example might be for the individual to emphasise the good points about herself or himself, or try to be more realistic about the situation she or he is in. When used in a structured, elaborated way, such an approach can be effective for treating conditions like depression (for example, see the work of Aaron T. Beck, 1967, 1983), and often appears most effective in combination with other forms of treatment such as behavioural methods, drug therapy, etc. (Sue et al., 2002), as well as proving applicable for a range of other conditions (see Seligman et al., 2001).

The cognitive perspective has also been criticised. For example, one early criticism of cognitive psychology was its heavy reliance on a laboratory-based approach to studying cognition. Inevitably, when testing phenomena in a laboratory setting – where a high degree of control can be achieved – the findings are said to lose their external validity; i.e., their relevance to real-life situations. These days, cognitive researchers carry out laboratory and field-based studies, and even combine the two – as is the case with quasi-experimental approaches discussed later in the book (see, e.g., Eysenck, 1994, 1998). Of course, the major limitation with taking too strict a cognitive perspective is that the human being cannot be understood just by exploring their thought processes (although these are important). This is why cognitive psychology is often combined with other perspectives to provide a multidimensional approach to studying humans (see also Sternberg, 1998).

Social psychology

Since we all live and function within a social world, it is not surprising that many theorists and researchers have studied what effects the social environment has upon the thoughts, emotions, and behaviour of the individual. Although there are some exceptions, humans actually like contact with others. Social psychology is the study of what effects groups have on individuals, and how being a part of a group or, in a wider sense, a society, affects a person's thinking, feelings, and behaviour. Social psychology has emerged as a major focus of study both from an experimental and a non-experimental approach, as well as offering viable explanations about real-world phenomena (see, e.g., Aronson, 2003; Baron & Byrne, 2004; Myers, 2001). Some of the major topics covered in social psychology include the study of social influence – which covers conformity, obedience, and compliance (Baron & Byrne, 2004, chap. 8); social cognition (Myers, 2001, chap. 5); group dynamics – such as polarisation, leadership, and decision-making processes (Sabini, 1995, chap. 3); attitude formation and attitude change (Taylor, Peplau, & Sears, 1997, chaps. 5 and 6); and aggression (Aronson, 2003).

Let us take one example from this and provide some insights into theoretical and research developments within the field – that being the work produced on the phenomenon generally known as "aggression". Aggression is usually defined in terms of an "intentional infliction of some form of harm on others" (Baron & Byrne, 2004). Violence can be seen as a deliberate act to inflict physical harm on some other person. There is a vast literature on the nature and origins of aggression, ranging from an "ethological approach" (see the work of Konrad Lorenz, 1966); to a "motivational approach" (see the work of J. Dollard and colleagues; Dollard, Doob, Miller, & Sears, 1939); to a "psychoanalytic approach" (see the work of S. Freud). All these approaches provide interesting insights into aggression, but they falter when it comes to explaining questions such as "What role might society play in mediating aggression?" Social psychology offers a different, and arguably more viable, explanation of factors that might mediate aggression.

Social learning theory (Bandura, 1977) has been applied to the study of aggression and includes the work on "social modelling", which suggests that aggression can be learned via an individual (quite often a child) observing aggressive behaviour in another person, who is called a social model and who might in this case be a parent. Thus, a child might copy aggressive and violent behaviour from observing such behaviour in other people. Indeed, increased levels of aggressive and violent behaviour have been seen to occur in an experimental setting where children were exposed to aggressive "models" (Bandura, 1973; Bandura, Ross, & Ross, 1961, 1963). Such findings have offered useful insights into some of the potential causes of aggression and have had an impact on wider issues such as the relationship between viewing violence on television and film, and elevated levels of overt aggression. Indeed, some researchers have suggested that violent viewing does in fact lead to increased and long-term manifestations of violent behaviour (Eron, 1982; Leyens, Camino, Parke, & Berkowitz, 1975). However, it should be noted that other researchers have discovered mixed findings on the effects of television viewing on aggression (see, for example, Freedman, 1984). It has also been noted that other psychological factors, such as cognition, also play a role in determining aggressive behaviour (Berkowitz, 1993).

In addition to the development of social psychology as a major perspective within psychology, applied social psychology has also recently developed. Applied social psychology is the application of theoretical and research aspects of social psychology to everyday, real-life phenomena (Baron & Byrne, 2004). Applied social psychologists study a number of topics, but away from the traditional laboratory-based studies that dominated psychology before the mid-1970s. These topics include: social behaviour and environmental factors, such as the work carried out on "personal space" and the effects of crowding; the study of health-related behaviour, such as the social dynamics involved in doctor–patient interactions; social psychological factors and ill-health; and work within a legal forum, such as eyewitness testimony, courtroom dynamics, and jury size – all of which represent current, active areas of research in applied social psychology.

Further reading: Baron and Byrne (2004), Sabini (1995), Saks and Krupat (1988), and Taylor et al. (1997).

Twenty-first century psychology

Before finishing this consideration of the major perspectives and methods within the study of psychology, it might be useful to consider some of the current interdisciplinary approaches to studying human behaviour. As stated, increasingly psychologists are taking a multidimensional approach to studying psychology and this is reflected in some of the developing areas within the study of twenty-first century psychology. Before completing this chapter we will consider some of these major developments. Three current areas are considered here briefly: *cognitive neuroscience, evolutionary psychology*, and *positive psychology*.

Cognitive neuroscience refers to the study of cognitive processes from a neuroscience perspective (that area of biology that deals with the brain and nervous system). This means studying cognitive processes (e.g., memory) using the methods and findings from neuroscience. Essentially, the aim of cognitive neuroscience is to explain how our mental processes operate, or are executed, within the brain. Cognitive psychology may provide the hypotheses (e.g., how do we remember names) and neuroscience provides the methods and findings about how these processes are organised and executed within the brain (e.g., what brain mechanisms and/or networks are involved in this process). Cognitive neuroscience is distinctive because one can use its methods to focus on the intact brains of "normal" participants (as opposed to studying brain-damaged patients). Thus, using modern brain-imaging techniques, such as PET or CAT, we can study the different mechanisms involved in short- and long-term memory systems. (See, for example, Gazzaniga, Ivry, & Mangun, 2002.)

Evolutionary psychology is basically the study of the biological origins of psychological mechanisms. This approach involves the interrelationship between biology, psychology, anthropology, and psychiatry. The principal idea behind evolutionary psychology is that, just like biological mechanisms, psychological mechanisms have evolved over time (millions of years) and are subject to the process of natural selection. Thus, the psychological mechanisms we possess today have been selected on a genetic basis and on the premise that they are beneficial to the survival of our species. Topics studied within evolutionary psychology include how we select our mates and what attracts us to specific others, how we behave when reacting to particular emotions, human aggression, work, and even certain types of criminal activity. As well as providing a flourishing framework for future research, evolutionary psychology (like its founding Darwinian framework) has generated much critical debate as to the nature of humans and their psychological functioning. Many people believe that human behaviour is strongly influenced by factors other than biological ones, such as cultural norms and a range of environmental factors (Carlson, 2004). Other contentious areas include the "uniqueness" of humans, and the origins of human processes such as language are hotly debated within this field. (See e.g., Rossano, 2003; *The Psychologist*, 2001.)

Positive psychology has, at least in part, developed in response to the study of abnormal psychological functioning. Seligman (2002) suggested that to balance what we know about mental illness (which constitutes quite a sizeable literature) we need to develop our knowledge of what and how humans "flourish" – what makes people "happy" or facilitates a sense of well-being. This is essentially what is meant by positive psychology. The study of positive psychology shares common ground with the humanistic approach outlined earlier, but the former relies more heavily on empirical methods to study the traits and mechanisms associated with its content. Thus, subjective experiences – such as happiness and optimism, potential "positive personality traits" – such as wisdom and courage, and the study of "positive institutions" – the social structures that might promote feelings such as happiness, can all be scientifically studied within this branch of psychology. The study of positive psychology leads one to conclude that positive emotions are worth cultivating in order to achieve states of happiness and well-being, but can also point the way to further personal growth. This has led to a range of focuses on internal and external factors that affect happiness, how organisational and work systems that affect our sense of well-being, as well as a range of psychotherapeutic interventions. (See e.g., Seligman, 2002; special issue of *The Psychologist*, 2003.)

Finally

It should be clear from this introduction that psychology is a *multi-dimensional subject*, drawing from a number of perspectives and methods. This is inevitable given the wide range of forces that impact upon the individual and is also reflected in the specialisms studied at postgraduate level in psychology.

Further reading: For good introductory texts on the main perspectives within psychology see, for example, Eysenck (1994, 1998), Gleitman et al. (2003), Hayes (1994), Smith et al. (2003), and Sternberg (1998).

In addition to understanding relevant theory and research findings in psychological literature, you will be expected to develop the knowledge and skills needed to carry out research yourself. You will be given tutoring in the research components of psychology on your course. The research component is reflected throughout the study of psychology; and is represented here in several parts throughout the remainder of this book. This chapter has provided a basic coverage of the major perspectives within psychology. The remaining chapters focus on the more practical aspects of studying psychology, as well as applied fields in psychology.

A study guide to lectures, seminars and tutorials 2

This chapter considers the types of skills that are developed on a course of study in psychology, and what the major modes of presentation are on a course. In addition, guidelines on effective note taking and on how to summarise materials encountered on the course are also considered.

Before progressing on to the more practical aspects of the book, it might be useful to consider some of the types of skills one expects a student to develop on a psychology course (as well as other academic courses).

Skills developed on a psychology course

In higher education in general there has been an ever-increasing focus on facilitating the development of a number of key skills in students. Two groups of skills are referred to here: *core* and *transferable* skills. Core skills is a term used to refer to particular skills developed throughout a course of study in psychology. Transferable skills is a term used here to refer to certain skills that are deemed desirable for all graduates to develop by the time they leave college or university – and is part of the notion of "student graduateness". These skills are considered here in general terms. Students are advised to consult with their own course leader, or study skills adviser, at their own institute for specific guidelines on skills relating to that college or university. All college and university institutes will have developed guides or a model of how such skills should be developed on their courses.

In reality, many of the core skills developed throughout a course of study become transferable skills that can be used beyond the course, in future careers. So, although a distinction is made here, these skills form part of the same group of skills utilised both on a psychology degree, as well as being transferred beyond the degree and into a prospective career.

Core and transferable skills

The types of skills one is encouraged to develop on a course include:

1. *Oral, visual, and written communication.* These skills can be developed through interactions during workshops, tutorials, seminars, and (to some extent) lectures.
2. *Numeracy.* Developed through courses such as research methods and statistics, as well as demonstrating numeracy in projects.
3. *Computing skills.* This includes basic transferable skills such as working on a computer; it does not mean that you have to become a "computer expert".
4. *Critical and creative thinking.* These skills can be developed through a number of routes – learning how to evaluate literature, presentation and discussion of competing theory and research in seminars, tutorials, as well as for essay writing and report writing, and, of course, in the examination assessment.
5. *Problem-solving ability.* On a psychology course the ability to look at a task or problem and make decisions about how best to reach a solution is encouraged across a wide variety of sessions (e.g., laboratory classes, tutorial meetings, personal tutor meetings, etc.).
6. *Decision-making ability.* Making decisions regarding module/unit choices, how to prepare work, and even making decisions within a group setting (e.g., on a joint project) are all course-related skills that are encouraged.
7. *Team work.* Working as part of a team (e.g., on a joint project or seminar presentation) is actively encouraged on psychology courses, and can lead to the development of leadership skills.
8. *Organisation and self-discipline.* The ability to organise your study time and discipline yourself to attend learning sessions, work independently, and meet deadlines, are actively encouraged when studying for a degree in psychology.
9. *Self-evaluation.* Being able to judge your own abilities and progression, and knowing where and how improvements in your performance can be achieved, are all encouraged on a course and specifically dealt with in relevant study skills sessions.

Transferable skills refer to personal skills that can be utilised in situations beyond the course of study a student is taking, such as in a future career. If the student is alerted to these skills at an early enough stage, and actively develops them, then transferable personal skills can be of great benefit throughout the rest of his/her life. It is generally accepted that these are skills which future employers are attracted to when considering graduates for employment. In an increasingly competitive job climate, having these "value-added" skills, as well as having demonstrated your ability to study at degree level, can be of enormous benefit to a graduate.

So, in this sense, all the skills referred to earlier can become transferable skills: oral, visual, and written communication; numeracy and literacy; basic and advanced computing skills; critical and creative thinking; problem-solving ability; confidence and experience in decision making; working both as part of a team and independently; self-discipline and organisation; self-evaluation; and demonstrating leadership qualities. All of these skills are attractive to future employers. They enable a future employer to develop within the recruit, through training, aspects of this skills base that are necessary for a given job.

Many of these skills can be developed through formal learning sessions such as practical classes, seminars, tutorials, and (perhaps to a lesser extent) in lectures. These skills are also developed through preparing, compiling and presenting your work throughout the course. Having said this, it is the student who is ultimately in control in terms of the development of these skills; it is she/he who has to see the importance of the acquisition of such skills. In addition, developing your ability to negotiate, present a persuasive argument, or act diplomatically when necessary, and being able to deal with the setbacks one inevitably experiences in life, are all qualities that are looked for beyond the degree; e.g., in applied psychology and in the general careers market (see Chapter 8).

As a student, your contact time – the amount of time you are required to attend formal academic sessions – will be made up mainly by your attendance at lectures, seminars, and, in some cases, tutorials. The only exception to this is the time spent in practical-related classes.

Practical classes

For research methods courses on a psychology degree, particularly where the degree is a Bachelor of Science (BSc), practical classes can make up a substantial component of the course. In practical classes you are taken through procedures for conducting literature searches, designing and running studies, analysing the data from those studies, and producing a final report on the research. The aims of a research methods course are to enable you to learn the basic skills involved in carrying out research, to familiarise you with the different approaches to research and with relevant statistical analyses and other methods of measurement, to help you to develop report-writing skills, and to provide you with hands-on experience of running experiments and using appropriate laboratory equipment, as well as relevant computer packages.

Typically, for practical classes, your contact time will include a lecture component, a laboratory class component, and in many institutes, a related seminar/tutorial class. The lecture component will provide you with the necessary theory and empirical knowledge; the practical class component will provide you with the practical experience of researching; and the seminar component can be used to provide a forum for discussions related to your whole experience of research methods. The exact organisation of practical classes will vary from institute to institute, and it is therefore difficult to provide guidelines on how best to prepare for such sessions. At the beginning of each research methods course, you should be provided with a timetable for the lectures, practical classes and (where appropriate) seminars. In addition to this, you should be given advice about what preparation you need to do for these sessions. For example, if you were at the "design" stage of research you might be given a lecture on designing experiments, experience in designing an experiment in class, and be asked to come along to the seminar to discuss different types of designs (having first been directed to reading sources). It might be a good idea to ask the research methods tutor at the beginning of the course to explain the exact interrelationship between the different components of the methods course.

The aim of the remainder of this section is to provide guidelines on how best to prepare for and study during lectures, seminars, and tutorials.

Contact time

Local education authorities often require that you attend at least 80 per cent of all course contact sessions (lectures, tutorials, seminars, etc.). Those students who do not meet this requirement run the risk of having their funding withdrawn (which includes any course fees paid by the funding body). The amount of contact time will vary from institute to institute, but a contact time of between 10 and 14 hours or so each week can be expected. You are expected to engage in self-directed study in addition to this. In general, the amount of class time is reduced as you progress through the course. Thus, at the final-year stage it is highly likely that you will be working independently, outside formal contact sessions, for much more of the time than would, say, a first-year student. There are a number of reasons for this: For example, the research methods classes are replaced by your undertaking a self-directed (but supervised) psychology project or dissertation in the final year of an undergraduate degree. The rest of your contact time is likely to be spent attending lectures, seminars, and tutorials. So, what do these sessions involve?

Before going on to look at what these sessions involve and how best to prepare for them, it might be useful to consider two approaches to learning that can be used in such sessions. Over the years these different approaches to learning have been referred to as the *having* or *being mode* of study, or as *passive* and *active* learning, and, more recently, as *deep* and *surface* processing (Barnes, 1995; Fromm, 1979; Smith & Brown, 1995). These approaches can play a crucial role in learning during contact sessions on a degree, as well as for any preparatory work a student does for examinations, etc.

Active and passive learning

In 1979, Eric Fromm distinguished between those students who were in a *having* mode of study and those who were in a *being* mode of study. The *having* mode is used to describe those who merely obtain a body of knowledge through a relatively passive mode of study: The lecturer imparts a body of knowledge on a subject, the student listens, takes notes, and reproduces part of that body of knowledge for some future event (e.g., an exam). The being mode of study refers to where the student becomes actively involved in the material being presented, thinking through the material, making notes of relevant points from the material presented, and posing questions that allow her or him to develop an understanding of the concepts and issues involved in the topic, as well as its relation to other subject matter; for example, how the research/theory compares with other research findings and/or theory in the literature. The mere accumulation of knowledge will not by itself stimulate thought processes, whereas an active participation in the material itself will enable the perceiver to assess critically, analyse, and draw conclusions from that material.

Active learning, then, is a skill that should be developed throughout a course of study (for example, in lectures, seminars, and tutorials) and should be used when carrying out coursework, as well as revision for examinations. When preparing for coursework in the form of essays (see Chapter 3) and practical reports (see Chapters 4, 5, and 6), organising the literature in relation to the task can facilitate active processing (i.e., organise the literature around a particular question/ topic in an essay, or around the aims of the research project). Also, when revising for examinations (see Chapter 7), organising information taken from the literature can provide a powerful cue for recall. Active study is also about a student using the information in such a way so that she or he analyses the information, thinks critically about the information, develops and/or links ideas together from various sources, and presents a critical account of the information in relation to the particular topic, issue, or question being addressed. This is quite different from a passive approach to learning, where a student merely collects information and regurgitates it at some future event (e.g., an exam). A student who develops active learning skills will benefit from this in terms of their ability to organise, remember, and use information picked up on the course, and through their own literature searching.

Current research has shown that using different approaches to learning does lead to different outcomes. Specifically, it has been found that using a deep approach to learning has a more beneficial effect than using a surface approach. These different approaches can be summarised as follows (see Smith & Brown, 1995).

A surface approach involves:

- focusing purely on the discrete components of the text (e.g., describe a phenomenon; recall facts)
- memorising and regurgitating information
- forming associations between concepts and facts without reflection
- failing to draw relationships between, or distinguish between, new or previous evidence and argument
- seeing the task as an imposition placed upon you by some external agency (i.e., your tutor).

A deep approach involves:

- focusing on what you think the main argument(s) are in an author's piece of work (or what is required by the tutor setting your work)

- drawing relationships and distinguishing between new ideas and previous literature
- drawing relationships and distinguishing between evidence and argument
- relating the evidence to everyday life
- organising and structuring the content of a piece of work.

The more adept you become at using an active or deep approach to learning, the more you will come to understand the material you are reading and writing about, and the more of that material you will remember. Also, by using such an approach your marks and final degree classification can be improved (see, e.g., Ramsden, 1988). The first year of an undergraduate degree course can be the ideal time for you to acquire and develop these learning skills. Such skills should be utilised, as much as possible, in all your contact sessions (lectures, seminars, tutorials) as well as in on-course assessments.

Lectures

During a lecture you will be presented with a range of materials (for example, lecture notes, slides, diagrams, etc.) and you are responsible for taking concise, easily understood notes that you can elaborate on at a later date. Some lecturers provide handouts containing the main points about the lecture topic, and, in some cases, a full set of references cited for that lecture. Be sure to ask where the references can be found if you have not been given the full reference source by your tutor (e.g., are they from a particular book or particular journal article?). Most lectures will be a 1-hour affair, but sometimes you may be asked to attend a 2- or even 3-hour lecture (in which case there is normally a break halfway through). It is normally left up to the student's own conscience whether to attend a particular lecture. However, if the attendance at lectures is consistently low, the lecturer may decide to take a formal register.

Lectures are seen as a very important part of the psychology course because it is here that you are presented with a framework of the phenomena studied on that particular part of the course. During this time, relevant theory and research are presented in a concise and coherent form. You should refrain from asking questions during the lecture, but do ask questions outside the lecture venue, in a related seminar or tutorial session. Although lectures may seem like a very one-sided affair (lecturer talking and student listening), students can enthuse a lecturer by appearing interested, alert and attentive.

However, do bear in mind that not all lectures will be fascinating. Very often, what you get out of a lecture depends not just on how it is presented, but how much you enjoy the particular topic under consideration and your own preparation. So, how can one study effectively during lectures, and what behaviours should be avoided? What follows is a list of activities likely to occur (on the part of the student) during a lecture, and brief comments as to their likely effectiveness as a learning strategy.

Copying down lecture notes from the overhead projector or from what is said by the lecturer. This is often seen as a passive strategy because, although you are getting the information down, you are probably not thinking a great deal about that information.

A much more effective strategy would be to rewrite the information into a form that has more meaning to you, perhaps accompanying each paragraph with a question or two (which you can either use as a basis for questioning the lecturer afterwards, contemplate yourself at a later date, or discuss with fellow students after the lecture).

Asking the lecturer questions about the topic being considered in the lecture. This is a very useful and active strategy because when asking questions you become alert and are actively thinking about the subject.

Although a recommended strategy, asking questions during a lecture is usually discouraged by lecturers. It is probably best to wait until after the lecture has finished. If everybody in a lecture hall containing 100 students wanted to ask questions, there would be little time left to complete the lecture itself!

Answering the questions posed by the lecturer. This is seen as an active process because again it requires you to think critically about the topic.

Remember, you are not expected to know all the answers, so even if you find that your answer is not quite accurate, do not be put off answering questions.

Writing down your own ideas and thoughts on the subject. This is a very active strategy and is highly recommended during lectures. It will help you to distinguish between lectures and may make a particular lecture more memorable (i.e., it can help with what is known as the consolidation process in memory).

Asking yourself relevant questions. Ask yourself the following questions about the material (see, e.g., Barnes, 1995):

> **1.** How does that part of the literature compare with other parts covered?
> **2.** How can the literature be organised or structured?
> **3.** What is worth noting and what is not?
> **4.** What are the major issues or topics of controversy?
> **5.** Are there problems/limitations with the information presented?

Remember, the main aim of a lecture is to provide you with a framework of the topic under consideration from which to work. This means that you must spend some time outside the lecture on fleshing out your lecture notes. As you progress through your course, particularly at degree level, you will be expected to search for information sources such as textbooks (which are called secondary sources) and journal articles (which are called primary sources) that may fall outside those to which you have been referred in the lecture. You must do this by reading around the literature the lecturer has referred to in the lectures, and summarising relevant theory and research before adding this to your own set of notes. As you progress through your degree, you will be encouraged to look at sources beyond what you are provided with during contact sessions, i.e., to conduct your own computer or journal search. If you do this as an ongoing task you will find that it makes revision much more manageable, rather than leaving it all until nearer the deadline for the assessment or examination.

Further reading: For further advice on studying in lectures, see, for example, Marshall and Rowland (1998), and Saunders (1994).

Seminars

A seminar can take one of a number of forms. It can be where you as a student are expected to prepare and present some piece of work to the rest of the seminar group. Alternatively, it can be where a group discussion ensues about particular phenomena (e.g., a theory, piece of research, etc.), and students are encouraged to provide their own informed opinions about the topic under discussion. The precise format of the seminar will be determined by the course tutor. A seminar group will usually consist of the lecturer and several students. The number of students in a seminar group can vary, depending on the numbers enrolled on a particular course and the nature of that course. A seminar group will normally consist of the same group of people throughout the whole year and each one typically lasts for about 45 to 50 minutes. The lecturer will provide the initial briefing, during which you should be fully informed about what is expected of you in terms of your preparation and the amount of time for which you should aim to speak during the seminar itself. For example, you may be asked to read a chapter from a book or a journal article and prepare and present a summary of that piece of work to the seminar group. You will also be expected to handle some questions from the group about the material you have prepared, so make sure you prepare well for such a session.

Quite often there will be ground rules laid down about whether or not you can use visual or audio equipment in support of your presentation, such as slides, or acetates on an overhead projector. Again, your tutor should fully brief the group as to the guidelines and/or ground rules at the beginning of the course. Normally, there will be a number of presenters (i.e., students), each of whom submit a summary of a piece of work, the aim of which is to address one part of a topic or question under consideration. Once these presenters have finished, group discussion follows with the lecturer there to guide the seminar through its various stages. If you are at all worried about an impending seminar presentation or not sure how to organise your presentation, the tutor should be willing to meet with you beforehand and provide some guidance.

Preparing for a seminar

As stated earlier, your tutor will provide you with a full briefing sheet and/or explain to you what you are required to do for the seminar. The briefing (written or oral) should (ideally) tell you what question or topic is to be addressed in the seminar; what your contribution is expected to be; which piece of work you are expected to consult and summarise; and for how long you are expected to talk. Advice on actually preparing for the seminar can be provided by the tutor on request.

Once you know what the topic is and what material you need to access, start preparing sooner rather than later by collecting the information from books and journal articles well in advance of the seminar. Read the material and make brief notes about the main points of the information, always trying to relate it to the question set in the seminar briefing (or topic to be addressed). DO NOT prepare exhaustive notes that amount to a rewrite of the whole material: This is not what the seminar is about and will not look good on the day. Your fellow students and the tutor will not appreciate your sitting through reading of several notebooks on the topic!

If you feel happier, and the facilities are available to you, use some visual aid such as an overhead projector, but make sure the notes you place on the acetates are brief and contain the salient points only (assuming that your tutor agrees to this). Many people like using visual aids because they take the attention away from them as the presenter and onto the projected image, therefore reducing the anxiety of having several people watching their every move. If you do use transparencies, make sure they are clear and that you do not put too much information onto one transparency. Also, make sure they are legible.

Using handouts is also a good way of diverting attention and can actually help the other students by allowing them to think about the subject rather than hurrying to take down notes about what is being said. Handouts provide permanent reminders of the information discussed in seminars. Remember, it is possible that the material you cover in seminars will be part of the assessment (e.g., the final examination). You might wish to check this point with your tutor.

Perhaps the most daunting part of the seminar process is when you are asked questions on the topic, either by your tutor or your fellow students. Most students, of course, will not be looking to ask too difficult a question – after all, they will have to take their turn as presenter! If you are asked a question, take your time, think for a moment, perhaps repeat the question (it gives you more thinking time), and try to make some informed answer. Remember, psychology is ultimately to do with human experiences, so even if you forget all the grand theories, you should be able to come up with something from your own past experience (but this is not as good as providing an informed answer based on the literature). If you really do not have a clue what the answer might be, admit it and ask if others might make a contribution.

In some institutes attendance at seminars will be monitored by the tutor taking a register, in others it may not. In most cases you will be asked to present perhaps only once or twice throughout the particular course (or module), such as an Introduction to Psychology course in your first year – *but you are expected to attend all seminar sessions*. In some institutes, seminar presentations are marked and contribute to your overall assessment on a particular course.

Why bother with seminars?

Presenting to small groups is a very useful skill to develop, not only because it is part of your learning experience, but also because it has a great deal of relevance to other aspects of your life. So what are the uses of seminar presentations?

Presenting at conference. Some of you (for example, in your final year of study) may go on to present your work at a conference. Indeed, there are a number of undergraduate conferences each year to which you could be invited to present a summary of your final-year project/dissertation. Presenting your work at a conference will enable you to gain respect in your particular field and have your work published in conference proceedings. Conferences are good places to impress other people in your field, so presenting your work at a conference can be a good way of "networking". It also looks good on your curriculum vitae (CV).

Improving social skills. Developing the skill of presenting to small groups can help to overcome the nerves many people experience when discussing things with a group of individuals who are familiar with the topic. The more you learn to control those nerves in a group discussion setting, the easier it becomes.

Good practice for job interviews. Presenting at a seminar can be very good practice for performing at a job interview. The interview is somewhat like a seminar in that you will be asked questions about material you have prepared (i.e., your CV or application form) by a number of people. You will be expected to present a concise and coherent argument as to why you are best suited for that job. The more practised you are at seminar presentation, the better you will come across at interviews.

Some don'ts in relation to seminars:

- Don't panic! most academic institutes will have an adviser who can provide guidance on how to control panic.
- Don't leave the preparation for a seminar until the last minute.
- Don't rush things; take the time needed to get the information across clearly in the seminar.

- Don't just miss the seminar. This will not only annoy your tutor, but will cause problems for the rest of the seminar group (you'll probably be asked to present another one in its place).

It would be wrong to try to make out here that seminars are easy to do. They can (as indeed tutorials can) be a somewhat daunting experience. However, nobody is out to make the student look a fool, or induce any unnecessary angst, so do not act as though you were going before a firing squad. Prepare well, accept that you do not know all the answers, and deal with the situation. Seminars can play a very important part in the learning process (if they are organised correctly), and they do get easier with practice.

Tutorials

A tutorial is typically an event where either a small group of students and the lecturer get together, or sometimes a single student meets the lecturer on a one-to-one basis. The main aim of a tutorial is to offer the student the opportunity to follow up material covered in the related lecture course and to ask the lecturer questions relating to that material. A tutorial can provide the student with the ideal opportunity to ask the lecturer to clarify theory, research, or general points about the topic under consideration, rather than trying to pin down the lecturer outside formal contact time. Where you have a very busy lecturer, such as a professor who spends a lot of her or his time preparing for publications or attending conferences or busy meetings, a tutorial may be the only chance for you to question her or him at any length.

So the tutorial differs from the lecture in that you are not just one of a large lecture audience listening to the lecturer expounding views on a particular topic, nor is it like a seminar where you are expected to prepare and present some piece of work. But you are expected to come to a tutorial prepared to question and to make active, spoken contributions (the same expectation applies to the lecturer). With ever-increasing numbers of students in further and higher education, tutorials can tend to get a little large in their numbers. However, this format still provides you with the opportunity to ask questions about the topic and engage in discussion.

Another problem arising from the large numbers might be a situation where a part-time lecturer is hired to take some of the extra tutorial (or seminar) load away from the course tutor. When this happens it can sometimes be a little off-putting for students having to question one lecturer about material presented by another lecturer. If this happens, do not be put off. The lecturer who takes the tutorial or seminar should be familiar with the area or fully briefed by the main lecturer running the course and presenting the lectures. One major problem students have with tutorials (and with seminars) is their feeling that, because they are not experts in the field, they are afraid of looking stupid in front of the lecturer and other students if they get the information wrong, or have to admit that there is something they are not sure about. Tutors are fully aware of this and know that even the brightest of students sometimes find it very difficult to master new material (after all, your tutor will have had to learn the material in a similar way!). So do not be put off asking questions you think are relevant, or offering what you think are useful contributions to the tutorial (or seminar). In fact, your fellow students will probably be silently thanking you for asking a question that they were too afraid to ask!

Some final points about seminars and tutorials

In some institutes of higher education, seminar and tutorial work is marked and may contribute towards your final grade, whereas in others it is not marked – a point that is worth checking with the relevant course tutor. It is felt that attending and contributing to seminars and tutorials will help you develop learning skills that cannot be acquired in the traditional lecture setting, and will therefore help you to improve your performance in your coursework (and examinations).

Taken together, seminars and tutorials will help you to:

- clarify ideas and literature that you have not understood
- evaluate material by looking at different viewpoints
- summarise material (e.g., a journal article) into a manageable form
- relate the information you (and your fellow students) have read to the specific question/topic under consideration
- express yourself clearly and coherently when taking part in discussions
- discuss related topics not necessarily covered in lectures, such as applied aspects or everyday aspects of the phenomena.

Developing these skills can help enormously on the course. In particular they can *help you to develop the type of critical thinking necessary to become an active learner and promote deep processing*. If you are able to develop such skills, you should find that your coursework – be it an evaluative essay, a critical appraisal of a piece of research, or your performance in a final examination – will benefit. Developing and enhancing these skills in the first year of study can have a positive effect on the two subsequent years that typically make up the bulk of an undergraduate degree in psychology. Remember that in most institutes years 2 and 3 usually determine your final degree classification. These skills are not only crucial for studying for your degree, but will also help in your personal development. So, make the most of your contact time.

Further reading: For preparing for and studying during seminars and tutorials, see, for example, Barnes (1995), Marshall and Rowland (1998), and Saunders (1994).

Effective note taking

Note taking is a skill that you are likely to use during lectures, seminars, and perhaps even tutorials. In addition, note taking can form an important part in preparing for a written essay (see Chapter 3), preparing the groundwork for writing an empirical report (see Chapter 6), and as part of the revision process for exams (see Chapter 7). When studying at college and university level, often you are expected to look at what you are studying in greater depth and more critically than at any other stage of your education. Becoming more effective in your note-taking skills can only enhance your learning and improve the final product – your coursework and exam work. So what are the key aspects of effective note taking? *Effective note taking involves making informative, brief, accurate, clear summaries of the information you are listening to, or reading about*. In order to develop effective note-taking skills you need to: *identify* what purpose the notes will serve, be *selective* in what you record, and use an *effective* method for recording the notes.

At college and university level it is generally expected that the student progresses from pure detail (e.g., recording and retrieving mechanical details of something, such as a theory), to showing knowledge (and detail) and understanding of the topic. The latter is achieved by posing questions about the phenomenon under consideration, looking at alternative ideas, assessing validity, and so on.

These skills develop over time, but are available to all students who are willing to spend some time trying to understand the material to which they are referred.

Identify the purpose of note taking

By identifying what purpose the notes will be used for, it is possible to identify what type of notes should be taken. If you are taking notes for an impending assignment (such as an essay or practical) then the notes need to: accurately depict the relevant theory and/or research related to the topic under study, provide a format that can be used to help structure the assignment, and provide good supporting references related to the topic. In addition, good critical/discussion points can also be added to these notes: How does the theory/research compare with other competing theory/research? Are there any flaws in terms of the evidence/arguments in the literature presented? Are there any logical extensions to the theory/research, etc.?

If the notes are for revision purposes, for say, an impending exam, then they should contain the main points related to that topic, should be structured, should be accurate and include supporting references. In addition, the notes should be in a form that can be easily understood by the student after some time has elapsed. Various techniques can then be used to enhance your learning of the information before the exam itself (see Chapter 7).

Being selective in your note taking

Being selective in what you record means that your notes focus on the main points of the lecture material (or seminar or revision material). On the one hand you do not want to end up with a verbatim account of what has been said during the session (indeed, this would be difficult to achieve), whereas on the other your notes should not be so patchy and omitting of detail that you find it difficult to make sense of them at revision time. As pointed out by Drew and Bingham (1997), it can help if you think about three categories of information when taking notes. *First*, you need to consider what main principles, concepts, theory(ies), and arguments are postulated in the literature. *Second*, you need to take sufficiently detailed notes of these components so that you can understand key principles/arguments/ theory afterwards, or can follow up important sources. *Third*, you can add your own questions to the notes – this will enable you to evaluate the material and be critical of that literature.

For example, if you were taking notes on Sigmund Freud's theory of the personality you would need to include in your notes:

1. What ideas/principles/concepts underpin the theory, and what the essential components and/or stages of the theory were.
2. What the main line of argument is with regards to Freud's theory, and what supporting evidence there is for the theory (including noting key texts and research).
3. What conclusions can be drawn from the literature presented, what contradictory evidence there is, and judge how accurate (and/or applicable to the real world) the theory appears to be.

As stated earlier, as a student progresses from their first through to their final year on a psychology course, better grades can be achieved by showing evidence of understanding underlying principles, concepts, arguments and being able to criticise the literature. Being selective in what you record as notes is critical to this process.

Recording your notes

How you choose to record the notes should be partly determined by how you intend to use them: What format should the notes take to fit the purpose? If you wish to remember the basic facts and main points of argument about a particular theory, then perhaps a brief sketch of these components in the form of a set of linear notes would be helpful. Linear note taking basically refers to where you break down lengthy sentences (either from a lecture or piece of written work) into a more manageable form. For example, the theory of working memory (see Example 3.1, in Chapter 3) could be broken down as follows:

- *Title of theory*: Working Memory.
- *Key references*: Baddeley and Hitch (1974), Baddeley (1986, 1997), Logie (1986, 1999), Parkin (1993), Smyth and Scholey (1994).
- *Components of model*: Central Executive – responsible for incoming information from a range of sensory modalities, redirecting that information to the other subslave systems, and maybe involved in control processes within the subslave systems; Articulatory Loop – responsible for storage and maintenance of auditory and verbal information (e.g., sounds and words), comprised of a phonological loop system (for passive storage of information) and active rehearsal processes; Visuo-spatial Sketch Pad – responsible for storage and maintenance of visual and spatial information (e.g., static images and movement), may have the ability to redraw images as a form of "visual rehearsal".

- *Effects associated with model*: Phonological similarity effect reflects passive storage in loop system; word length effect reflects active rehearsal in loop system; visual similarity effect reflects passive storage in sketchpad system; dynamic visual interference reflects active process in sketchpad system.
- *Validity of model*: Model explains effects outlined previously; much research in support of components of model; applications of model include, developmental applications, neuropsychology (e.g., amnesia), everyday tasks (e.g., playing games such as chess, finding your way around in the dark), and applied aspects (e.g., reading, and writing). Shortcomings of model.
- *Conclusions*: Model is robust, useful in applied terms, and provides a useful theory of short-term memory.

Such linear note taking is helpful because it contains clear headings, subheadings, and so on. The notes also contain the key words, phrases, references, and explanations needed to summarise the topic. They could have been improved by using simple techniques such as underlining, circling, boxes, or forming a distinct pattern to them (such as a visual diagram of how the notes interrelate, perhaps even using arrows to signify the interrelationships).

Getting the most from your lecturer

Note taking in class can be aided by asking your lecturer (before the class has started) to: explain the aims of the lecture, explain what information will be covered in class and in what order, indicate important aspects of the material, be willing to explain key areas that you do not understand, provide key reference sources in sufficient detail for them to be traced, and pace her/himself so that there is time for notes to be taken.

Taking notes within a lecture

Within a lecture, when you need to be attentive and think about what is being presented, elaborate note taking might not be possible. It may be more effective for you to take brief notes about the main information provided by the lecturer: for example, noting key terms, basic details, names of researchers, and critical points about the topic, then writing these notes up more fully after the lecture. By doing this you will allow yourself enough time in the actual lecture to think about the topic critically, as well as having the necessary information (in note form) so that you can elaborate upon these notes at a later date. It might be a good idea to elaborate upon the notes sooner rather than later after the lecture. In addition to this, you can also summarise related material using the procedures outlined in this chapter and adding these summaries to your notes. Rewriting and expanding upon lecture notes (and notes from other sessions, e.g., seminars, your own research) can be an effective way of consolidating the material.

Finally

Write notes in your own words and adapt the method to suit your own particular needs – what you feel most comfortable with. Review your notes periodically, updating, highlighting and expanding where necessary. Make sure you organise your notes effectively so that you can retrieve them easily when they are needed – perhaps place them in an A4 file under the course title, with headings, titles, and dates. Organising revision notes early (whether they be for coursework or examination preparation) can save you time later and help overcome the angst some people experience when deadlines are approaching.

Reference materials

When studying on a psychology course, a range of reference source material is encountered. The main types of material used as reference sources are books and published research papers. As the student progresses through the years on a course, particularly at under-graduate level, she/he will be expected to read and report on selected books and papers. These sources provide description and explanation of major theory and research in psychology, and can provide the impetus for further thinking and research in the area. The three most common forms are empirical reports, theoretical papers and literature reviews.

Empirical reports

These are reports on pieces of research that are either entirely original or have original components in them. Such reports are relatively concise, to the point and subsectioned into the areas outlined in Chapter 6 of this book on report writing. Empirical reports are very important in that they enable researchers to test the assumptions derived from a theory or model in psychology, compare method-ologies, and can ultimately extend our knowledge of psychological phenomena (see, as an example, Hitch et al., 1991).

Theoretical papers

Theoretical papers typically review the published literature on a particular psychological model or theory, and attempt to evaluate and advance our understanding of that theory. Typically the author of the paper begins by stating what theoretical problem is to be addressed, and will summarise the theoretical contributions made by various previous authors. The author might then go on to discuss any shortcomings of current theoretical thinking on the subject matter and may suggest how the theory might be changed or advanced – to account for discrepancies between the theory and current thinking or empirical research. For example, Jean Piaget's theory of cognitive development has undergone a number of changes over the years due to alternative theoretical thinking and empirical results that are inconsistent with his original thesis. It is now accepted, for example, that social context and cultural factors play important roles in cognitive development. For example, Doise's (1990) paper reviews evidence of how social factors can intervene in cognitive development in children.

Literature reviews

Literature review papers often focus on a particular psychological phenomenon and summarise what is known about that particular phenomenon. In such a paper, previously published research will be summarised and presented (usually) in chronological order. Comparisons of old and new evidence are made and the author will attempt to establish how new ideas have acted to change or extend our view of the topic under consideration. The paper may be sub-sectioned into discrete parts: for example, a review of literature up to a certain time, contemporary literature, current thinking; or laboratory studies, field studies, combined approaches. For example, the Freedman (1984) article reviews the available field and correlational research up to that period on the effects of viewing television violence upon subsequent aggressive behaviour in people.

To some extent books such as those used as reference sources on a psychology course can also be included in one of the previous categories. General textbooks provide a review of the main theories and research in psychology. For example, Smith et al. (2003) provides comprehensive coverage of all the major areas of study within psychology, with at least one chapter devoted to each of these areas. On the other hand, more advanced texts can review literature about a particular psychological phenomenon and theories and/or present empirical evidence that is used to evaluate the phenomenon. For example, Baddeley's excellent book *Working Memory* (1986) reviews the literature on memory, proposes a model of short-term memory, and evaluates this in light of historical and contemporary findings (up to that date).

Summarising a piece of work

Being able to summarise a piece of work (e.g., a journal article) can be the key to effective study and revision. Cuba (1993) breaks down the process of summarising a piece of work into a number of components. This is a useful process and forms the basis for the following list of details that should be included in a good review.

1. Begin the summary with sufficient bibliographic information – a formal reference of the work being summarised. This will allow you to clearly identify the source of the work and will be useful when compiling a reference section. For example:

   Freedman, J.L. (1984). Effects of television violence on aggressiveness. *Psychological Bulletin*, 96, 227–246.

2. The major hypothesis(es) or question(s) posed by the study: you need to be clear and specific about this. Record the formal hypothesis/question posed by the author and, if you wish, include your own interpretation.

3. What method of investigation was adopted. Identify whether the study was predominantly qualitative or quantitative. Note what mode of observation was used in the study, e.g., interviews, questionnaires, experimental manipulation (if so, what conditions were created in the experiment?), a field study, etc.

4. List the major variables or factors, with a brief description of each. Include here the dependent, independent and control variables (see Chapter 4 for more details).

5. The participant sample: define the sample in terms of age, sex, type of sample (e.g., random sample, chosen for a particular reason, stratified sample), other details which might be important (e.g., social status, job status, etc.).

6. The findings drawn from the study. List here the main results and significance levels. Provide statements about whether the

results support the hypothesis(es)/question(s) posed in the introductory section of the report. Be brief.

7. The conclusions reached by the author. Note what evaluations the author has made with regards to how the findings can be interpreted, what implications these might have for future studies and any shortcomings about the study.

8. Note your own comments on the report. You may wish to make comparisons between this and other reports you have read. Or perhaps you can think of your own criticisms or shortcomings about the report. For example, can one infer a cause and effect relationship between the independent and dependent variables? Use this space to make additional notes of your own. Questioning and evaluating pieces of work are essential components in the progression to the "deep processing" referred to earlier in the chapter.

You might organise your reviews in chronological order or in a topic-based order. For most essays and practical reports, one typically reads and reviews reports for a particular topic (e.g., memory).

Finally, remember to be somewhat selective in what you review, say, for an assignment. You do not have to feel the need to read an exhaustive amount of literature for a particular topic. Often, a good review of a topic can be worth several empirical articles on that topic. Effective note taking and the effective reviewing of materials referred to on a psychology course can be the key to performing well in course and examination work.

A guide to essay writing and referencing 3

This chapter describes the various stages in essay writing, progressing from carrying out a literature search on the topic, to planning the essay, and finally through to the stages of writing drafts of the essay, as well as referencing procedures. A coursework essay can be found in Example 3.1.

Essay writing is a skill that an undergraduate student needs throughout the whole of a psychology course. In fact, in most institutes of further and higher education essays can make up a large part of a student's coursework, so taking the time to get it right is time well spent. The composition of an essay can take any one of a number of forms, depending on what key phrase or phrases are contained in its title. Some key phrases likely to appear in essay titles are provided further on in the chapter. The size of essays on undergraduate courses varies, but usually the word length increases from about 1200 to 1500 words in the first year of a course to about 2000 to 2500 words in the second year, and up to around 3000 to 3500 words in the final year. An example of a good coursework essay can be found in Example 3.1, which follows the information provided here.

What follow, then, are guidelines on the main stages of essay writing and on writing style within an essay, and a guide to referencing in psychology. The guidelines on writing style were provided by, and reproduced here (with some modifications) with the permission of Neil McLaughlin Cook. The guidelines on referencing were provided by and reproduced here (with some modifications) with the permission of Sue Thomas and Keith Morgan. All three lecture at Liverpool Hope University College.

Stages in essay writing

A good essay, particularly one focusing on an academic subject, is rarely completed in one great sweep. General study skills advice suggests that the craft of essay writing needs to be learned over time, and that one good way of learning about the process is to break it down into clearly identifiable stages (see Northedge, 1997). The following are therefore brief notes on the stages involved in writing an essay.

Giving some thought to the title

This sounds obvious, but it is a fact that some students rush headlong into an essay without giving enough thought to what is required for that essay. The title can tell you what is required (see the major keywords included later in this chapter). One useful strategy might be to jot down, in one or two sentences, what you think the title means. For example, is it a request for a descriptive essay where you are required to provide a detailed account of the topic under consideration, or are you required to write an argumentative type of essay, where a particular point of view is stated and the writer attempts to defend (or disprove, if appropriate) that viewpoint by looking at the evidence on balance?

Keywords to look out for in essay titles

What follows are some keywords typically used by tutors when setting essay questions, and what these terms mean.

Account for	Reason why something is as it appears
Analyse	Examine (in detail) the components of something
Assess	Estimate what value can be attached to something (this definition can also be used for the term *Evaluate*)
Comment	Make remarks/explanatory notes on something
Compare	Estimate the similarity of one thing to another
Contrast	Estimate the differences between two or more things
Consider	Weigh up the merits of something (or *Deliberate*)
Define	Provide some meaning of
Describe	Provide details of something
Discuss	Examine by argument
Distinguish	Differentiate between two or more things
Evaluate	Judge the importance of in the light of criteria
Examine	Investigate the phenomenon in detail
Explain	Clarify some phenomenon(a)
Illustrate	Provide detailed analysis to make a point clear
Interpret	Explain the meaning of something
Justify	Provide support for an argument or action

Outline	Detail the most essential aspect(s) of something
Relate	Make some connection between things
Summarise	Provide an account of the main points

Further reading: For further consideration on the differences between descriptive and argumentative essays, see Smith and Smith (1990).

Literature searching

Before attempting to write the essay, you must first gather together the relevant information and organise it in some way. Fortunately, most tutors will provide some supporting references when setting essay questions (or may provide starter references), so you need to access these sources. In addition, you could carry out a computer search in the library using specific keywords that are in the essay title. If you do carry out a computer search, make sure you have combinations of keywords to hand, so that you can be more specific in the search process (otherwise you might end up with hundreds of citations from the computer!).

If you already have notes from relevant lectures, organise these by perhaps rewriting the relevant parts of the lecture notes in relation to the specific topic covered in the essay title. For example, if your essay title was: "Discuss how effective behavioural therapy is as a treatment or intervention for anxiety disorders", then you need to look through your lecture notes for Abnormal Psychology and pick out those most relevant to the essay topic. Make additional notes from the extra sources you have accessed and add these to the extracted lecture notes. Finally, add to these any relevant supporting references (e.g., Seligman, 1992; Sue, et al., 2002) and organise under subheadings (for example, definition of phenomena; supporting evidence; counter arguments). Carrying out a fairly thorough literature search is a very important part of preparation for essay writing and should not be done superficially. Some more time is spent here on searching the literature.

Searching and evaluating the literature available on a particular phenomenon provides the best source of ideas that can guide a research project. It also enables the researcher to discover what research others have carried out in the area and what they have found. Ultimately, the scientific approach is about testing some formal hypothesis (or set of hypotheses). What is a hypothesis? The term *hypothesis* refers to an operational definition about the exact comparison that makes up the aim of the study (Bausell, 1986). An *operational definition* is the definition of some variable or psychological construct (phenomenon) in terms of the procedures employed to measure that variable or construct. In this sense it enables the reader to focus on exactly what the study is about – which is to provide some answer to a research question or to test a particular prediction. All research, regardless of whether it is "quantitative" or "qualitative", should be guided by some overall hypothesis(es) or research question(s) that needs to be addressed. Before reaching the stage of hypothesis formation, or the development of overall research questions, the researcher must first come up with a source for the idea. Research is not developed in a vacuum.

The source can be some common-sense notion of what one expects to happen – what we believe to be true or false. Relying on pure common-sense notions to guide research can be problematic; they could be wrong. An idea could come from our observations of the world around us. Observations of personal experiences and social events can provide a hypothesis that merits testing (Cozby, 1989). However, on a degree course it is likely that you will be expected to consult a formal body of literature (books and published articles) based on established theory and research. Established theory and research can be used to generate ideas for further research and as a basis for a particular research project. Theories can provide the impetus for research. *A theory is a formal set of statements that summarise and explain a particular phenomenon* – for example, a theory of memory. A theory can act as a guide to how we can make sense of what we observe in our world and can generate new knowledge about real-world phenomena. Theory can also be modified by what is discovered through research.

A formal literature search can begin with the references provided on course – that is, by the course tutor for a particular topic (e.g., a course reference list on, say, abnormal psychology). Good reference sources in the form of books provide useful lists of relevant primary and secondary source material in their reference sections. As a student progresses through the psychology course, she or he should become less dependent on a standard set of references provided by the tutor and more familiar with library searching. This is particularly true for the final-year dissertation/research project. Library searches can provide a wealth of critical information with regard to what research has already been carried out in the area of interest and can come in a number of forms. Some of the major sources of library searching are outlined below.

Psychologists report their work in three ways. First, research findings can be presented at one of the many conferences organised periodically. Conferences can be general, such as the BPS Annual Conference, or specialist, such as the Clinical Psychology Conference. Conferences can be a useful source for accessing current research, but can be costly and time consuming. A second way of communicating research findings is via the use of books. These may be general text-books, say on social psychology, or specialist texts, say on working memory. Third, psychologists can communicate their current research findings via the use of journals. Journals provide the most up-to-date source of literature, so some time is spent on considering these next.

Journals

Journals are collections of work, both theoretical and research-based, that are published at regular intervals (e.g., on a monthly basis or quarterly basis). These are sometimes referred to as periodicals. In these journals, theorists expound their latest views on some phenomenon (for example, a theory of personality) and researchers will publish their latest findings. The majority of these journals are "peer reviewed", which means they have been scrutinised by other researchers in the field and judged worthy of publication for the wider research population. These journals are usually listed in a library catalogue under specific headings, depending on the nature of the articles they contain. Each library will have a limited stock of psychology journals, but articles from journals not held by your own library may be ordered through an inter-library loan system. It should be noted that the eligibility of students to use this system may differ between institutes, and first-year students are not normally eligible for free inter-library loans. A number of journals may now be accessed through the Internet. The department of psychology or campus library should be able to offer advice and guidance on how to access these journals. The major listings include the following.

General psychology. Subsumed under this area are journals that include literature reviews, theory, and other general topics within psychology. See, for example: *American Psychologist, British Journal of Psychology, European Journal of Psychology, International Journal of Psychology, Journal of General Psychology, Journal of Psychology, Psychological Bulletin* and *Psychological Review*.

Behavioural psychology. These journals contain articles pertaining to behavioural approaches to psychology, and also include interdisciplinary research that links behavioural psychology with other areas of psychology (e.g., the biological bases of behaviour, clinical conditions). See, for example: *Behavioural Neuroscience, Behavioural Science, Behaviour Therapy, The Behavioural and Brain Sciences.*

Cognitive psychology. Subsumed under this heading are journals that contain articles on a range of topics related to cognitive psychology. These include: cognition, cognitive development, experimental investigations into cognition, perception, attention, memory, thought, reading and language. See, for example: *Cognitive Psychology, Cognitive Therapy and Research, Journal of Memory and Language* and *Journal of Reading.*

Clinical and counselling psychology. These journals contain articles pertaining to clinical and counselling psychology (e.g., mood disorders, schizophrenia, anxiety neurosis, addiction, behaviour therapy, counselling theory and application, and so on). See, for example: *Journal of Abnormal Psychology, Journal of Counselling Psychology, British Journal of Psychiatry, Journal of Clinical Psychology* and *Journal of Consulting and Clinical Psychology.*

Developmental psychology. Subsumed under this heading are journals that contain articles on a range of developmental issues. These include: child development, experimental investigations into child psychology, infant behaviour and cognition, gerontology, applied areas of developmental psychology, and so on. See, for example: *British Journal of Developmental Psychology, Child Development, Developmental Psychology, Developmental Review, Journal of Experimental Child Psychology, Human Development* and *The Gerontologist.*

Experimental journals in psychology. These journals contain experimental articles on a range of psychological phenomena (e.g., memory and cognition, perception, animal and human behaviour, genetics, learning and motivation, cognitive science, psychophysics, neuroscience, and so on). See, for example: *American Journal of Psychology, Journal of Experimental Psychology* (including the subdivisions of General, Human Learning and Memory, Perception and Performance, and Animal Behaviour Processes), *Memory and Cognition, Journal of Verbal Learning and Verbal Behaviour, Cognition, Perception* and the *Quarterly Journal of Experimental Psychology* (Parts A and B).

Personality and social psychology. These journals contain articles on research into personality and social psychological phenomena as separate topics, but also combinations of the two, as well as applied research in these fields. See, for example: *European Journal of Social Psychology, Journal of Applied Social Psychology, Journal of Experimental Social Psychology, Journal of Personality, Journal of Personality and Social Psychology,* and the *Personality and Social Psychology Bulletin.*

Applied psychology research. These journals contain articles on a range of applied areas of psychology, such as educational psychology, applied behaviour analysis, applied cognitive psychology, occupational psychology, environmental psychology, criminological psychology, and so on. See, for example: *Applied Psychological Measurement, Journal of Applied Behaviour Analysis, Journal of Applied Behavioural Science, Journal of Applied Developmental Psychology, Journal of Applied Psychology, Journal of Educational Psychology, Occupational Psychology* and *Psychology in the Schools.*

Further reading: See Cozby (1989) for further listings of journals in these areas.

Searching the Internet

The Internet represents a vast collection of computer networks linking every part of the world. It contains a hive of information on almost everything, including facts, statistics, documents, articles, lists, discussions, video and sound tracks. This information can be accessed via the various Internet sites (websites) – the trick is to find those sites relevant to your needs. The degree of organisation and how user-friendly these sites are will vary enormously. Some sites can be accessed free of charge, whereas others will impose a cost for access. Use your course information and campus library to access those sites that are essential for searching current literature in psychology. The Internet sites most relevant will include: your own university website, online journals, computer-based literature searches (e.g., BIDS), the BPS website, and websites for any specialist groups or organisations related to psychology.

It should be noted that in the first year of a degree course a student is not expected to have a full grasp of literature-searching techniques, but will be expected to learn more and more about such techniques as they progress through their course with the help of their tutors.

Web of Science – accessed via Web of Knowledge (WOK)

The Web of Knowledge for UK education is a new platform by which users can obtain multidisciplinary and subject specialised knowledge.

The Web of Science can be accessed via the Web of Knowledge and allows you access to the *Science Citation Index*, which contains cited references and author abstracts from 1981 onwards, and the *Social Sciences Citation Index Expanded*, which contains cited references and author abstracts from the social sciences, again from 1981 onwards (web address: http://wok.mimas.ac.uk/).

Social Science Citation Index (SSCI)

The Social Science Citation Index (SSCI) is a comprehensive index of researchers who have cited other researchers in their work. The index is organised by author (e.g., Heffernan, T.M.) and also by the subject cited (e.g., Working Memory). When looking up the author or subject you will find a list of persons who have made the particular citation in their work. This index is updated annually and should be available from the university library. The SSCI is also available via a CD-ROM computer-based system. This source is now available via the Internet and can be accessed via the WOK.

Bath ISI Data Service (BIDS)

The Bath ISI Data Service (BIDS) provides access to three citation indexes which are multidisciplinary (social science, science, arts and humanities), and is widely used by psychologists. This service allows access in excess of 7000 journals worldwide. BIDS allows you a range of search options, such as author, journal, date, or typing in key-words. Typing in keywords is a common method of searching. One should bear in mind that a general term(s) (e.g., memory) may attract several hundred if not thousands of sources or "hits", so refining your key term(s) (e.g., rehearsal and memory) can reduce the number of hits significantly. Students on a psychology degree are encouraged to use this search procedure by the time they complete their second year, and are expected to use such a search (or an equivalent search procedure) in their final year, for example, for their final-year project. This source is now available via the Internet (web address: http://www.bids.ac.uk).

Psychological Abstracts

Psychological Abstracts is a source that lists the abstracts from the major psychology journals in a non-evaluative way (i.e., without judging the content of the article). This can prove to be a very fruitful way of searching a large literature source, but provides you with only a summary of the piece of literature in the form of an abstract, and its source.

This source is available on computer format, via a CD-ROM reader, and is referred to generally as *PsycLit*. PsycLit is accessible in most university libraries, where a librarian should be able to advise you how to operate this system.

PsychINFO is another information retrieval service, offering computerised assistance in search of the *Psychological Abstracts*, and was developed by the American Psychological Association. PsycLit and PsychINFO will be updated periodically. These sources are now available via the Internet, for example, PsychINFO can be accessed via BIDS.

Scirus

Scirus is relatively new and provides one of the most comprehensive science-specific search engines on the Internet. Like other search engines, you are required to type in key terms or authors names. Scirus searches more than 150 million science-related pages to provide you with quick access to relevant information from a number of sources. It pinpoints scientific, technical and medical data on the web, finds the latest reports and peer-reviewed articles and journal sources, and locates university sites and scientists' home pages that some other search engines miss. You can identify which sources you wish to access, e.g. journal articles, and/or other web sources. When I have failed to find information on a particular subject from other search engines, I have found that Scirus almost always comes up with something (web address: http://www.scirus.com/).

Further reading: For further reading on searching the literature, see e.g., Barnes (1995), Breakwell, Hammond, and Fife-Shaw (2001), Cozby (1989), Elmes et al. (1995), Marshall and Rowland (1998), and Saunders (1994).

Devising an essay plan

Once you have thought about the title and organised your notes you might decide to draw up a plan of the essay. This will entail your putting down on paper a series of ideas, suggesting how the essay will flow from the introduction, on to the main body of the essay, and through to the conclusion stage. Be prepared to change these ideas or scrap what you have written and start again (e.g., if, on a second look at the plan, you feel it is not the best way to organise the information). However, research has found that using an essay plan, or even several essay plans, does not lead to higher marks for the essay itself (Norton, 1990). Having said this, an essay plan can be of some use in providing a structure around which to organise the essay.

Example of an essay plan. The following simple essay plan could be used to organise an essay on "Discuss how effective behavioural therapy is as a treatment for anxiety disorders".

1. *Introduction*: Definitions of keywords; explaining what is meant by the question set (if appropriate); briefly suggest how the essay will attempt to address the question/topic.
2. *Main body of essay*: Definition of "clinical" anxiety; examples of anxiety disorders; what types of treatment are available; relevant theory underpinning treatment(s); the efficacy of the treatment(s); supporting references; criticisms/limitations of treatment(s).
3. *Concluding section*: Overall conclusion(s); overall comments which directly address essay question/topic in the light of previous literature cited.
4. *Reference section*: Citation of primary and secondary sources (see final section of this chapter for further details on referencing).

Writing a first draft of the essay

Once you reach this stage in the process you are just about ready to begin writing the essay itself. The first draft does not have to be one great sweep from introduction to conclusion(s), it can develop in parts. You might write part of the introduction section on one page, move on to describing the concepts under study on another page, and so on. This stage is aimed at getting down on paper, in a basic essay form, the information you have collected in note form. You should write the draft in a fluent and convincing manner, as if you were trying to persuade the reader that your views are the most valid. Once you have begun writing, try to carry on and finish the draft. Stopping and pondering over every few sentences will throw you off track and interrupt the flow of ideas you should be experiencing (you will still refer to your notes for supporting theory and research). You need to give your full attention to this draft, as though you were thinking through a talk you were giving to an attentive audience.

Correcting the first draft

Once you have written the first draft, you should read through the essay, analyse its structure and content, and make the necessary changes.

You should check that the essay:

- has a coherent structure
- flows from one part to the next: Are there link sentences between paragraphs? Does one paragraph follow logically from the previous paragraph?
- has enough support for your arguments (i.e., references)
- has enough up-to-date literature (as well as historical literature)
- shows evaluation of relevant theory/research
- has fully addressed what was set out in the title (e.g., have you answered the question posed in the title?)
- has reached some conclusion(s) about the topic
- incorporates a complete reference section.

Please note: It is reasonable to say that failing to address the topic/answer question set in the title of the essay is one of the most common causes of receiving a poor mark (this applies to exams also).

Final modifications

When you finally reach this stage, what may be needed is no more than a rewrite of the essay, incorporating the changes proposed at the previous stage. If you can, try to get some independent source to provide critical feedback, such as another student. You can always reciprocate by reading a draft of her or his essay. If you do seek another student's feedback on your work, be sure that you don't become the victim of plagiarism (where one person presents another person's work as their own). Do not spend any more time on this than you must. If you feel you have done the job properly, submit it and move on to the next task.

Example 3.1: A completed coursework essay

Here is a completed example (the final draft) of a first-year essay (coursework, as opposed to examination) which is 1500 words in length and would be expected to achieve a mark in the high 60s to low 70s assessment range. Please note that a second-year essay, and particularly a third-year essay, would be significantly longer (approximately 2000 to 2500 words in the second year, and approximately 3000 to 3500 words in the third year), would contain more primary source material (e.g., journal articles), particularly up-to-date articles, would cover research in depth and evaluate that research, and be more discussion based. The precise nature of the essay will depend on the essay question/title.

Subject area:	Abnormal Psychology
Year:	First year
Word length:	1500 words
Title of essay:	Define what is meant by the term "anxiety disorders" and evaluate behavioural treatments for such disorders.

This essay will begin by defining anxiety disorders, before going on to outline and evaluate the major aspects of behavioural therapy. The essay will assess how effective behavioural therapy has been as a form of treatment for anxiety disorders.

The *Diagnostic and Statistical Manual of Mental Disorders* (4th ed. Revised, APA, 2000) defines anxiety disorders as a group of disorders in which anxiety and avoidance are the main symptoms. These disorders include: Phobic disorders, Panic Disorder, Generalised Anxiety Disorder, Obsessive-Compulsive Disorder, and Post-traumatic-stress Disorder (Davison, Neale, & Kring, 2003). As an example, phobic disorders are considered here in greater detail.

A phobic disorder is defined as "a disrupting, fear-mediated avoidance, out of proportion to the danger posed by a particular object or situation and is recognised by the sufferer as groundless" (Davison et al., 2003). An example of a phobia is an animal phobia. These phobias are highly focused (i.e., on a particular animal), are thought to begin in early childhood, and make up about 10–20% of all phobias (APA, 2000). People who suffer from animal phobias are often able to recall what specific event led to the phobia, but some people cannot recall any potential "trigger" (Marks, 1969). Inanimate object phobias include an extreme fear of things such as heights, closed spaces, dirt, thunderstorms, etc. The triggering stimulus for inanimate object phobias can be the experience of a traumatic event (Laughlin, 1967; Sue, Sue, & Sue, 2002). The phobic symptoms are typically focused around one specific object or event, but can become generalised to other, similar, objects or events (Gleitman, Fridlund, & Reisberg, 2003). Individuals who suffer from these types of phobias are otherwise psychologically sound (i.e., they don't suffer from any mental illness). The symptoms experienced by a phobic person include: physiological symptoms (as outlined previously);

psychological symptoms (e.g., a feeling of loss of control; a strong desire to escape from the situation, etc.), and behavioural symptoms, e.g., avoidance of the object/animal/situation (see, e.g., Mischel, 1999).

Fear and avoidance are the major symptoms with phobias. These symptoms can be in relation to actual objects or animals (e.g., a spider); environmental (e.g., lightning, earthquakes); blood, injection, or injury; situational (e.g., travelling in a car/train/aeroplane, heights, etc.); or some other type. The most common types include the fear of small animals, heights, being in the dark, and lightning (see, e.g., Agras, Sylvester, & Oliveau, 1969; Sue et al., 2002). Theories of how phobias emerge vary, and include psychological models (such as the psychoanalytic perspective; behavioural ideas) as well as biological approaches (see, e.g., Davison et al., 2003; Mischel, 1999; Seligman, 1992; Seligman, Walker & Rosenhan 2001; Smith, Nolen-Hoeksema, Fredrickson, & Loftus, 2003).

So what kinds of behavioural treatments are there? And how effective are these? The following paragraphs outline three such treatments and evaluates them.

Behavioural therapy is based on the idea that the irrational fear and maladaptive behaviour accompanying this (e.g., avoidance) is caused by environmental factors. These factors can trigger the onset of the phobia (i.e., cause the phobia) and reinforce the phobia (i.e., maintain the phobia). Three types of behavioural treatment are considered here: "systematic desensitisation", "flooding", and "modelling". These three approaches to treatment have the same overall goal: to change or modify the maladaptive behaviour to make it adaptive and therefore reduce the levels of fear in the individual (Mischel, 1999, Pt. V).

Systematic desensitisation is the most commonly used behavioural therapy (see Wolpe, 1973). In this approach the patient is asked to formulate a "fear hierarchy", which is comprised of the most feared situation, to the least feared situation. Once a hierarchy is formed the patient and therapist can work through it from least feared to most feared scenario. The patient is taught to use relaxation methods beforehand (e.g., the patient sits with their eyes closed, relaxes muscles, etc.). When fully trained in its use, relaxation can be brought about almost automatically by the patient. The basic assumption is that as the patient works through the hierarchy of fears, the relaxation training will counteract the feelings associated with the extreme fear, and that once each stage is conquered the next can be overcome in a similar way. This approach to treatment can take several weeks or months before the final, most fearful stage in the hierarchy is reached, but is very successful (Sue et al., 2002).

Some of the advantages of this type of intervention are that it works quite quickly in reducing the fear and is inexpensive to carry out (Carver & Scheier, 2004). Patients undergoing this therapy can find it a frightening experience and some patients may therefore drop out of therapy.

Flooding is where the patient confronts the feared stimulus by either imagining it or being in its actual presence (e.g., confront the spider that induces the fear), but the exposure would be persistent so that the patient cannot avoid the fearful stimulus. For example, a spider phobic (a person afraid of spiders) would be put in an enclosed space with the spider for several minutes or even hours. The principle here is that when the patient is forced to face their fear, that fear will subside and the person will return to normal. Again, relaxation training can be given to alleviate some of the physical symptoms associated with the phobia. This form of treatment requires great courage on the part of the patient and is not always best suited to some patients (e.g., if the patient has a heart condition). Flooding, like systematic desensitisation, has a high success rate (see Marks, 1969; Serling, 1986). It is clear that one drawback of this approach is the potential for causing extreme fear in the patient who is exposed "all at once" to the fearful stimulus. One must be careful when selecting which patients are best suited for this technique, e.g., their health status should be checked (Sue et al., 2002).

Finally, modelling can also be used as a form of behaviour therapy. Modelling involves the copying of behaviour from another person (the "model"). Thus, the phobic will watch another person (who is non-phobic) as they confront the fearful stimulus without reacting in a mal-adaptive way. For example, someone who has a spider phobia might watch the therapist as she/he interacts with a spider stimulus – perhaps allowing a live spider to crawl on the therapist's hand without appearing alarmed. The idea behind this is that the patient will see either that the spider (or whatever the fearful stimulus is) is not harmful, or can be tolerated, and will then go on to mimic the behaviour themselves. Again, this procedure requires great courage on the part of the phobic person and a good rapport between therapist and patient, since the patient must place her/his trust in the therapist. Overall, this form of therapy appears as effective as the previous two (see, e.g., Bandura, Adams, & Beyer, 1977; Rachman, 1976; Sue et al., 2002). Once these modelling techniques are learned, the patient can practise these adaptive behaviours on their own without the need for the therapist to be there. This approach is useful because many researchers believe that anxiety disorders (like phobias) are the product of learning and the product of association of some sort (see, e.g., Mischel, 1999).

The common principle underlying all three therapies outlined here is the process of extinction. In all three treatments the phobic person is exposed to the feared stimulus, and this exposure is repeated and enduring. Extinction can take place because the patient is taught to relax in the presence of the fearful stimulus, and therefore reduce and extinguish the symptoms associated with phobias (see, e.g., Mischel, 1999; Sue et al., 2002).

Although they are effective, behavioural treatments have their drawbacks and limitations. First, they are best used in combination with other forms of therapy (e.g., relaxation therapy or drug treatment). Second, it is clear that cognition plays a role in phobias – just the mere thought of a fearful object/situation can bring on a fearful response. So learning is not the only way a person develops a fearful response. Third, phobias on the whole appear to be selective in their development – they are focused on certain things (like those outlined earlier in the essay). This goes against the learning principle because virtually anything you come into a negative contact with should have equal chance of developing into a phobia (e.g., knife phobias are rare even though knives are often the cause of injury). See Davison et al. (2003) and Sue et al. (2002) for more consideration of the advantages and limitations of using behavioural methods.

Finally, there is a large body of support for the view that behavioural methods might be effective at dealing with the symptoms of the disorder (i.e., the behavioural manifestations), but may not actually get to the underlying cause, which many believe lies in deep-rooted problems during a child's development. One example of this would be the psychodynamic approach to anxiety and fear (see, e.g., Gleitman et al., 2003, chap. 18).

So, on the whole, behavioural methods do appear to be effective at treating anxiety disorders, but they do have their limitations – not least of which is their being based on the assumption that all things are learned via the environment. I believe this problem is reflected in the fact that behavioural techniques are not entirely successful (they don't work 100% of the time), so other factors must play a role. Clearly, some disorders may have biological, cognitive, social, or some type of psychodynamic roots that cannot be ignored, which is why therapists tend to use a combined approach.

References

Agras, S., Sylvester, D., & Oliveau, D. (1969). The epidemology of common fears and phobias. *Comprehensive Psychiatry, 10,* 151–156.

American Psychiatric Association. (2000). *Diagnostic and statistical manual for mental disorders* (DSM-IVR; 4th ed. Revised). Washington, DC: Author.

Bandura, A., Adams, N.E., & Beyer, J. (1977). Cognitive processes mediating behavioural change. *Journal of Personality and Social Psychology, 35,* 125–139.

Carver, C.S., & Scheier, M. (2004). *Perspectives on personality* (5th ed.). Boston: Allyn & Bacon.

Davison, G.C., Neale, J.M., & Kring, A. (2003). *Abnormal psychology* (9th ed.). New York: Wiley.

Gleitman, H., Fridlund, A.J., & Reisberg, D. (2003). *Psychology* (6th ed.). New York: W.W. Norton.

Laughlin, H.P. (1967). *The neuroses.* Washington, DC: Butterworth.

Marks, I.M. (1969). *Fears and phobias.* New York: Academic Press.

Mischel, W. (1999). *Introduction to personality* (6th ed.). Orlando, FL: Harcourt Brace.

Rachman, S.J. (1976). Therapeutic modelling. In M. Felman & A. Broadhurst (Eds.), *Theoretical and experimental bases of behaviour therapy.* Chichester, UK: Wiley.

Seligman, M.E.P. (1992). *Helplessness on development of depression and death.* New York: Freeman.

Seligman, M.E.P., Walker, E., & Rosenhan, D. (2001). *Abnormal psychology* (4th ed.). New York: Norton.

Serling, R.J. (1986). Curing a fear of flying. *USAIR,* 12–19.

Smith, E.E., Nolen-Hoeksema, S., Fredrickson, B., & Loftus, G.R. (2003). *Atkinson & Hilgards' Introduction to psychology* (14th ed.). New York: Wadsworth.

Sue, D., Sue, D., & Sue, S. (2002). *Understanding abnormal behaviour* (7th ed.). New York: Houghton Mifflin.

Wolpe, J. (1973). *The practice of behaviour therapy* (3rd ed.). Elmsford, NY: Pergamon Press.

Critical evaluation

This essay represents a very good essay of a high upper-second class to a low first-class piece of work for a first-year coursework essay. There are a number of strengths and weaknesses in the essay that, taken in combination, affect precisely what mark such as essay might achieve.

Strengths

- It has an opening paragraph stating the structure and, for the most part, it follows this structure.
- It addresses the topics well, focusing on the two key points raised in the title of the essay.
- It is well supported in terms of references (classic and current).

- There is a flow to the essay: from definition, to examples of phobias, to evaluation of treatments, to conclusions.
- It shows critical consideration of the area in key places.
- It answers the essay question set in the essay title.
- It has a very good reference section, clear and complete.
- It ends with some fairly good conclusions and shows evidence of independent thinking in parts.

Weaknesses

- The essay adheres to a fairly standard approach to the topic/argument.
- More up-to-date primary source material could be offered (i.e., journal articles). *This is particularly important when students reach the second and final years of their course.*
- More evidence is needed of reading around the topic (i.e., include references from outside main lecture references). Most of the primary sources cited in the essay could have been derived from references provided in a few key texts on the topic. *This is particularly important when entering the second year, and is crucial in the third year of the course – where you are expected to show signs of independent literature searching.*
- The overall conclusions reached could have been strengthened.

> *Please note*: **By improving on the weaknesses described, the final mark/grade could have been improved significantly.**

Important points about coursework essays

Norton's (1990) research on the relationship between strategies used by students to write essays and tutors' strategies for marking has produced some findings relevant to this section. In addition to her finding that essay plans do not lead to higher marks, she also found that those essays providing relevant support in the form of citations of theory and research (which, in the first year of a degree, are often derived from books) produced higher marks. Whilst the majority of students thought that providing good content and structure were the main things to aim for in an essay, rather than putting forward an argument based on the literature addressed, tutors' marks indicated that it was those essays that produced an argument on the basis of research evidence (which can be derived from secondary sources, i.e., books) that achieved high marks. Structure and content do feature in marking, but not nearly as highly as argument, critical analysis, and so on. Norton concludes, amongst other things, that students should:

1. Be clear about what the tutor who is marking the script is looking for in the essay.
2. Concentrate on presenting their essay in the form of an argument, rather than relying on factual or descriptive accounts.
3. Support their arguments with research-based literature.
4. Spend several hours (six or more) preparing and writing the essay.
5. Discuss their mark with the tutor in order to gain feedback.

By developing these strategies further, the student can improve her or his essay writing skills enormously, and should, of course, achieve better marks.

A guide to writing style

Neil McLaughlin Cook

Several stylistic conventions apply to academic writing in Psychology. This guide outlines four such conventions, which you should try to follow in your essays. It concludes with a warning about the consequences of substantially deviating from two of them!

1. Using appropriate terminology

When writing essays, you are expected to choose your words carefully, and you should try to avoid phrases that are *imprecise*, *ambiguous*, or imply *irrelevant value judgements*.

- An example of an *imprecise phrase* commonly found in students' essays is: "Psychologists argue that . . .". A more appropriate phrase might have been: "Several psychologists (e.g., Bryant & Bradley, 1985; Cashdan & Wright, 1990) argue that . . .". Similarly, your tutor will expect you to use precise technical terms (such as "mean", "median", or "mode") instead of relying on more general terms used by the person in the street (such as "average").
- An example of an *ambiguous phrase* is "man's achievements", where "man" is intended to refer to human beings of both sexes,

but might be interpreted as referring to males only. A better essay would use a less ambiguous phrase like "human achievements".

- An example of a phrase that implies an *irrelevant value judgement* is "man and wife". A better essay would use parallel terms such as "husband and wife", or "wife and husband".

Note that two of the problems shown here were eliminated by using non-sexist language. The British Psychological Society (1990) has published a very helpful set of guidelines for using non-sexist language, which also considers how to avoid ethnically biased language. This document is well worth consulting and contains much practical advice that will help you to ensure that your writing meets the three criteria outlined here.

2. Infrequent use of the first person

New students often use the first person ("I" or "we") in their essays. However, this is rarely appropriate in formal academic writing in psychology, and you should seek to adopt a more impersonal style. (An exception to the "avoid the first person" rule might be when discussing your own personal experiences. Note, though, that arguments in psychology essays should normally be based on published theories and research, with personal experience being used at the most as supplementary information.)

Shown next are two reasons why students use the first person, together with an indication of alternative ways of achieving the same goals.

Signalling

One reason for using the first person is to signal the structure of an essay (e.g., "We will now discuss Freud's theory of personality"). Certainly, there is evidence that including signals in the text can be a sensible strategy. For example, Spyridakis and Standal (1987) have shown that signals can have a positive effect on reading comprehension, and so it is reasonable to infer that they might help a tutor to understand your essays! However, it is possible to incorporate signals into an essay without using intrusive phrases like "We will now discuss . . .". For example, here are some phrases that signal a move to another section of an essay:

Another important theory of personality was developed by Freud . . .

> Therefore, laboratory experiments imply a negative answer to the question. However, a different picture has emerged from the results of field studies . . .

Indicating that an idea is your own

A second common reason for using the first person is to indicate that an idea is the student's own (e.g., "I think Blogg's experiment is invalid because . . ."). Certainly, tutors' marking criteria often imply that it can be fruitful to include your own ideas in an essay. For example, at Liverpool Hope the criteria for first-class honours include "clear evidence of originality". Fortunately, originality can be indicated without using the first person in academic writing. You are expected to cite your source for all the ideas you include in your essay, so your tutor will assume that any idea for which no source is cited is your own! Therefore, although the first extract following implies that an argument has been obtained from a student's reading, the second implies that the argument is the student's own:

> McKay (1996) argues that these findings are ambiguous because . . .

> These findings are ambiguous because . . .

3. Expressing ideas in your own words

When marking your essays, your tutor will want to know if you understand the material you are writing about. Indeed, Norton (1990) found that "understanding" was judged by tutors to be one of the most important criteria they used when marking essays. One good way to demonstrate understanding is to *express ideas in your own words*. If instead you write an essay that consists merely of extracts copied or paraphrased from books, you are giving your tutor no information about whether you understand the material. For example, take the sentence: "Wherever Gestalts intervene, they do not do so as autochthonous factors, but as assimilatory schemata" (adapted from Piaget & Inhelder, 1973, pp. 402–403). It is an easy matter to copy the sentence, or paraphrase it to "Wherever Gestalts intervene, they do so as assimilatory schemata, not as autochthonous factors", without trying to understand any of the technical terms. Therefore, you should try to write your essays, as far as you can, in your own words. (If you feel that you do have to include an extract from a published source, then also include an accompanying comment to demonstrate that you have a good understanding of it! For example, one explanation of the quote might read: When subjects perceive an unusual figure as having characteristics of a regular shape, this is not the result of an innate tendency to perceive stimuli that have regular features, but instead the subject's use of previously encountered shapes as a framework to guide their perception of new figures.)

When asked to write essays in their own words, students sometimes raise the following objections.

Textbooks express ideas so much better than I can

This may be true (but do not underestimate your own writing abilities). However, your tutor wants to assess *your* work, not Glassman's (1995) work. Nevertheless, you may occasionally feel that the force of the author's point would be lost unless the point was quoted verbatim. In this case, you should cite the full source of the quote, including page number(s), as follows:

> Watson (1980) argued that the experiments outranked most others "when it comes to cruelty, deception, ingenuity and sheer absurdity" (p. 23).

I don't deliberately keep to the wording in a text; I base my essays on my notes, and forget which notes were copied verbatim

This reveals a need to improve your skills in note taking from texts. Try making notes mainly in your own words rather than in complete sentences; where your notes do follow the same wording as a text, try writing your essay in different words, rather than merely copying your notes.

4. Organising ideas in your own way

It can be tempting to let your essay follow the ready-made structure in a book. However, simply to copy someone else's structure gives no indication that you have understood what you have to do, and will probably result in a structure which does not meet the demands of the question set. The only way to show your tutor that you understand the demands of the question is to organise the material yourself. Such a strategy may well reap rewards in terms of marks, because Norton (1990) found that "answering the question" was judged by tutors to be the single most important criterion when marking an essay!

What happens if a student's essay does keep closely to the wording and structure of the student's sources?

Nobody will bother about the odd phrase being the same as a phrase in a book. However, if a large part of the essay appears to stick too closely to your sources, your tutor will notice it and take action. If the material taken from your sources is properly acknowledged as such, your tutor might simply comment that it would be preferable to rely more heavily on your own words.

However, if a large proportion of your essay consists of copied or paraphrased extracts from sources you do not properly acknowledge, this will be regarded as *plagiarism*, which means presenting other people's work as your own. Plagiarism derives from the Latin word *plagiarius*, which translated into English more or less means "kidnapper", a form of literary theft, stealing another person's work. This can be done deliberately or inadvertently. Plagiarism could involve copying material from other students' essays as well as copying material from books, or even from material on the Internet. In all universities it is treated very seriously, no matter what source the material has been taken from. The detailed procedures for dealing with plagiarism will vary across institutions, and the penalty imposed in any individual case would depend on the extent of the plagiarism and the circumstances involved. Typically though, the penalties available to the examiners might range from a reduction in the marks awarded for an essay to a recommendation that the student not be allowed to graduate. The simple rule in relation to plagiarism is: Don't do it!

A guide to referencing

Sue Thomas and Keith Morgan

The term referencing means the citation of information sources referred to by the essayist (or experimental researcher). Referencing is a method of providing your reader with the evidence and/or sources that you have used to support your arguments or statements, etc., in a piece of written work. Referencing enables the reader to find the original evidence so they can check your interpretation or read further. Referencing falls into two parts:

1. *Citing* the source in the text.
2. Giving full information in the *Reference section* on how to find the source.

A reference section is NOT the same as a bibliography. A reference section must include EVERY source cited by you in the text, and NOTHING ELSE. A bibliography is just a list of the sources you consulted while preparing your piece of work, whether you cited them or not. *In psychology you have to give only a reference section.*

There are several referencing systems in use. *In psychology you must use the Harvard system.* (Since the American Psychological Association [APA] uses the same system, you may find this referencing system referred to as either APA or Harvard. In this book I have used APA, with a few variations to suit the preferences, or "house style", of its publishers, Psychology Press.) When you have your psychology degree it will be assumed that you can freely communicate with all the other qualified psychologists. Using a common referencing system is part of our shared language. Other subjects use different systems, but you must use the Harvard (APA) system for all your psychology assignments. Because this is so important, some psychology departments (or sections) penalise students for poor referencing, *which means that you may lose marks for poor referencing.* Check what the policy is in your own psychology department/section. If you follow this guide you should not have any problem with referencing correctly. It may be laborious, but it's not hard.

The two most common types of sources referred to in psychology are books (in part or in whole) and journal articles. This section provides a brief guide to the acknowledgement of reference sources both within the text of and at the end of an essay or practical. If you have thoroughly searched through the whole document without finding what you need, then you should ask a psychology lecturer (preferably the tutor who will mark your piece of work) for assistance. Check you have read this guide carefully first! One of the features of academic writing, and one that distinguishes it from more informal styles (e.g., when writing a newspaper article) is that you are expected to indicate fully your source for all the material mentioned throughout your work.

Citing sources in text

Using the Harvard (APA) system means that every time a reference to a particular source is made, the author's surname and year of publication are given. If the author's surname appears naturally in the sentence, the year is given in brackets; if not, both surname and date are given in brackets. For example:

> Freud (1936) was mistaken in thinking . . .

> This was considered to be correct at the time (Freud, 1936)

If you have given the date in the text, you don't have to repeat it in the brackets:

> In 1936, a summary of the yearly conference (Freud) . . .

Common sense dictates that in the rare circumstances that both the name and the date are clear in a well-written sentence, then a citation in brackets can be omitted:

> 1936 was also the year in which Freud published his summary of the yearly conference.

But if you are in any doubt, cite.

If you have cited more than one source by the same author from the same year (anywhere in the whole piece of work), these are distinguished by adding lower-case letters (e.g., a, b, c, etc.) after the year, within the brackets:

> Baddeley expounded his theory on memory (1983a) . . .

> Baddeley reinforced the notion of the applicability of his theory (1983b) . . .

If there are two authors, the surnames of *both* should be given before the date every time the source is referred to:

> It will now be understood how it is that the psycho-therapeutic procedure we have . . . (Freud & Breuer, 1955).

The use of "et al." If there are more than two authors, but less than six, then the first time the source is referred to *all* the authors must be given, but subsequent citations can be referred to by the first surname followed by "et al." (not italicized):

> [1st time]: A nominal scale measures just the property of difference and nothing else (Elmes, Kantowitz, & Roediger, 1995).

[2nd time]: A nominal number does not assist in measuring a person's attributes . . . (Elmes et al., 1995).

Where there are six or more authors, the first surname followed by "et al." is used for *all* citations.

When giving multiple citations they must appear in *alphabetical order*:

Psychology has often been likened to a "science of the mind" (Gleitman et al., 2003; Sternberg, 1998).

More than one citation of the same author should be given in *chronological order*:

Beck (1967, 1983) showed that . . .

Direct quotations

Direct quotations must include the following: the author's name, date, and page number. Short quotations should be presented within quotation marks as part of the text (Example 1), longer quotations should be indented (Example 2).

Example 1:

Personal Construct Theory has questioned the validity of Freudian or behaviourist theories; for example: "In the theory of personal constructs the person is not segmented into 'learning', 'cognition', 'motivation', 'emotion' . . ." (Fransella, 1981, p. 147).

Example 2:

Thus, Fay Fransella (1981) claims that:

In the theory of personal constructs the person is not segmented into "learning", "cognition", "motivation", "emotion" . . . (p. 147)

which is typical of the Construct Theory approach.

Omissions from a quotation (as at the end of these two examples, where the quotation ends before the sentence in the original) are indicated by an ellipsis (three dots). Words added to the quotation by you to improve the sense are enclosed in square brackets:

> Alvin Stardust (1974) has claimed hegemony over youth groups with soundbites such as: "I [Stardust] am the leader of the gang . . ." (p. 1), which echoes the rhetoric of Glitter (1972).

Presentation of a reference section

Your reference section must come at the end. Always give it a clear heading. The format of references included here is dependent on whether you have consulted a *primary source* or a *secondary source*. So what is the difference?

A *primary source* basically means that you have read the original, whole text (e.g., an article in a journal, chapter in an edited book contributed by the author, book by the author, etc.), which you have found and consulted. A *secondary source* refers to where you have found an original piece of work mentioned, discussed or described (e.g., textbooks are usually full of citations of articles and books), so the textbook is a secondary source for these papers, etc. Note that almost every academic piece of work will cite other items, as can be seen from the reference sections.

It is important that you give the reference for the source you have actually used (i.e., if you read about Sigmund Freud's work in Atkinson et al., then you should reference Freud in such a way that the reader knows that you have read about his work only in a textbook, rather than in the original).

For example, if you are writing an essay on Freudian theory and you go to your departmental library and find Freud's book *Totem and Taboo*, which you take notes from and cite in your essay, then in the reference section you would give a straightforward reference to that book:

> Freud, S. (1912). *Totem and Taboo*. London: Routledge & Kegan Paul.

However, if you had read about *Totem and Taboo* elsewhere, such as in another text or book (as in the example used here), then you would list the secondary source in the reference list, and refer to the primary source in the text citation, for example:

> *Text citation*: Freud's (1912) book *Totem and Taboo* (cited in Strachey, 1958).

Reference list: Strachey, J. (Ed.). (1958). *The standard edition of the complete psychological works of Sigmund Freud, Vol. XIII*. London: Hogarth Press.

Different types of sources (e.g., books, journals, edited collections) are presented in slightly different ways in your reference section. Information on each of these methods is given next. Remember, your reference section should be organised so that the references appear in alphabetical order by first author. If the same author appears on more than one occasion, then the order of referencing for that author is by date of publication of work. If one author has produced several pieces of work in the same year, indicate this by alphabetical suffixes (a, b, c, etc.), listing alphabetically by title. For example:

Baddeley, A.D. (1983a). Working memory. *Philosophical Transactions of the Royal Society of London, Series B, 89,* 708–729.

Baddeley, A.D. (1983b). *Your memory: A user's guide*. Harmondsworth, UK: Penguin.

Listing a reference for a book

For books, each entry should give certain basic information as follows:

1. Author's surname followed by initials as given on the title page of the book (not from the spine or cover). As this is the vital reference for location of work in a library, make doubly sure that the name is correctly spelled. If the writer edited a collection rather than wrote the book, indicate this by placing (Ed.) after their name (Eds.) if more than one editor.
2. The year of publication, in brackets. This is usually shown on the imprint page (reverse of title page) of the book you have consulted.
3. The full title of the book, including any subtitle. Use a capital letter for the first word of the title and the subtitle, and for any proper nouns. This title should be underlined or in italics if word processed. If it is a revised edition or a second/third/etc. edition, follow the full title with (Rev. ed.) or (2nd ed.) or (3rd ed.), etc., as appropriate, but do not italicise this. If you have cited a new edition, remember to give as the publication date the date of the

edition you used. Reprints, impressions, etc., are not important because they do not involve any changes in the text.

4. The place of publication (if more than one is shown on the title page of the book, check the imprint page, which will usually give details of which office actually published this volume) in the form of town/city and country/state, and the name of the publisher (the place and the name are separated by a colon [:]). It is not necessary to add details such as "Limited", "Inc", or "& Sons" etc.

For example:

>Becker, H.S. (1966). *Social problems: A modern approach*. New York: Wiley.
>Paivio, A. (1979). *Imagery and verbal processes*. Hillsdale, NJ: Lawrence Erlbaum Associates.
>Paivio, A. (1983). *Imagery and verbal processes* (2nd ed.). Hillsdale, NJ: Lawrence Erlbaum Associates.

Listing a chapter from an edited book

The chapter is described first, followed by a description of the book it is taken from:

1. Chapter author's surname, followed by initial(s).
2. Date of book, in brackets. Usually this is the same as the text in the chapter, but not always, as for example, where there are collections of material that has been previously published, in which case the reference is followed by "(Original work published 19XX)", and the citation is "(19XX/19YY)", where 19YY is the publication date of the book.
3. Title of the chapter in full, using a capital letter for the first word and any proper names.
4. The word "In" followed by the initial(s) and surname(s) of each of the editors of the book from which the chapter comes, and the abbreviation (Ed.) or (Eds.) in brackets, followed by a comma.
5. The full title of the book, including any subtitle, using a capital letter for the first word of the title, the subtitle, and any proper nouns. This should be underlined or italicised. In brackets give edition if appropriate, and page numbers of the chapter if possible.
6. The place of publication (if more than one is shown on the title page of the book, check the imprint page, which will usually give details of which office actually published this volume) and the name of the publisher (the place and the name are separated by a

colon [:]). It is not necessary to add details such as "Limited", "Inc.", or "& Sons".

For example:

> Hobfoll, S.E., Banerjee, P., & Britton, P. (1994). Stress resistance resources and health: A conceptual analysis. In S. Maes, H. Leventhal, & M. Johnston (Eds.), *International review of health psychology, Vol. 3*. Chichester, UK: Wiley.
>
> Reyna, V.F. (1985). Figure and fantasy in children's language. In M. Pressley & C.J. Brainerd (Eds.), *Cognitive learning and memory in children: Progress in cognitive development research*. New York: Springer-Verlag.
>
> Rogers, C. (1990). Motivation in the primary years. In C. Rogers & P. Kutnick (Eds.), *The social psychology of the primary school*. London: Routledge.

Listing an article from a journal

For an article from a journal, adhere to the following format:

1. Author(s) surname(s) and initial(s).
2. Date (in brackets).
3. Title of paper (initial capital letter only).
4. Full name of journal (this should be underlined or italicised). It is better if you write the title of the journal in full: Do not use standard abbreviations. Capitalise all major words.
5. Volume number, in *italics*, followed by the issue number, in brackets, if relevant. Do not italicise the latter, or the surrounding punctuation.
6. Page numbers (first to last).

For example:

> Heffernan, T., Green, D.W., McManus, I.C., & Muncer, S. (1998). Comments on network analysis and lay interpretations: Some issues of consensus and representation by S.J. Muncer & K. Gillen. *British Journal of Social Psychology, 37*, 253–254.
>
> Heffernan, T.M., Moss, M., & Ling, J. (2002). Subjective ratings of prospective memory deficits in chronic heavy alcohol users. *Alcohol and Alcoholism, 37,* 269–271.

Hitch, G.J., Halliday, M.S., Schaafstal, A.M., & Heffernan, T. (1991). Speech, "inner speech", and the development of short-term memory: Effects of picture-labeling on recall. *Journal of Experimental Child Psychology, 51*, 220–234.

Norton, L.S. (1990). Essay-writing: What really counts? *Higher Education, 20*, 411–442.

Roediger, H.L. (1980). Memory metaphors in cognitive psychology. *Memory and Cognition, 8*, 231–246.

If you cannot obtain part of the information needed to write a full reference, then give what details you know and indicate that the omission is deliberate. The most common element missing is the date: it is convention to use the letters "n.d." to show this. For example:

Squid, G.Y. (n.d.) The ethnography of adultery in royal clans. *Monarchy and Monarchs, 13*, 32–48.

Listing an electronic journal article:

For an article from an electronic journal, adhere to the following format:

1. Author(s)/editor(s) surname(s) and initial(s).
2. Year (in brackets).
3. Title of article (initial capital letter only).
4. Full name of journal (this should be underlined or italicised). It is better if you write the title of the journal in full: Do not use standard abbreviations. Capitalise all major words.
5. Type of medium i.e. [Internet].
6. Date of publication (if applicable).
7. Volume number, in *italics*, followed by the issue number, in brackets, if relevant. Do not italicise the latter, or the surrounding punctuation.
8. Where the information is available from: the URL (i.e. http://www. . . . . .).
9. Date accessed.

For example:

Baddeley, A.D. (2003). Working memory and language: an overview. *Journal of Communication Disorders*. [Internet]. *36*, pp. 189–208. Available from: http:/www.sciencedirect.com/science [Accessed 3rd December, 2003].

Referencing information from the Internet

If the piece of work is an article or book extract then use the procedure outlined previously for that particular source. If not, then cite the following information: name of author/editor (if known), date of publication (if no date is given then may assume it is current), title of paper (if known), and state in brackets [Internet], Edition (if applicable), Place of publication (if known), where the information is available from: the URL (i.e. http://www. . . . . .), you should also include the date the information was downloaded from the website (since the information posted on websites can change and may no longer be available after a particular date). For example:

> British Psychological Society. (1997). *Criteria for membership.* [Internet]. U.K., Leicester. http:/www.bps.org.uk./ [Accessed 15 July, 1999].

Online images

For an online image, adhere to the following format:

1. Title of image.
2. Year.
3. State: [OnLine image].
4. Available from (state URL).
5. Filename including extension.
6. [Date accessed].

For example:

> The Tyne Bridge, Newcastle-upon-Tyne. (2001). [online image]. Available from: http:/www.freefoto.com/preview. jsp?id=1043–28–17 [Accessed 3rd December 2003].

Listing a conference paper

For a paper from an unpublished set of conference proceedings, adhere to the following format:

1. Author(s) surname(s) and initial(s).
2. Date (in brackets; year followed by a comma and the month of the conference, if known).
3. Title of paper or poster (initial capital letter only) (this should be underlined or italicised), followed by a full stop.

4. Full name of conference, preceded by the words "Paper presented at the . . ." .

5. Location of conference.

For example:

> Coates, R., Hamilton, C., & Heffernan, T.M. (1997, July). *The development of visuo-spatial working memory: Effects of interference tasks on passive and active VSWM components.* Paper presented at the Spatial Cognition conference, Rome.
>
> Heffernan, T., & Muncer, S. (1999, July). *Applying network analysis to perceived causes of crime: A comparison of offenders and non-offenders.* Paper presented at the VI European Congress of Psychology, Rome.

Where a paper has been published in a volume of "Proceedings", use the following format:

> Heffernan, T.M. (1996). Task predictability and rehearsal: A developmental perspective. In *Proceedings of the British Psychological Society*, *Vol. 4*(2). Brighton, UK.

Listing general media

Weekly and monthly (and some other) publications (often called periodicals) may number each issue from page 1 (instead of carrying on from the page number that the previous issue finished at). If so, it is very useful to give the exact date of the issue. For example, the exact date for a weekly *New Scientist* will be something like "(1993, December 4)" (the date will be given after the author as usual); for the monthly *Scientific American* the exact date might be "(1993, December)". For example:

> Horgan, J. (1994). Can science explain consciousness? *Scientific American*, *271*(July), 72–78.
>
> Kingman, S. (1994, September 17). Quality control for medicine. *New Scientist*, *143*, 22–26.

References to articles from magazines, newspapers, etc., can often use the same structure as scientific papers, although "p." or "pp." should be used before the page number(s). For example:

Highfield, R. (1994, January 19). Great brains fight for your mind. *Daily Telegraph*, p. 14.

References to sources like television programmes, radios, videos, audio-cassettes, and newspapers/magazines/etc., for which you do not have enough information to use the earlier styles, should be written so as to give all the help that you can in tracing the source. For example:

Equinox. (1992, February 21). *Born to be gay?* Channel 4.

Listing tests and other materials

Questionnaires, scales, stimuli, etc. all need to be referenced. This is easy: You simply treat them as books, chapters, or journal articles, whichever is appropriate. If the scale comes from a chapter, reference as a chapter. Test manuals are regarded as books for this purpose. For example:

Dickman, S.J. (1990). Functional and dysfunctional impulsivity: Personality and cognitive correlates. *Journal of Personality and Social Psychology, 58*, 95–102.

Eysenck, H.J., & Eysenck, S.B.G. (1969). *Personality structure and measurement*. London: Routledge.

A guide to research methods 4

This chapter introduces the reader to research methods in psychology.

Since psychology is ultimately about the scientific study of behaviour, it is necessary to consider what methodological tools are used in order to gain a fuller understanding of that behaviour. These different methods of investigation should be seen in terms of each one serving a particular purpose, rather than in terms of one method being "better" or "worse" than another. Eysenck (2002) likens it to a golfer selecting a particular golf club for a particular type of shot: It is simply a matter of selecting the one that is best designed for that purpose, not because one club is "better" than the other.

On a Bachelor of Science (BSc) psychology degree course (as well as on many other types of psychology course), research methods and associated analysis comprise a large component of the course, culminating in a large-scale final-year research project. The reader is now introduced to the fundamentals of hypothesis/question formation, research methods, and associated analysis. Having a knowledge of research methods and analysis serves a number of functions:

- It enables you to assess the value of findings reported in various sources, such as newspapers, formal reports, magazines, etc.
- It enables you, as a researcher, to assess the value of existing lines of research (such as, for example, the long-term efficacy of a particular drug treatment).
- It provides the motivation for new research projects, which can be aimed at furthering our knowledge of relevant theory/research.

The quantitative/qualitative distinction

Social scientists in general, and psychologists in particular, make a distinction between *quantitative* and *qualitative* research. *Quantitative* research involves the collection of numerical data in order to answer questions about some phenomenon (for example, the use of questionnaires to estimate how many people use alcohol or other substances, or the administration of cognitive tests to estimate how well people remember under certain conditions, and so on). Statistics are applied to the data in order to summarise the findings and enable the researcher to draw inferences about the wider population from which the sample is drawn.

Qualitative research is best suited for situations where the phenomenon under study does not lend itself easily to quantitative methodologies (such as attempting to find out why a person uses addictive drugs, why people commit crime, and so on). In reality, many researchers combine both approaches. For example, a "qualitative" researcher may collect some data in order to bolster her or his argument; and a "quantitative" researcher may first ask a series of general questions in order to guide hypothesis formation, before going on to test these hypotheses using a quantitative methodology. Whatever approach is used, a researcher will normally carry out a literature search in order to provide some basis for the study. Literature searching was dealt with in the previous chapter.

Once the researcher has conducted a literature search and decided what research hypothesis(es) or research question(s) they wish to address, then they need to decide who they will study and what method of study will be used. The first part of this relates to sampling procedures and the second part relates to the type of methodology adopted by the researcher – both of which are considered here.

Sampling procedures

Sampling refers to the selection of a group of participants (selected for the study) from a wider population. Since no researcher is likely to have access to all the people in a given population, they must rely on a sample of participants from the wider population. The sample must be as representative as possible of the wider population, otherwise the generalisability of the findings to the wider population will be reduced. There are a number of sampling techniques from which the researcher can choose; these include *random sampling*, *quota sampling*, and *opportunity sampling*.

Random sampling
Random sampling is a technique whereby participants are chosen from the wider population using some random method, which can

range from the flip of a coin to computer-generated random selection. Random sampling is seen as a very good method for achieving a representative sample, and is sometimes referred to as "probability sampling" because everyone in the wider population has an equal chance of being selected for inclusion in the sample. However, random sampling does have its limitations: for example, it can be time consuming, and those who are selected for the sample might refuse to participate when asked.

Quota sampling

Quota sampling is a technique whereby the researcher chooses a sample that reflects the makeup, in numerical terms, of the wider population (Cozby, 1989). So, for example, if a researcher wanted to study gender differences in first-year undergraduate psychology students, and the wider population comprised a 60/40 per cent split females/males, then the sample must be comprised of this same ratio of females to males. Thus, in a sample population of say, 100 participants, the sample would contain 60 females and 40 males. This quota system can also be used for other factors, such as age, ethnic background, etc. Like all techniques, quota sampling does have its drawbacks. For example, it can be time consuming and the researcher would still need to consider exactly how the subgroups that make up the sample are selected: e.g., what if those who are selected refuse to participate – how might this affect how representative the sample is?

Opportunity sampling

Opportunity sampling is a technique whereby participants are selected purely on the basis of their availability at that particular time. So, for example, if a third-year undergraduate walks into a canteen and asks if anyone would be willing to participate in an experiment and they agree, this would constitute an opportunity sample. It would be an opportunity sample because the people had been selected purely on the basis that they happened to be in the canteen at that particular time. This approach is least likely to produce a representative sample, but is a sampling procedure commonly used by undergraduate students. The approach also has a number of drawbacks to it, not least of which is the problem of just how representative the sample is to the wider population. These issues should be borne in mind when using such a sample and should be considered when discussing any findings from a study based on this type of sample.

The sampling method used for selecting participants for a study is very important and should be considered when planning the study, as well as in any subsequent critical consideration of the findings (e.g., in an experimental write-up).

Further reading: For further consideration of a range of sampling techniques see, for example, Breakwell, Hammond, and Fife-Shaw (2001, Pt. II), Cozby (1989, chap. 8), Elmes et al. (1995, chap. 5), and Robson (1994, 2002).

Once the sampling technique has been chosen, the researcher must then decide which method to adopt. These methods include the *experimental method*, the *quasi-experimental approach*, *non-experimental methods*, and *qualitative approaches*, each of which is considered here briefly.

The experimental method

The experimental method offers perhaps the most rigorous approach to testing a hypothesis or set of hypotheses. This approach incorporates the following key components:

- a literature search (as outlined in the previous chapter)
- the formation of a hypothesis(es)
- testing the hypothesis(es) in a controlled environment
- the manipulation of one or more independent variables
- the measurement of one or more dependent variables
- the specification of a particular design of the experiment
- the inclusion of at least one control and one experimental condition
- the inclusion of control procedure(s) in order to overcome potential confounding factors
- a causal inference drawn from the findings.

The hypothesis

As stated earlier, a hypothesis is a statement about what is likely to occur between two or more factors in the experiment. For example, if you expect that watching televised violence will lead to increased aggression in the viewers, this could form a hypothesis that you wish to test. A null hypothesis is always that there will be no link between two factors. Typically, when writing your report, you would not include a null hypothesis(es). You could check this point with your tutor.

The independent and dependent variables

The *independent variable* (IV) refers to some factor that is manipulated by the experimenter. This factor can have two or more levels – normally an *experimental condition* and a *control condition*. An experimental condition is where the participants receive some form of experimental manipulation or intervention. This is usually the group in whom the hypothesised change is expected to take place. The control condition is the counterpart to the experimental condition, and is labelled "control" because it is where the participants do not receive any experimental manipulation. Its inclusion provides a baseline measure of performance. Having both conditions enables the researcher to assess any change in performance across conditions, as measured in the *dependent variable*. The dependent variable (DV) refers to some measure of performance in the participants of the study.

Experimental design

The notion of design in research refers to the specific organisation or plan of a study: the relationship between the participants and the conditions (e.g., whether or not each participant performed in all the conditions) and the number and type of variables under consideration in the study. Broadly speaking, designs are divided into three types: *between-subjects*, *within-subjects*, and *mixed* designs.

   A *between-subjects design* is one in which participants are assigned to either the experimental or control condition – but not to both. Where there are more than two conditions, again the principle is that each participant is assigned to only one of these conditions. This type of design is also known as an independent-groups design. Assignment to one or other of the groups can be based on *simple random assignment*. This is where each participant is assigned to a group based purely on chance; e.g., the flip of a coin. Assignment to a relevant condition can also be based on *matched random assignment*. This is where pairs of participants are matched on some important feature(s) (e.g., intelligence) and each one in that pair is assigned to a different condition – either the control or the experimental condition. The advantages of using such a design include the fact that no carry-over effects occur (considered later in the confounding variables section). The disadvantages of using this design include an increase in the number of participants needed for the study and the possibility of some individual variation between conditions.

   A *within-subjects design* is where each participant performs in all of the conditions – the experimental and control conditions. It is also known as a *repeated-measures design*. There are a number of advantages to using such a design: It lowers the number of participants needed for the study, and the use of the same participants across conditions reduces the possibility of individual variation between conditions. Potential problems with this design include the possibility of order effects and practice effects (considered later in the confounding variables section).

A *mixed design* is where there is at least one between-subjects factor and one within-subjects factor incorporated into the experimental design. This is a more complex design than those outlined earlier and provides a good method for testing the potential interaction between two variables. For example, providing practice versus no-practice (this could be the between-subjects variable), and assessing what effect this has on students' performance in two different modes of assessment, examinations and coursework (this could be the within-subjects variable). When using such a design one must incorporate all the relevant control procedures (considered next).

Confounding variables and control procedures

In addition to the IV and DV, there is a third class of variable that needs to be considered in research; that is, the confounding variable or factor. A confounding variable is where an extraneous variable systematically changes alongside the main independent variable (the variable of interest) so that it leads to the same outcome. For example, this can be illustrated by the finding that men are more likely than women to purchase a magazine from the top shelf of a newsagent. A conclusion might be drawn that the top shelf magazines were subject to a gender preference. However, it is also possible that because men are taller on average they can more easily reach the top shelf. In this case, height would thus be a confounding variable (confounded with the main variable of preference, with which it is systematically linked).

When this occurs the internal validity of the experiment is open to question; i.e., the experimenter cannot be sure which factor has caused the change in performance – is it the experimental manipulation or variable of interest, or some confounding variable? There are a number of techniques developed to overcome or reduce potentially confounding factors; these include *matching, randomisation*, and *counterbalancing*.

Matching is where participants in the experimental and control conditions are matched on a factor, or range of factors, that the experimenter suspects is likely to affect the scores on the dependent variable. Matching is a useful control measure where a between-subjects design is used. Thus, in a problem-solving task, it would be possible to match participants in terms of intelligence (Robson, 1994).

Randomisation refers to a technique whereby the researcher assigns participants to one condition or the other in a random fashion, and is therefore used in a between-subjects design. Thus, participants may be chosen at random to serve in either the experimental or the control condition. Randomisation assures that any extraneous variable is just as likely to affect one condition as it is the other condition. This technique ensures that the characteristic composition of the two groups is likely to be very similar (Cozby, 1989).

Counterbalancing is used in a within-subjects design in order to overcome order effects. An order effect can occur when participants are required to perform in two or more conditions. This can lead to a number of possible extraneous effects. For example, there may be a learning or "carry-over" effect in that some participants' perform-ances may be affected in a later condition by their having participated in an earlier condition. Counterbalancing basically refers to develop-ing some system whereby participants are assigned different orders of carrying out the different treatment conditions, so that any order effect is balanced out (Robson, 2002). Thus, the first participant would receive the conditions in one particular order, whereas the next participant would receive the conditions in another order, and so on (e.g., as in an ABBA design, see next paragraph).

As suggested earlier, a potential problem associated with a within-subjects design is the potential for *practice effects*: a change in the participant's ability at a given task (or tasks) with repeated testing. Thus, a person may get better and better across trials when a particular skill is required, or their performance might decline across trials if the task causes fatigue. One method of controlling for practice effects is a procedure referred to as *ABBA counterbalancing procedure*. In this example, the A and B represent two conditions. This pro-cedure involves presenting the series of trials, say two presentations of condition A and two presentations of condition B, in one sequence followed by the opposite sequence. This procedure is seen as a useful way of reducing practice effects and can be used in experiments where there are more than two conditions. Other methods to reduce practice effects include the *Block randomisation procedure* (see Shaughnessy & Zechmeister, 2002, chap. 7).

Causal inference and the experimental method

In a well-controlled experiment, where the researcher has manipu-lated the independent variable, adequately controlled for confounding (or "nuisance") variables, and predicted the direction in which a change should take place, then there is a very plausible argument for claiming that a change in the dependent variable is due to the experimental manipulation. The ability of the experiment to ascertain a causal relationship (that A caused B) is its big advantage over other techniques (Robson, 1994). The probability of this relationship between the IV and the DV being a true reflection of what happened in the experiment can be measured using appropriate statistical analysis (considered later in the section on data and statistical analysis).

The quasi-experimental method

The quasi-experimental method (or approach) can be used in a situation that does not meet all the requirements for controlling the influence of extraneous variables (Christenson, 2004). Most commonly, the requirement that is not met is that of random allocation of participants to groups, such as randomly allocating to either the control or experimental group. This approach can be used either within a laboratory environment or outside the laboratory (e.g., within a "real-world" setting). You might equate these groups on certain criteria. This approach incorporates the following key components:

- a formal literature search, as outlined in Chapter 3
- the formation of a research question(s) or hypothesis(es)
- its use in situations that do not meet all the requirements for controlling extraneous variables
- the approximation of control features incorporated into the experimental method, so that the researcher can infer that a given treatment did have its intended effect (Cozby, 1989)
- a causal inference can be made.

There are a number of quasi-experimental designs from which the researcher can choose. Those most commonly used include: the *non-equivalent control group pre-test/post-test design*; a *time series design*; or a *control series design*.

The non-equivalent control group pre-test/post-test design

This design incorporates an experimental and control group, but participants are not randomly allocated. Each group is tested prior to some treatment/manipulation stage (the pre-test phase) and after the treatment/manipulation stage (the post-test phase). The *experimental group receives the actual manipulation, whereas the control group does not –* this would constitute the independent variable. The actual measure(s) taken at the pre- and post-test stages (for both groups) would constitute the dependent variable. The two groups could then be compared on their differences between pre- and post-manipulation measures. This design is called non-equivalent groups because it allows the researcher to select the separate samples for experimental and control groups on a non-random basis. This could be seen as a weakness in the design, but is acceptable because the design allows the researcher to *observe any changes from pre- to post-manipulation/ treatment stages within the same group* (i.e., control pre-post; and experimental pre-post). Since there is a manipulation taking place (in terms of the IV) this design allows the researcher to argue that any change across pre-post stages is due to the manipulation itself.

Although this design can be particularly useful when you cannot guarantee random of participants' allocation to the groups, it does have its drawbacks. One problem with this design is the possibility of some sample selection bias entering the study; for example: On what basis were the particular participants recruited for the study? Did they participate for any particular reason, such as those in the experimental group wanting the treatment/manipulation? What of those who refused? Thus, the researcher has to be aware of possible cohort effects: Those people in the control group might be quite different from those in the experimental group. Another drawback is the possibility of subject mortality, a term which refers to participants leaving the study for whatever reason.

The time series design

The time series design involves testing only one sample or group of participants – those who receive some treatment or manipulation – but involves testing these people over an extended period of time. Usually, this means assessing/testing them on several occasions (at least three times) – therefore measuring the dependent variable on several occasions before and after the manipulation has taken place (e.g., a number of times before and after a drug treatment has been given). The idea here is to gauge what effect the manipulation/ treatment has had on the participants' psychological state/behaviour (e.g., Has there been a significant improvement in biological function? Has their behaviour changed?). Typically, the researcher will use multiple measures of psychological phenomena – but always administering the same assessments each time the participants are tested.

The main advantage with using this design is that it can reduce the sample bias which can occur when using two different groups. It can also provide a powerful argument for any changes that take place being due to the manipulation – since it involves the same participants being tested on each occasion. The major disadvantages with this design include the possibility of a practice effect (covered earlier in the chapter); problems with subject mortality; fatigue and boredom effects; and "instrumentation effects" (see, for example, Breakwell et al., 2001).

The control series design

The control series design is really a combination of the previous two designs: It has elements of both. It includes a time series analysis – that is, multiple measures are taken before and after a given treatment/manipulation has taken place – but it also includes both an experimental group and a control group. This design has the advantage of having both an experimental and control group, as well as the opportunity to observe changes across pre- and post-manipulation stages within each group. This allows the researcher to make inferences about any changes that occur. The problems with this design include many of those previously outlined earlier, including subject mortality, possible instrumentation effects, and so on.

Although referred to here as "designs", quasi-experimental techniques should be seen as somewhat flexible approaches to studying psychological phenomena that cannot easily be tested using a strict experimental approach, rather than rigid designs that should be followed by the researcher. Many researchers adopt a combination of techniques that fall under the heading "quasi-experimental".

Further reading: For more on quasi-experimental approaches, see, for example, Aronson, Ellsworth, Carlsmith, and Gonzales (1995), Breakwell et al. (2001), Christensen (2004), Elmes et al. (1995), Kantowitz, Roediger, and Elmes (1994), and Robson (2002).

The non-experimental method

The non-experimental method offers a way of assessing non-manipulative factors, or phenomena that are naturally occurring. Such an approach can be used to provide a description of the phenomena under study, or can be used to study the relationship between factors. This approach incorporates the following key components:

- a formal literature search, as outlined in Chapter 3
- the formation of a research question(s)
- sampling procedures, such as: random, quota, and opportunity sampling
- a more naturalistic and less contrived approach to studying behaviour; i.e., no manipulation of variables
- a number of approaches including: observations, case studies, surveys, and the correlational method
- a causal inference cannot be drawn from the findings.

Formation of research questions

Since non-experimental methods do not typically involve the manipulation of variables, often they will not involve the specification of experimental hypotheses. There may be an overall research aim or statement that is to be verified. As with other approaches, a literature search can provide the basis for the overall aim/statement the researcher wishes to address using a non-experimental approach. The major non-experimental approaches included here are: *observational methods*, *case studies*, *surveys*, and the *correlational approach*.

Observational methods

Observational methods are ones in which the researcher observes naturally occurring behaviour outside the laboratory setting. Typically, such observations take place over an extended period of time. This approach can involve *non-participant* or *participant observation*.

Non-participant observation. This is where the researcher remains an outsider to the group she or he is studying and observes naturally occurring behaviour in that group. Therefore, the researcher does not become an active participant in the situation under study. The advantage with this specific approach is that because the researcher is "on the outside" she or he can observe the phenomena objectively and impartially.

Participant observation. Where this is used, the researcher becomes very much an active member of the group to be studied, observing the phenomenon as it occurs from inside the group itself. The advantage of this approach is that the researcher can study the phenomenon "from the inside and as it naturally occurs", often gaining access to groups that otherwise would be difficult to observe.

With either approach, there are considerations that have to be borne in mind. With non-participant observation, the researcher has to consider the exact method to be used to observe things. For example, does the researcher conceal her or himself from view? If so, what implications might this have on the ethics of the approach, such as an invasion of privacy? On the other hand, being an *active participant* of the group under study might mean that the researcher loses her or his objectivity, and thus the whole validity of their findings might be adversely affected. A method for observing the behaviour, coding that behaviour into a form suitable for data analysis and selecting an appropriate set of analyses so that the data can be interpreted, must be decided upon beforehand (see e.g., Robson, 2002).

Once an overall approach has been decided upon, and sufficient consideration has been given to the advantages and/or disadvantages of the approach, the researcher then has to decide on the precise method used for data collection. Typically, these include: *case studies*, *interviews*, *surveys*, or *correlational methods*, each of which is briefly considered here.

Case studies

A case study is often described as the study of an individual or small group of individuals with a view to studying their history, characteristic behaviours, reactions to given situations, and responses to particular manipulations (e.g., drug treatment) (Cozby, 1989, p. 39). However, in a wider sense, it can also be used to refer to a strategy for carrying out research involving an empirical study of a contemporary phenomenon within its real-world context. In this latter sense, a case study can refer to the scientific study of an individual, a given situation, a group, or some other phenomenon. A case study therefore focuses on the development of a strategy for studying some phenomenon within its context, and the use of multiple techniques for collecting evidence about the case. It also involves an interpretation of findings in relation to the context and other issues, such as issues of validity, what generalisations can be made from the findings, and so on (see, for example, Robson, 2002).

For example, a case study can consist of an individual being monitored on a single characteristic or a whole range of characteristics; or it can consist of the study of several individuals in a series of single-case studies. An example of the former scenario might be where a clinician studies the effects of a particular treatment on a patient. The clinician might observe certain behaviour before treatment; during the course of the treatment; and after the removal of the treatment (as is the case with an A-B-A design). An example of the latter might be where several individuals are assessed, each of whom may be suffering from a similar condition (say, for example, some brain pathology). The aim of such a study might be to test a particular approach to rehabilitation – as is the case with a number of areas, such as the study of amnesia (see, for example, Barlow & Hersen, 1987; Kazdin, 2003; Solso, Johnson & Beal, 2002). The main advantage of using a case study approach is that the researcher can look at a particular individual or phenomenon in depth, obtaining a multitude of information about the case. The major disadvantage with this approach is in the lack of generalisability of the results to the wider population, though this, of course, depends on why the researcher has chosen to use the case study approach.

Surveys

Surveys generally refer to a group of techniques for gathering information from large numbers of people. The survey method is often used to gather data on people's opinions about certain phenomena (e.g., smoking habits, preference for particular brand names, voting behaviour, etc.), but can also be used to gauge specific attitudes, personality characteristics, and so on. This approach often involves assessing large numbers of participants (hundreds, or even thousands in some cases). Typically the methods used include interviews, attitude scales and questionnaires (see, e.g., Eysenck, 2002; Oppenheim, 2000). So what are *interviews*, *attitude scales* and *questionnaires*?

Interviews. An interview generally refers to a conversation between two persons, which is aimed at one person extracting information from the other. Researchers use interviews to find out about people's attitudes, opinions, habits, and so on. Within this general framework, the three main types of interview are: the *completely structured interview*, the *semi-structured interview*, and the *unstructured interview*.

The *completely structured interview* is where the researcher asks a series of predetermined questions and records the interviewee's responses on a standardised response sheet. Thus, the topics, precise questions, and response sheet are all produced in advance, and the researcher will keep to a strict agenda.

The *semi-structured interview*, as the title suggests, is where some predetermined structure is used. The researcher might use a series of predetermined questions, but could deviate from those questions if she or he decides (during the interview) that there is some other interesting line of enquiry to pursue. Normally the researcher will record the interviewee's responses. Any changes the interviewer makes will be based on her or his perception of the situation (the interview) as it unfolds. The more experienced the interviewer, the better the semi-structured interview will be.

Finally, the *unstructured interview* refers to a situation where there is no set agenda. It does not have a series of predetermined questions, but might consist of the researcher freely pursuing a number of topics with the interviewee.

Together, completely structured, semi-structured, and unstructured interviews are the most commonly used forms of the interview process. Interviews can be very useful in that they can be flexible and adaptive methods for discovering things about a given sample of people (for example, not only their verbal responses, but also their non-verbal behaviour can be recorded). On the other hand, they can be very time consuming and some people find them intrusive (which might affect their willingness to participate, thus affecting how representative the sample might be).

Further reading: For a range of interview techniques, information recording techniques, validity and reliability issues/techniques, as well as interpretation of interview "data", see, for example, Breakwell et al. (2001), Elmes et al. (1995), Oppenheim (2000), and Robson (2002).

Attitude scales. Attitudes are concepts used to describe the way in which a person thinks, feels, or behaves towards a particular object or situation. Since attitudes are essentially hypothetical constructs, measuring them inevitably involves using indirect measures, from which the researcher infers a given attitude to an object/situation. One way of measuring such constructs is by using attitude scales.

An attitude scale typically consists of sets of statements or series of words, which assess an individual's like or dislike of a particular object or situation, or series of the same. Depending upon their responses, the researcher can place each individual somewhere along a particular point on the scale, representing their degree of positive or negative feelings towards the given attitude focus. The precise types of scales differ depending upon a number of things, such as the items used in the scale, but most scales will approximate to the well-established scales such as the Likert or the Thurstone scales. Only Likert scaling is considered here in greater detail; for Thurstone scaling the reader is referred to Cronbach (1990), Oppenheim (2000), and Robson (2002).

Likert scales, developed during the first half of the twentieth century, involve two essential aspects – the construction of the scale itself and the use of a scoring key. The procedure for the construction of the scale and the scoring key are as follows:

1. The collection of a large pool of positive and negative statements about the attitude object/situation. Also neutral statements.
2. The use of a standard scoring key. For positive statements, where the participant "strongly agrees" with the statement she or he is given a score of 5; where she or he "agrees" then a score of 4 is given; where she or he is "neutral" on the subject, a score of 3 is assigned; where she or he "disagrees" with the statement, then a score of 2 is given, and, finally, where she or he "strongly disagrees" with the statement, a score of 1 is given. For negative statements pertaining to the attitude object/situation, a reverse scoring mechanism is used. Thus, an overall positive/neutral/negative score can be assigned to each participant.
3. Administering the scale to a group of participants, in order to gauge whether they have a positive or negative attitude towards the object/situation. This could constitute "piloting" the scale and could be used to test validity and reliability (two issues that are covered next).
4. Testing the scale for validity. Validity basically refers to how well the scale actually measures what it sets out to measure (i.e., positive or negative attitudes to the object/situation). For this, the researcher can use any one of a number of techniques, or a combination of these. These techniques include: *face validity*, *content validity*, *construct validity*, or *item analysis* (see, e.g., Cronbach, 1990; Oppenheim, 2000; Robson, 2002).
5. Testing the scale for reliability. Reliability basically refers to the extent to which the attitude scale provides a consistent measure over time (i.e., does the same participant respond in a similar way when the same scale is administered again?). Again there are a number of ways this can be assessed, including *test–retest reliability*, and *split-half reliability* (see, e.g., Cronbach, 1990; Oppenheim, 2000; Robson, 2002).
6. Once validity and reliability have been established, administering the scale to a group of participants in the main study.

Please note: Points 3–6 from this list refer to general procedures for compiling and testing attitude scales, and are not unique to the Likert method.

Using attitude scales are useful ways in which the researcher can assess attitudes towards particular phenomena (for example, smoking, abortion, etc.). Attitudinal research can also be used to look at wider issues such as how attitudes might be formed and prejudiced attitudes, as well as how these might be changed.

Questionnaires. Questionnaires are general techniques used in research to test current opinions and patterns of behaviour (Coolican, 1990). As with other survey methods, questionnaires can be used in quasi-experimental settings as well as in more naturalistic settings (e.g., field studies). The exact make-up of a questionnaire will depend upon a number of things such as the aim(s) of the research, what precisely the researcher wishes to measure, and so on. Therefore, rather than giving the impression here that a single, precise format for questionnaire use is available, the rest of this section will consider the major features of questionnaire design. These are based on the key features outlined by Coolican (1990).

1. *Minimise the information required from respondents.* Keep the information required to a minimum and make the questions highly pertinent to the research topic. Avoid general "chit-chat" as this can be time consuming, and avoid questions that are vague. The responses the researcher gets may vary simply because the nature of the question is open to different interpretations. Also, avoid questions that are not necessary, such as the sex of the respondent (unless, of course, it is not obvious, e.g., if the questionnaire was sent by post).

2. *Keep the questions fairly simple.* Try to ensure that the questions used can be answered fairly easily. Do not include any that might require a great deal of knowledge on the topic (unless the sample of respondents used are "experts" on a particular subject).

3. *Choose questions that should produce "truthful" answers.* If the researcher chooses questions that the respondents might find difficult to answer entirely candidly, the responses may not be valid. For example, some people might find it difficult to be open about topics such as "Do you believe in smacking your child?", particularly if the political climate is one in which this is seen as unacceptable. Try to formulate questions that avoid such scenarios, or reassure the respondents that their views are entirely confidential, are not going to be judged, etc.

4. *Ensure that the questions will be answered.* Make sure that the questions used are such that they will ensure a response from

the person who is being interviewed. Sensitive topics should be avoided or else the interviewee should be fully aware of the sensitive nature of the interview.

5. *Use fixed and open-ended questions appropriately.* Fixed questions refer to those that are designed in such a way that the respondent must choose one answer from a range of possible answers. An open-ended question is one which can be answered in whatever way the respondent wishes to answer. Fixed questions are useful because they can be easily coded and numerically analysed. Open-ended questions can be useful because the respondent can provide their own response, instead of choosing from a set of pre-determined responses, thus eliciting a more naturalistic response. Most questionnaires contain predominantly fixed questions, but many researchers also use open-ended questions.

With regard to the final point (5), the following are examples of fixed and open-ended questions:

- Fixed questions:

    Question 1. Did you vote for the Labour Party at the last election?
    Answer (circle one): Yes/No
    Question 2. How may cigarettes do you smoke each week?
    Answer (circle one):
       (a)   between 1 and 20
       (b)   between 21 and 40
       (c)   between 41 and 60
       (d)   61 or more
       (e)   I do not smoke cigarettes

- Open-ended questions:

    Question 1. What are your views on abortion?
    Question 2. How do you think the Chancellor of the Exchequer should handle the economy?

Like other forms of measurement, questionnaires should be tested for their *discriminatory power*. This means that they should be structured in such a way as to identify those individuals with extreme views, whilst not producing a wide range of scores in those people who are not at one extreme or the other. Also, as with other scales, questionnaires should be tested for validity and reliability, and should be standardised, preferably via a pilot study or several pilot studies (see also Coolican, 1990; Oppenheim, 2000).

Correlational approach

A correlation basically refers to the degree of association between two factors. To take an example from Chapter 1, if a researcher wished to study the relationship between viewing violent television programmes and levels of overt aggression in children, they might use a correlational method to establish whether the two factors (i.e., viewing violent television programmes and overt aggression) are linked. Thus, if the researcher found that, as the amount of violent TV viewing increased, so did levels of overt aggression in child viewers, then they could say the two are correlated. It is worth noting that the correlational approach/method is quite different from an experimental approach. This is because in an experiment the researcher manipulates a variable and predicts a change in behaviour: Thus, a *causal link* can be established. With a correlation it is quite different: *The researcher can look only at the degree of association between two factors* – not knowing exactly which factor caused a change in the other (e.g., Is it that violent TV viewing leads to increased aggression? Or do aggressive people watch violent TV?). Thus, *with a correlation*, no causal link can be drawn.

The association itself is assessed in terms of the nature and the degree of association. The nature of the association refers to whether a systematic change taking place in one factor is related to any systematic change taking place in another factor. For example, a positive correlation is where an increase in levels of one factor accompanies an increase in levels of another factor. The degree of association refers to a numerical estimate of how well associated the two factors are. For example, are the measured increases in one factor incrementing by the same amount as the measured increases in another factor? Both of these types of information can be established by the application of relevant correlational statistics and are reflected in the correlation coefficient (see, for example, Greene & D'Oliveira, 1999; Robson, 1994).

There are a number of advantages to using a correlational approach, for example, the fact that the researcher can look at factors that do not easily lend themselves to experimental manipulation (for example, intelligence, smoking behaviour, etc.). Also, this approach often involves assessing large numbers of participants – a task that would be very time consuming if they had to be tested in a laboratory setting. There are, however, disadvantages, not least of which is the inability to draw any causal link between factors (i.e., just because two factors are associated, it does not mean that one caused a change in the other; it could be that a third factor has affected them both). For example, increases in the accuracy of prospective memory (memory for future events) for everyday activities is related to an increase in age from young adulthood through to old age (65 years +) (Baddeley, 1999). But this appears to be mediated by a third factor, that is, the use of more strategies to aid memory (such as making notes) in the older people. Merely looking at a correlation between prospective memory and age would have given one a false picture of what was truly happening.

Further reading: For good coverage on the correlational method/approach and related statistical analysis, see, for example, Breakwell et al. (2001), Elmes et al. (1995), Greene and D'Oliveira (1999), and Robson (1994). See also, Clark-Carter (1997) for good coverage of research design and reporting.

Data, statistical analysis and causal inference

Although there are instances in research that do not require the formal measurement of psychological phenomena (as is the case with a number of qualitative research paradigms), there are many instances where measurement of data is desirable (as is the case in all quantitative research). Measurement basically refers to the numerical classification and manipulation of some phenomenon(a). The precise method of measurement is dictated by particular sets of rules (i.e., a particular statistical procedure and its underlying philosophy). Since psychological phenomena are not normally open to direct measurement, it is often the case that indirect measures are used to classify and quantify such phenomena. Statistics are applied to the data collected so that the researcher *can describe the data* collected *and make inferences about that data* (Cozby, 1989). Statistics are techniques that enable the researcher to identify characteristics of a sample of data drawn from a larger population. Thus, statistics can be used to summarise, describe, calculate differences between, and demonstrate associations between, sets of sample data.

Since the realms of statistical theory, the procedures for applying them, and the precise outputs that are produced by them, could fill volumes of texts, and since the precise statistical procedure depends upon many aspects of the study (e.g., the precise aims of the research, the design, the number of factors/variables, etc.), an exhaustive trawl of statistical procedure will not be carried out here. What will be considered are three important aspects that enable the researcher to judge which statistical procedures are most applicable to the data she or he collects. These aspects are: *the level of measurement used; the distinction between parametric and non-parametric tests*; and *the distinction between descriptive and inferential statistics*. A flow chart of the major statistical tests used in psychological research is presented at the end of this section (Figure 4.1).

It should be noted that as you progress through the first two years of study on a research methods course, many more issues in relation to methods and statistics (other than those considered here) may be covered.

Levels of measurement

Levels of measurement are ways in which the researcher can classify raw data, before going on to decide what statistical tests can be applied in order to make sense of the data. Thus, different levels of measurement will produce different types of data, which in turn will affect the types of statistical analysis(es) open to the researcher. Generally, there are four levels of measurement/types of data. These are: *nominal, ordinal, interval,* and *ratio*. So how do these differ?

Nominal level data

A nominal level of measurement is where the researcher categorises information by placing it into one category or another. For example, where the researcher is interested in looking at what frequency of male and female students fall into either the mature or non-mature student categories (mature traditionally being over the age of 21 upon entry to a university). The items are grouped together on some characteristic or set of characteristics (e.g., gender and entry status), producing simple, nominal data. Nominal data can include several categories of information which can be given arbitrary labels (e.g., categories 1, 2, 3; or A, B, C, etc.) – *but these do not represent any differences in size of the data*: i.e., category 3 is not three times greater than category 1. The numbers that fall into the relevant categories are referred to as frequencies (e.g., 12 male mature students/8 female mature students, and so on).

The nominal level of measurement presents the least amount of quantitative information (Coolican, 1990) and therefore places limitations on the types of statistical analyses that can be carried out on that data. Thus, the researcher can describe relative frequencies of occurrence, but cannot test for differences in performance between, say, females and males, matures and non-matures, etc.

Ordinal level data

An ordinal level of measurement involves the use of some type of ordered scale; categories of information can be placed at some point along that scale in an ordered fashion. Ordinal data refers to numbers that are placed on that scale in order of preference, with the implication that one category is "better" or "worse" than another category. So, for example, if a lecturer were to order her or his students on a scale of ability using categories such as very good, good, medium, bad, very bad, this would constitute an ordinal measure because it involves rank ordering the information. However, one drawback of an ordinal level of measurement is that the intervals between scale points (i.e., the categories themselves) cannot be assumed to be equal in value. So, for example, those students falling into the very good category cannot be assumed to be five times better than those falling into the very bad category. The nature of ordinal data places limitations on the statistical analyses that can be applied to the data.

Interval level data

An interval level of measurement is one that "assumes equal intervals between the data on a continuous numerical scale" (Greene & D'Oliveira, 1999, p. 26). What this entails, then, is data that is numerical in form, is measured along some continuum or scale, and has equal intervals between each scale point, such as the Fahrenheit temperature scale. One thing to remember about interval data is that it does not have to have a zero starting point, as, for example, with Fahrenheit temperature. Because interval scales require numerical data and because the differences between each point on the scale represents equal distance, interval level data can be subjected to more complex statistical analyses than can nominal or ordinal data.

Ratio level data

A ratio level of measurement is where there is an exact zero starting point to the scale (e.g., as in the case of some memory tests), but it is the same as interval data in all other respects. This exact zero starting point would be meaningful if the researcher were, for example, testing pulse rate in humans (a zero pulse rate might well be important to the researcher!). Since the greatest difference between interval and ratio levels of measurement is the fact that the latter has a zero starting point, the statistics that can be applied are the same in either case. Thus, many researchers do not distinguish between the two types of data for statistical purposes.

Parametric and non-parametric tests

Parametric tests are those that make assumptions about the population from which the sample is drawn. The data obtained from an experiment or study should meet these assumptions before parametric statistics can be applied to the data. These are:

1. The data itself should be at least interval level data.
2. The amount of variability in each data set should be similar. This is known as homogeneity of variance.
3. Each sample set of data should approximate a normal distribution (a theoretically expected distribution in which the data is assumed to be continuous, symmetrical, and unimodal, with the mean, median, and mode all appearing at the same value).

Strictly speaking, if these criteria are not met then parametric statistical tests should not be used. The advantage of using parametric tests includes the fact that they are powerful tests. *Power* refers to the ability of the test to detect experimental effects from the data produced; the more powerful the test, the greater its ability to detect an effect that is present (Elmes et al., 1995). The power of a statistical test can be affected by other factors as well, such as the size of the sample – the greater the sample size, the greater the likelihood of detecting an effect. Where one or more of these assumptions cannot be met (say, for example, the data is only nominal level) then the researcher should use a non-parametric test.

Non-parametric tests are, by definition, those that can be used on data that do not meet the assumptions for parametric testing, and are sometimes referred to as "distribution-free tests". These can be useful in situations where, for example, the researcher has collected very simple data (e.g., data based on categories [nominal data]). Non-parametric tests lack the power ascribed to the parametric tests, but are equally acceptable forms of statistical testing.

Descriptive and inferential statistics

Descriptive statistics are ways in which the data yielded from an experiment or study can be summarised. This is why they are also referred to as "summary statistics". Descriptive statistics include those that describe the most typical value – as measured by some averaging procedure – and those that describe the amount of variability in a set of data. These two classes of statistics are known as *measures of central tendency*, and *measures of dispersion*. Usually, a researcher will choose only one measure from each class (typically the mean and standard deviation) per set of data, since these two measures can tell you what trends are emerging in the data and how widely dispersed the data is around the mean.

Measures of central tendency

These refer to those sets of statistics that describe the average of a set of data and include the *mean*, the *mode*, and the *median*. The *mean* represents the average score for a set of data and is calculated simply by dividing the total of a set of data by the number of numbers in that set of data. The mean can provide a good indication of the typical value in a set of data, particularly when there is not a great deal of dispersion in the data (i.e., all the numbers are clustered closely together) – but can be thrown out by extreme scores entering the data set. Having said this, the mean is the most frequently used descriptive statistic in psychology and is thought to be the most representative of the average of a set of data.

The *median* is a way of establishing what the central value is in a given data set. This can be estimated by arranging the numbers in the data set in ascending order of size and seeing which number appears in the central point: this is said to be the median. Using this procedure can be time consuming and the median can be affected by a change in any number near the central point itself (whereas the mean is not).

The *mode* simply refers to the most frequently occurring number (or score) in a given data set and, in this sense, it provides some measure of the most typical value in the data set. You can have a bi-modal distribution (where there are two numbers appearing with equally high frequency), or a tri-modal situation (three modes), and so on. The major drawback with the mode is that it can vary greatly with the introduction of few numbers to the data set; it is said to be unstable, and is rarely used in psychological research.

Further reading: Coolican (1990), Greene and D'Oliveira (1999), and Robson (1994).

Measures of dispersion

These provide summary information about the spread of numbers or scores in a given data set and should be used in conjunction with one of the descriptive statistics. There are three commonly used measures of dispersion: These are the *range*, the *mean deviation*, and the *standard deviation*. The *range* gives the researcher some idea of the spread of scores within the data set and represents the difference between the lowest and highest scores in that data, described in a single number (the higher this number, the greater the range is for the data). The range is useful when the scores in the data set are clustered closely together, but can be thrown out by extreme scores in the data.

The *mean deviation* is calculated by estimating how many points each number or score is away from the mean (the mean deviations). A total of these mean deviations is calculated and then divided by the total number of numbers in the data set, thus giving a mean deviation across the data set. The higher the mean deviation, the greater the spread of scores. The mean deviation is rarely used in psychological reports because it ignores some of the mathematical properties of data sets (for example, it does not take into account pluses or minuses).

The *standard deviation* again estimates the spread of scores from a central point (the mean), but also takes into account positive and negative numbers – an advantage over the mean deviation. This is achieved by using a different statistical procedure, which has more powerful mathematical properties than the formula for the mean deviation.

Further reading: Coolican (1990), Greene and D'Oliveira (1999), and Robson (1994).

Inferential statistics are a branch of statistical procedures which allow the researcher to "present the probability of whether the observed differences between the various experimental [and control] conditions have been produced by random, or chance, factors" (Elmes et al., 1995, p. 82). This means that inferential statistics can tell the researcher whether any differences in the results (which can often be intimated by trends in the data) are effects due to the manipulation, or whether chance cannot be ruled out. Inferential statistics also estimate the probability of such results appearing again in future experiments of a similar kind (see Coolican, 1990; Greene & D'Oliveira, 1999; Robson, 1994). For a range of the major inferential statistics used in psychological research, see the flow chart in Figure 4.1.

A final note on data and statistics

Figure 4.1 contains an easy-to-follow flow chart of the major statistical analyses used in psychology. These tests are classified according to the number of variables/factors in the study, the level of measurement used, and the type of design of the study; and are given with the parametric and equivalent non-parametric tests used.

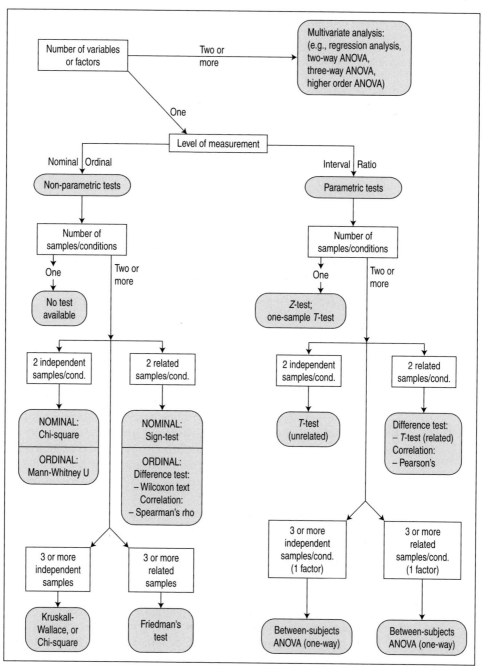

Figure 4.1. Flow chart of major statistical tests for psychology.

Further reading: On data, statistical formulae, and procedures, see, for example, Clark-Carter (1997), Coolican (1990), Ferguson and Takane (1990), Gravetter and Wallnau (1996), Greene and D'Oliveira (1999), Heiman (2000), Hinkle, Wiersma, and Jurs (1998), and Robson (1994).

Qualitative approaches

Qualitative approaches to the study of behaviour do not follow conventional modes of analysis like those apparent in the other methodologies, outlined previously (Robson, 2002). However, there are a number of characteristics that are key elements in qualitative research. These are:

- a formal literature search, as outlined in Chapter 3
- the formation of a research question(s) that is to be addressed
- a method used for generating qualitative data
- a method used to code the data
- a method used to conduct some form of content analysis
- some conclusion specific to the phenomenon under study.

The literature search and formation of a research question(s)

This can involve a formal literature search, as described in Chapter 3, and/or a pilot stage where the researcher formulates a research question or questions by observing some natural phenomenon she or he wishes to study. Typically, this will not involve a specific hypothesis(es), but can be a question, an overall aim, a focus point for the study, or multiples of all three. Often the research focus is flexible, in that it can change during the process of observing and assessing the phenomenon(a) under study.

The method for generating data

Once a particular research question or focus point has been decided on, the researcher will then decide what approach to studying the phenomenon(a) she or he will adopt. This refers to the methodology adopted by the researcher in order to gather data about the phenomenon(a) under study. Data, in the qualitative sense, does not necessarily refer to quantifiable amounts (although it can), rather it refers to the type of information gathered by the researcher. Such data can come in the form of language, non-verbal behaviour, or just about anything that is observable. The types of methods used for qualitative research vary, depending on the aims of the study, the nature of the study, etc. They can involve group study, as, for example, with participant or non-participant observation techniques, or they can be based on a single-case study method. Indeed, many of those approaches outlined earlier lend themselves to qualitative research.

Once a particular approach has been decided on, the researcher should, wherever possible, ensure that the approach is valid and reliable. Triangulation is one method used to achieve this. Triangulation is a technique whereby the data is assessed by using two (or more) methods of study in order to verify one's results. This can be problematic where the study is very time consuming and takes place over an extended period of time (e.g., where there is an exhaustive amount of observation taking place, looking at several aspects of human functioning). Other methods of data collection include interviewing, questioning, discourse analysis, repertory grid techniques, Q-sorting, role playing, focus groups, the study of archive data, and so on (see, for example, Breakwell et al., 2001; Coolican, 1990; Robson, 2002).

Coding and analysing the data

Once the data has been collected, some method for coding it should be employed. Coding data refers to reducing it to some manageable form; for example, generating categories of information and assigning the data to one of these categories. Once coded, the data can be described in some way (for example, this could be an account in a narrative form of what has happened). Recording the data may take the form of a detailed analysis of conversation, recorded in the context of an interview, or focus group discussion, or from naturally occurring conversation that has been recorded, for example, from a television interview. Once the data has been coded and described, then some form of content analysis can be carried out in order to complete the analysis of the data. Content analysis is a technique that allows the researcher to analyse the information in terms of units (which can be words, characters, themes occurring in a narrative, etc.), and estimate the relative frequency of each source of information.

Conclusions drawn from qualitative research

Once the analyses have been carried out on the data, the researcher can then refer what she or he has found back to the research question or focus of the study. Typically, the conclusions drawn from qualitative research should be specific to the sample included in the study and generalising to wider populations should be approached with caution. Like other approaches to research, a full report is normally written as a final stage to the research process.

Further reading: Regarding carrying out and writing up qualitative reports see, for example, Breakwell et al. (2001), Colman (1995b), Haworth (1996), Mason (2002), and Robson (2002). There are also many texts on how to carry out and write up quantitative research projects (see Breakwell et al., 2001; Christenson, 2004; Colman, 1995b; Elmes et al., 1995; Haworth, 1996; Jones, 1995; Robson, 2002; Shaughnessy & Zechmeister, 2002).

Ethics in research 5

This chapter highlights the major ethical considerations in research.

Before carrying out a piece of research in psychology, there are a number of ethical considerations that a researcher must bear in mind when designing a study. Some brief notes on the subject are provided here, but for a full consideration of formal criteria on ethics in research the reader is referred to the British Psychological Society (BPS, 2000) *Code of Conduct, Ethical Principles and Guidelines*, or the American Psychological Association (APA, 2003) *Research Ethics and Research Regulations*.

Ethical issues in research are to do with the way you conduct your research – the rights and wrongs. Psychologists are expected to conduct themselves in line with ethical guidelines that are set by bodies such as the British Psychological Society and the US equivalent the American Psychological Association. Not only do you have a duty to protect the rights of the participants in your study, but also to protect the reputation of the discipline under which name you are studying, psychology. In most cases, given the types of research conducted by the majority of psychology students, the only ethical considerations you need to ensure are that your subjects have consented to their participation in the study and that they are fully debriefed. However, in some cases where there is a risk of harming or causing psychological distress, then the researcher needs to adhere to the guidelines. Here are some of the major ethical considerations for a researcher.

Ethical considerations when testing humans

Considering the welfare of your participants

As a researcher you must ensure that the participants in your study are protected from physical harm or from suffering psychological harm as a result of your manipulation(s). In some cases there is inevitably a risk (e.g., if you were administering a drug – say, to a patient in care – which might have some side effects), in which case you must go through the relevant ethics committee associated with that particular institute. In short, it is your duty to ensure the safety of your participants.

Gaining the consent of the participants

Wherever possible, the researcher should ensure that all the participants are volunteers and have given their full consent. Often researchers have their participants sign a consent form before testing them. Ideally, you should explain all aspects of the procedure(s) to the participant before you gain their consent. You should also inform them how and where feedback will be provided, and, if appropriate, provide them with help lines or information sources, e.g., if your study were on substance misuse you may provide some useful help lines. In some cases, gaining the consent of the individuals you wish to study is difficult (if not impossible): for example, if you want to study very young children in the school setting, or disturbed patients in a psychiatric hospital. In such cases consent can be obtained from those who are in authority over those persons. For example, the consent of a parent of a young child (under 16 years of age) may be required, or from those in loco parentis: for example, the head of the school may take responsibility for agreeing to your having access to test the children; or the psychiatrist can give consent in the medical setting. It is a good idea to have a letter of introduction from your supervisor for the project. This offers some assurance to those outside your institute that your intentions are honourable and that you will conduct yourself in an appropriate manner. In longitudinal research, consent may need to be obtained at several stages throughout the research.

Deceiving your participants

Deceiving your participants should be avoided whenever possible. The BPS suggests that deception should not be used if, once the participants have been debriefed, they are likely to have objected to the study had they been told about it beforehand, or if this deception is likely to lead to discomfort, anger or objections. The notion of deception is sometimes difficult because, as a researcher, you might argue that informing the participants of what you are going to do may well cause a change in naturally occurring behaviour. The general advice on this is that if you have to deceive your participants you should take the matter before some form of ethics committee and debrief your participants as soon as possible after the study is complete.

Risk

You should always protect your participants from undue risk in psychological research. You may wish to carry out some form of risk assessment. For example, does the place of testing pose any safety risk to you or your participants? Are there any risks associated with the particular procedure you are using?

Debriefing your participants

You should always fully debrief your participants once they have participated in the research. This involves telling them the nature of the study, the aims, and what was found in the study – in terms of overall findings. Indeed, you should be willing to tell the participants anything they wish to know about their participation in the study. In some cases, a verbal description may not be sufficient to negate the after-effects of the study. In some cases it might be necessary to carry out some further procedure to restore the person's psychological well-being: for example, if the study induced a negative mood state in the participant, then one would be expected to induce a happy mood state before the participant has left. In addition, your participants should also have the following rights:

- *The right to withdraw from the study at any time*: forcing the person to take part in the study may reduce the validity of your results. In fact, the participant should be made aware that they have the right to withdraw their data from the study after their participation and have it destroyed by the researcher, if they decide that they do not wish their data to be used in the report after debriefing.
- *The right to anonymity and confidentiality*: you might "code" your participants instead of using their names, if this is possible. This will provide confidentiality and will allow the person to have their data withdrawn from the study afterwards (and destroyed), if

they so wish. Tell the person how anonymity/confidentiality will
be achieved before he/she consents to participate in the study.

- *Protection of participants*: you must protect your participants from
  mental or physical harm during the study. Assess the "risks"
  involved and inform participants of these beforehand. The simple
  rule here is to avoid such risks altogether.

Giving advice

During research, an investigator may obtain evidence of psychological or physical problems of which a participant is, apparently,
unaware. If the investigator believes that this may be of sufficient
seriousness as to damage the future well-being of the participant,
then that investigator has a responsibility to inform the participant if
the investigator believes that by not doing so the future well-being of
the participant may be endangered. The investigator should be careful not to offer advice outside his/her professional experience. If the
investigator does not feel qualified to offer assistance, the appropriate
source of professional advice should be recommended.

Observational research

Studies based on observation must protect the privacy and psychological well-being of the participant. Participants should ideally
give their consent to being observed. Where this is not the case, then
observational research is only acceptable in situations where those
who are being observed might expect to be observed by strangers.
Local traditions and customs must also be taken into consideration in
such studies.

Ethical considerations when testing animals

In general terms, it is estimated that each year millions of animals
are tested in order to carry out research into a number of areas
(Shaughnessy & Zechmeister, 2002, chap. 2). However, it should be
pointed out that, within psychology departments in the UK, the
participation of animals in research is low. The relative merits of
conducting research on animals is not debated here. What is outlined
here are some of the major ethical guidelines one should adhere to if
there is a need to carry out psychological research using animals as
subjects. These major guidelines approximate those outlined by the
BPS and APA, and are as follows:

1. The procurement of animals must be obtained under legal and governmental guidelines.
2. Psychologists should choose a species that is best suited for the intended use.
3. The researcher is legally required to use the smallest number of animals necessary and sufficient to accomplish the research goals of a given study.
4. When conducting your research you must treat animals humanely.
5. The care, use of, and (where necessary) disposal of animals should adhere to the state and local laws and regulations, and those laid down by the professional body under which you operate.
6. Psychologists should have appropriate training in the handling and testing of the animals under study.
7. Any assistants used by the psychologist must be adequately competent in the tasks they are expected to perform.
8. Psychologists must make every effort to minimise the discomfort to the animal that is being tested.
9. Animals under study should not be exposed to pain, unless there is no alternative procedure that is appropriate (i.e., the administration of a painful stimulus must be justified by the value of the research).
10. Any surgical procedures used must be carried out under appropriate anaesthetic and sterile conditions.
11. Where it is necessary to terminate the life of an animal, it must be done speedily, with the aim of reducing suffering, and must be done so according to appropriate regulations.

Further reading: See Kimmel (1996), for further consideration of these guidelines. Also, Shaughnessy and Zechmeister (2002, chap. 2) and Wadeley (1991), for further consideration of ethical issues in research.

Empirical research report writing 6

This chapter provides guidelines on empirical research report writing. A completed practical report can be found in Example 6.1. The final section provides brief guidelines on presenting your research at a conference. A research article can be found in Example 6.2.

For most psychology degrees you will be required to run experiments or studies throughout the first two years of the degree and, in your third year, to design your own experiment. Having conducted an experiment (or a non-experimental study) and analysed the data from it, the researcher is normally required to write a report on what the experiment was about; what the procedure was for carrying it out; what was found in the experiment; and a full explanation as to why the things occurred as they did during the experiment. Within the field of psychology, there are clear rules that have been developed for writing empirical reports. Such rules relate mainly to the particular format the empirical report should take, and should be adhered to by the report writer. Following a standard format for empirical report writing makes it easier for other researchers to comprehend the large numbers of research articles they are likely to access during the course of their work. It also allows report writers to get their ideas, procedures, and results across to others.

Academic written reports differ from essays, or other forms of narratives, in that the report must: (a) convey sufficient detail for the research to be replicated; (b) state clearly what the research was about and what was found in the study, so that it can be judged on its scientific merits. A third aspect to remember about written reports is that they may not be read in the same way as, say, an essay. The reader might well switch from one section of the report to another, in a non-linear fashion. Think of the time saved by reading through a series of abstracts before deciding which reports are most relevant to the topic under study. This is why academic written reports should follow a standard format.

Although, as a general rule of thumb, empirical reports should follow the overall format of an article in a journal (see, for example, *British Journal of Psychology*, *British Journal of Developmental Psychology*, and *American Journal of Psychology*), the types of reports written on an undergraduate degree course usually contain more detail than would be found in a journal article. For example, all the raw data is normally provided in an undergraduate practical, whereas they are not provided for a journal article. All too often undergraduate students fail to provide a clear, coherent or complete report and lose vital coursework marks as a result of an inadequate write-up of their work. So, again, the idea is to spend some time on writing the report before submitting it for marking. As previously suggested for essays, ask a fellow student to look at a draft of the report to check for any major omissions. You could reciprocate by doing the same for your fellow student.

What follows is a guide designed to cover the most important aspects of writing empirical reports within a psychological framework. Do bear in mind that this is meant as a piece of scientific writing and must be well structured according to a standard format. This standard format is set out in the remainder of this chapter. Guidelines about the length of a practical report are normally provided to students on particular courses.

Structure of the report

An empirical report is normally presented in a series of subsections, each of which begins with the title of the subsection as a heading. The relevant subsections are: a Front Page, the Title, Abstract, Introduction, Method, Results, Discussion, References, and Appendix. This is the order in which they are dealt with here. Example 6.1, later in the chapter, contains a completed write-up of an experiment and should be referred to in conjunction with these guidelines.

Title page

The title itself should convey information about the main aspects of the experiment (or non-experimental study). It should briefly identify the following aspects of the study: the independent and dependent variables, or factors under study; the subject population; and what particular method was used. For example, consider the following title:

The effects of overt rehearsal on recall in young and older children, using a serial recall task.

It conveys information about: the independent variable (the manipulation of overt rehearsal); the dependent variable (recall); the subjects (young and older children); and it mentions the particular methodological paradigm used (a serial recall task). The title will often be the first thing the reader encounters, so make it clear, short, and informative. Finally, avoid using phrases such as "An experiment that tests . . ." or "An investigation into . . ."; these types of phrases are not specific enough and take up valuable word space that could be used to include additional information relevant to the project. The title page comes before the main body of the report and should typically contain information about the following:

- your full name (if your department runs an anonymous marking system, provide your ID number)
- year of study/submission date
- course/module
- name of supervisor
- title of report
- type of report.

Title – general rules

1. Keep it short: Try not to exceed about 15–20 words.
2. Include sufficient detail so that the reader has a good idea of the major focus of the experiment.
3. Do not include too much detail: Report such detail in later sections.

Abstract

This section is called the Abstract because it contains information that is abstracted from other parts of the report: It is also referred to as the Summary. Having an Abstract section at the beginning of the report is useful for those people wishing to assess whether your particular article/report is relevant to their needs. If the report appears to be relevant, the researcher can spend time reading the whole thing. Indeed, most computer-based literature searches provide only brief details about the author, source, and the abstract, so it is important that this section of your article/report contains the essential details of your experiment. If you go on to submit a research paper for, say, a conference, you will be asked to forward an abstract of the article you wish to present. If your abstract omits important details, your submission will be rejected.

There are a number of undergraduate conferences each year where some final-year students choose to submit their work. The Abstract section should stand out from the rest of the report (indent it and use single-line spacing) and should be relatively brief (a maximum of 150 words). It should contain brief details about the following: the aim of the experiment; the citation of any major experiment and/or theory underlying the experiment; the hypothesis(es); general design features; a brief interpretation of results; and any overall conclusion(s) that have been reached. Thus, the Abstract will consist of brief details taken from the other major sections of the report – the Introduction, Method, Results, and Discussion (but do not include a reference section in the abstract).

Although the Abstract appears as the first major subsection in the completed written report, it is often not written until the rest of the report has been completed. This is because it is easier to extract information about the experiment after you have put it all down on paper in a report form, rather than trying to wade through the sometimes vast amounts of information you have collected, such as notes on articles, printouts of results, etc.

Abstract – general rules

1. Keep it relatively brief: up to a maximum of 150 words.
2. Include the most important details from Introduction, Method, Results, and Discussion sections of the report.
3. Use single-line spacing and indent this section.
4. Compile the Abstract after you have written the bulk of the report.

Introduction

A researcher may carry out an experiment for any one of a number of reasons. It might be that the experiment is purely "experimental" in nature, in that no one else (at least to your knowledge) has looked at what effects a particular variable might have on another, or it might be a replication of a new and important finding, or, as is the case with most final-year undergraduate projects, it might be an attempt to extend support for some existing hypothesis(es) and/or theory by manipulating a number of conditions in some way. As students progress through their undergraduate course, more emphasis is placed on experimentation that extends the literature, rather than the mere replication of previous work.

Whatever the motivation for carrying out an experiment, few experiments are conducted without there being some background information available to guide hypothesis making. Invariably, there will be a body of literature that is relevant to the experiment you wish to run. The Introduction should summarise relevant empirical and theoretical work done previously in the area under study. It should flow from a general consideration of the area, through to summaries of previous empirical and theoretical work related to the area (always concluding something about each piece of work), to a specific outline of the present experiment, and finally it should lead to a clear, concise set of statements about the hypothesis(es). In many ways, the Introduction sets the scene for the experiment itself. It is often seen as having a funnelling effect – going from the general, to the more specific sets of empirical and theoretical literature, and on to a very specific focus point in terms of the experimental hypothesis(es). A good introduction should enable the reader to anticipate the aims of the study and the hypothesis(es) you wish to test – because what you have written becomes focused upon those factors you wish to explore. The Introduction should also state what novel feature(s) there is/are in the experiment (if applicable).

Some tutors prefer to see the Introduction split into two discrete sections: (1) a *general literature review* that covers the general area and empirical/theoretical literature that is available; (2) a specific *introduction to the experiment*, which specifically outlines the aims of the experiment, cites briefly any major studies relevant to the experiment, stresses any novel features of the experiment, and states the hypothesis(es) to be tested. (You should check the preference in style with your tutor.) As suggested, the Introduction should finish by stating what *experimental hypothesis(es)* are to be tested. Do not include the *null hypothesis(es) – unless there is something unusual about this*. These hypothesis(es) should be stated clearly and independently of each other, and should mention the (dependent and independent) variables involved. Any student who feels there might be some problem with regard to a tutor's preference for the precise format of the Introduction can easily check with the tutor beforehand, or you could look at some journal articles in that area to see how researchers achieve this.

It should be noted that when submitting a manuscript for publication, say, for example, as an article to a journal or for conference proceedings, or, as found in many cases, for the final-year psychology project, a separate hypotheses section is not necessary. Rather, a statement about what is expected from the research at the end of the Introduction section is sufficient (see the examples of a practical report and conference report provided in Examples 6.1 and 6.2, later in this chapter).

Introduction – general rules

1. Move from a general consideration of the area to a more specific focus point of the experiment so that your Introduction has the so-called funnelling effect mentioned earlier in this section.

2. Provide summaries of theoretical and empirical literature relevant to the experimental paradigm.

3. Use historical and up-to-date material wherever possible, and provide link pieces between sections of the Introduction.

4. Point out any novel feature(s) to the experiment.

5. List the hypothesis(es) at the end of the Introduction, or provide a statement about what is expected from the research.

Method

The main aim of this section is to provide sufficient methodological detail about the experiment so that anyone who chooses to can evaluate the appropriateness of the method used in your experiment, or can easily replicate your experiment (or a part of your experiment) after reading your report. The Method section is subdivided into the following subsections: Design, Participants, Materials (and Apparatus), and Procedure. As well as having sufficient detail, the organisation (structure) of this section is also important and influences the tutor's assessment of this part of the report: so do adhere to the structure outlined here (unless your tutor advises otherwise).

Design

This section should provide concise information about the following:

- the type of design used in the experiment (such as whether it was an independent group or matched group design, a repeated measures, a quasi-experimental design, a correlational design, or some other design)
- what constituted the independent variable(s), or factor(s) under study, and what the different levels of this were. For example,

word length might be the independent variable, with two levels (long and short words)

- what constituted the dependent variable(s), or measures, with brief details of how this was measured. For example, total number of words recalled might be the dependent variable
- details of what methods were used to deal with order effects (e.g., was randomisation used, counterbalancing, etc.?)
- other control methods employed in the experiment (i.e., how the experimenter controlled for nuisance variables).

> *Note*: **In some published literature, the Design subsection is combined with the Procedure subsection.**

Participants

This section should provide brief details about the participant sample and should include details on the following:

- total number of participants, including numbers per condition
- age distribution: age range, mean age, and standard deviation, per group
- sex distribution: how many males/females per group
- brief details of population drawn from: for example, were they undergraduate students? If so, which course were they taking?
- other relevant details: for example, were they chosen at random? Were they volunteers? Were they an opportunity sample? (Most psychology experiments will use an opportunity sample.)

Materials (and apparatus)

The materials refer to those things that were needed to run the study. You should include here enough detail to enable the reader to reproduce (if they wish to) similar materials and apparatus for a future experiment. Give the relevant trade name of any apparatus used. If the apparatus is new or highly specialised, a diagram may be used to demonstrate such aspects. If this is rather detailed and is likely to take up much space, then it can be placed in an Appendix section at the back of the report and referred to appropriately. Exact descriptions of materials, such as word lists, must either be given here or in the Appendix section of the report and referred to appropriately in the Materials section. For example, you might write "See Appendix 1 for details of word lists".

Procedure

The overall rule of thumb here is simple: Describe what typically happened to a participant during the running of the experiment. What you should have here is a standardised procedure. The following details should be provided in enough detail for a researcher to easily replicate your procedure:

- details of how the stimuli were presented to the participant
- how the participants were expected to respond
- details of the relevant timing procedures (e.g., what the rate of item presentation was; what the interstimulus-interval [ISI] time was)
- whether the participants were tested individually or in groups
- a verbatim account of standardised instructions given to a participant (but if the instructions are very lengthy, these may be placed in an Appendix and referred to appropriately here)
- what the differences in procedure were between the conditions
- any other relevant detail; for example, were the participants debriefed.

Please note: The Procedure is the only section that includes detailed information about how the experiment was run. So make sure that you have included all these details. However, if you realise a flaw in your method/procedure after you have run the experiment, do not discuss it here (this is a common mistake made by undergraduate students). Leave any discussion of major flaws until the Discussion section.

Method – general rules

1. Subsection into Design, Participants, Materials (and Apparatus), and Procedure.
2. Provide sufficient detail so that the experiment can be replicated (in part or in whole) by another researcher.
3. Where the report writer feels there is too much detail (e.g., where several pages of exhaustive instructions have been used), put this information in an Appendix section and refer to it accordingly.
4. Do not discuss any flaws in the Design or Procedure here. Leave such discussion until the relevant Discussion section of the report.

Important Note: The format of the method section will differ depending upon whether you are carrying out an *experimental study*, *observational study* or *qualitative study*. The major differences in format are identified below:

Experimental study. As outlined above: Design, Participants, Materials (and Apparatus), Procedure.

Observational study. Follow the following format: Participants, Materials (and Apparatus), Procedure, Coding, Observer reliability, Data reduction (or data summarisation).

Qualitative study. Follow the following format: Participants, Sources of data (and procedure for gathering the data), Transcription (or transformation) of the data, Procedures for analysis and interpretation of data.

Results

In the Results section of the report, the data you have collected is summarised and the findings from relevant statistical analyses are reported. This section should include *descriptive statistics* and *inferential statistics*. Descriptive statistics allow you to present your data in a condensed form and describe trends emerging from that data. Thus, *descriptive statistics* are used to summarise the data so that a researcher reading your report can begin to understand what has actually happened as a result of running the procedure (i.e., what the emerging trends were).

Inferential statistics are a branch of statistics that allow the researcher to estimate whether the conditions created in the experimental method have actually caused a significant change in the performance of the participants. By inferring that the manipulation(s) in the experiment have had a significant effect on performance in the participants, the researcher can evaluate whether or not there is support for the experimental hypothesis(es). Please note that you do not discuss your findings here: That is the main purpose of the Discussion section that follows the results. Do not place your raw data in this section (raw data should be listed in a table in the Appendix section at the back of the report).

Descriptive statistics (also referred to as *summary statistics*), such as means and standard deviations, should be presented in a table, or can be presented in graph form, followed by a concise statement about the emerging trends in the descriptive statistics (e.g., how the mean of group A differs from the mean of group B). You *must not* infer whether or not a hypothesis has been supported on the basis of the descriptive statistics alone. Tables and/or graphs should be clearly numbered and labelled. (Examples of a descriptive table and graphs are provided in the practical write-up in Example 6.1, later in this chapter.) Check with your tutor what the convention is at your own institute: whether you should present a table or a graph, or both. You should ask yourself whether your graph is demonstrating something useful to the reader or merely replicating the descriptions given in the table. If it is the latter, then perhaps you do not need a graph. Where you might have a complex table, then a graph could be useful in extracting an important finding to show to the reader. Where you may have found an interaction effect, you should show this in the form of a graph (e.g., a line graph). Finally, the results of the *inferential statistics* applied to the data are reported. When reporting these in the Results section, report what test was used, what value was obtained from the statistic, the degrees of freedom (or some other appropriate figure) and the significance level. If you have calculated the statistics yourself, do not include the calculations here (they can be placed in an Appendix and referred to accordingly).

There is a standard way to write out the descriptive and inferential statistics in a report. *You include them both in a sentence for each finding.* For example, part of a Results section might read as follows:

> The mean score on the video-based everyday memory task for non-users of alcohol (11.0, SD 2.43) was higher than the mean score on the same task for the excessive alcohol users (8.57, SD 2.15) and this difference was significant $t(44) = 3.64$, $p < 0.05$ (one-tailed). Therefore, the experimental hypothesis which states that excessive alcohol use has a detrimental impact upon everyday memory can be accepted.

SD is the abbreviation for the standard deviation. The abbreviation (t) refers to the test you have carried out (in this example, a t-test). For an ANOVA you would use the abbreviation F instead of the t, for a Pearson Correlation r instead of t, and so on, depending upon which test you have used. The number in brackets refers to the degrees of freedom (for an ANOVA, there will be two of these separated by a comma). The number after the equal sign represents the value of your statistical calculation. The final part of the statement refers to the alpha level (p-value) of the test. This tests the probability that you are rejecting the null-hypothesis based on the value obtained from your test (e.g., the t-value in the example provided above). If you see $p < 0.05$ then this means significant at the 5% level, $p < 0.01$ means significant at the 1% level, and so on. Where your test reads $p > 0.05$

this means that your result is not significant and you can abbreviate it to "p = n.s." (although some tutors prefer it if you provide the actual p value – check with your own tutor).

Your Results section should not consist of pages and pages of computer printouts of statistics carried out on computer packages, such as SPSS printouts. Rather, you should summarise the relevant parts of the analyses and present it here formally. Remember, you *must not* discuss your findings in detail in the Results section. Such discussion forms part of the content of the Discussion section that follows.

Results – general rules

- Do not put raw data or full workings of statistical calculations in this section. These should be placed in an Appendix at the end of the report, labelled and referred to appropriately.
- Descriptive statistics are a way of summarising the data obtained and inferential statistics allow you to state whether a hypothesis has been supported or not.
- Combine your *summary* of the descriptive and inferential statistics in a sentence, described in words, for each effect and present *after* any table or graph.
- All results should be briefly described in words, regardless of tables or graphs.
- Briefly state what the relationship is between the results and the hypothesis(es) set out in the Introduction.
- Do not discuss the results here. Such discussion should take place in the Discussion section that follows.

Discussion

Having reported the findings from the experiment clearly and relatively concisely, the next step is to fully discuss your findings in relation to the relevant background literature and your specific hypothesis(es). The Discussion section should begin with a summary of the major findings in words, not repeating the statistics from the previous section. These findings can then be related back to the consideration of the area, as set out in the Introduction, and to the specific hypothesis(es) or statement about the research, set out in the Introduction – then widen your discussion and arguments. Try to address questions like: Do the findings support the hypothesis(es)?

Are the findings consistent with what other researchers in the area have found? If not, what are the major discrepancies between your findings and those from other researchers? Do the findings support a particular theory or model that might be dominant in the area? Can you identify any methodological shortcomings or flaws in the experiment? If there are flaws, how might these be rectified in future experiments?

Finally, you should address two other issues in the Discussion section: Are there any recommendations you can make for future research on this topic? Have your findings any implications for existing theory/research, or are they applicable in some way? Your Discussion can finish by stating some overall conclusion(s) about the experiment, briefly: What did you do? Why? What did you find? What should happen now in this research area? What further research is needed? Keep your Discussion relevant; there is nothing worse than a Discussion that goes off on a rambling tangent.

Discussion – general rules

1. Provide a written summary of the findings.
2. Relate the findings back to the hypothesis(es) set out in the Introduction.
3. Interpret the findings in relation to the literature in the Introduction (both theory and research).
4. Consider any shortcomings or flaws of the experiment, and make suggestions about improvements in design, procedure, etc.
5. Assess what implications and/or applications your findings might have in relation to the phenomenon/topic under consideration.
6. Make sensible suggestions for future research.
7. Draw the discussion to a close with some conclusion(s).

References

In the Introduction and Discussion sections of the report, you will have referred to a number of pieces of published work. All references cited in the report should be listed here. Your Reference section must come immediately following the Discussion section of the report, before the Appendices. In the Reference section, details of all publications referred to in the other sections of the report should be listed in alphabetical order of author. These days, people often access literature via the internet, or from website addresses. The guide on referencing in this book has catered for such referencing. For the specific format references should take, see Chapter 3.

Appendices

An Appendix is a section within which you can place very detailed information that you wish to include, but not in the main body of the report where its inclusion might interrupt the flow of things. Include here: full instructions given to the participant (if they have not already been included in the Method section), a full list of the stimuli used, computer printouts of statistical analyses (e.g., an ANOVA table from the SPSS printout), a master copy of any questionnaire (ask your tutor if this is needed), other forms used in the experiment (consent form, briefing and debriefing sheets, a completed ethics form if necessary, etc.), workings of statistical analyses you did by hand, a raw data table (containing the scores for each participant across conditions and measures), diagrams of unusual experimental equipment or building layouts, etc. If more than one Appendix is included, these are labelled numerically (e.g., Appendix 1, Appendix 2) or alphabetically (e.g., Appendix A, Appendix B) and thus referred to in the main body of the report (e.g., "See Appendix 1 for details of the word lists used"). Each Appendix must be numbered and labelled, and a brief explanation given as to its content (e.g., "Appendix 1 consists of the raw data from both the control and experimental conditions"). They are generically referred to as Appendices. Make sure each appendix is cross-referenced within your report (e.g., in the Procedure you might write, for example, "Refer to Appendix 6 for full debriefing information").

Summary

Remember, the more of the components (outlined in this section) you have in your practical write-up, the more credit (marks) you will be awarded. Writing empirical reports should become easier the more familiar you become with the relevant format used. It should be clear by now that each section of the report serves a particular purpose. The *Title* page identifies the report writer and provides relevant details about the project (e.g., course/module, title of project, when the study was written up, etc.); the *Abstract* is a summary of the whole report, detailing the most important components from each of the major subsections of the report; the *Introduction* is there to present the background literature and to set the stage for the experimental hypothesis(es) that is/are to be tested; the *Method* provides full details of exactly how the study was devised and how it was carried out; the *Results* section summarises the data, looks for any trends in the data, and analyses whether these trends are significant or not (e.g., are they replicable, or just a chance occurrence?); the *Discussion* looks at what was found from the study, how these findings relate to the hypothesis(es) and background literature, considers flaws/ improvements/future research paradigms, and states some conclusion(s); the *Reference* section is there to log all the primary and secondary sources of information you have cited in the report; and finally the *Appendices* are there to include other information that is relevant to the report, but which does not necessarily fit in neatly with any of the other sections.

Please bear in mind that your own initial attempts at practical write-ups may fall far short of the guidelines provided here. However, as you progress through your course, you should show improvements with regard to your report writing skills. Report writing itself should get easier with the guidance provided on courses/modules on research methods and, of course, with practice.

Summary of format for an experimental report: Title, Abstract, Introduction, Method: design, participants, materials, and procedure, Results, Discussion, References, Appendices. An example of a practical write-up can be found in Example 6.1.

Example 6.1: A practical write-up

Having covered basic research methods (Chapter 4), having briefly considered the major ethical issues in carrying out research (Chapter 5), and having identified the major subsections of an empirical report (Chapter 6) it would be useful to provide a written example of a completed practical report. Here is an example of a practical write-up of an experiment. The experiments in the first year of a course are normally tutor-led – that is, they are designed by the research methods tutor, who supplies background references and details of the method, and who may also collate the data for the results and discuss the findings with students. When progressing through to the second year, and particularly in the final year, of a degree course, the student is expected to engage more in their own literature searching, hypothesis making, design of the method, etc., but will be given good guidance on all of these aspects by her or his tutor.

This practical write-up is a medium-length (approximately 1800 words) first-year undergraduate practical, and would be expected to achieve a mark in the high 60s to low 70s assessment range at this level. It is stressed here that for a second-year practical, and certainly for a final-year practical, although following the same format, the write-up will be substantially longer than in the example given here. Thus, the Introduction and Discussion sections of a final-year project would be extended to include more coverage of the literature, critical discussion, etc. The format used in this example is the same as that identified in Chapter 6. However, the report writer should try to include as many aspects of the report as she or he can so that they might achieve as high a mark as possible when assessed by the tutor. Please note that for your own reports each subsection (Method, Results, and so on) should begin on a new page. Students should bear in mind that report writing is a skill that develops over time, and that their own initial attempts may fall short of the standard set out here.

Name:	Tom Heffernan
Year of study/date:	19 May 1985
Course/module:	Research Methods – Year One
Title of report:	Short-term memory and its development
Type of report:	A first-year practical write-up

Abstract

As children develop, their rehearsal capability also develops and increases their memory spans. It was hypothesised that there would be an increase in the amount of words recalled in the experimental condition (Rehearse Out Loud) when compared to the control condition (No Rehearsal Instructions) in the 5-year-olds. It was also hypothesised that there would be no significant difference between the conditions for the 11-year-olds. A between-subjects design was used, with two age groups – 5- and 11-year-olds. In one condition, all the children rehearsed words out loud (the experimental condition), in a second condition the children did not rehearse out loud (the control condition). The dependent variable was the total number of words recalled. The results showed significantly more words recalled in the experimental group in the 5-year-olds, which supports Hypothesis 1; with no difference in recall between conditions in the 11-year-olds, which is consistent with Hypothesis 2. These results are consistent with the notion that your children do not spontaneously rehearse and were discussed in relation to the literature.

Introduction

Human memory involves some mechanism by which we encode information about the world, store that information, retaining it in the memory system, and recall that information for future use (Smith, Nolen-Hoeksema, Fredrickson, & Loftus, 2003). Without this ability we would not remember who we are or what we are doing. We would be living literally one moment to the next. Memory then, is a means by which we hold information for long or short periods of time – referred to as long-term and short-term memory respectively (see, e.g., Atkinson & Shiffrin, 1968). Other researchers have looked at memory in terms of "deep" and "surface" processing (Craik & Lockhart, 1972). Current views still see memory as being made up of short- and long-term systems (see, e.g., Eysenck & Keane, 2000).

Much of the early research has been carried out on adults (Baddeley, 1997, 1999). Recently, work has looked at the development of memory and what processes might be involved (such as rehearsal) in this development, using children as a focus (see Kail, 1990). One development is the use of rehearsal in short-term memory – with a clear difference emerging between the ages of 5 and 12 years (e.g., Flavell, Beach, & Chinsky, 1966; Ornstein, Naus, & Liberty, 1975). For example, Flavell et al. (1966) found evidence that there was an absence of rehearsal in very young children (around 5 years), but that older children (from 9 upwards) seemed to use rehearsal to remember things. This has been supported by more recent research (see Kail, 1990). Rehearsal is a term used to refer to the repetition of information (like words) over and over, in order to remember that information. It appears that, as they develop, children learn the advantages of using things like rehearsal to improve their memory, and by the age of 10 to 11 years they are fully aware of this process (see, e.g., Flavell, Miller, & Miller, 2002). So, as children learn to use strategies such as rehearsal, there are increases in the amount of information they can recall (their memory span). This seems to be the case for a range of materials, such as words, pictures, numbers, and so on (Kail, 1990). It is this aspect of memory that was the focus of the study.

The experiment here examined the effects of rehearsing aloud on short-term memory across two different age groups: 5-year-olds and 11-year-olds. If young children do not use rehearsal by themselves, then getting them to rehearse out loud should improve their recall. If older children already use some form of rehearsal to aid their memory, then there should be no benefit in their rehearsing aloud. On this basis the following hypotheses can be made.

The hypotheses

1. There will be an increase in the amount of words recalled in the experimental condition (Rehearse Out Loud) when compared to the control condition (No Rehearsal Instructions) in the 5-year-olds.
2. There will be no difference in recall between the experimental and control conditions in the 11-year-olds.

> *Please note*: As pointed out in Chapter 6, when submitting a manuscript for publication, say for example as a journal article or a conference paper, or, as is found in a number of final year psychology projects, a separate hypotheses section may not be necessary. Rather, a statement about what is expected from the research at the end of the Introduction section is sufficient. For example, the following statement could be used to replace the set of hypotheses stated here: "If 5-year-olds do not spontaneously rehearse, then providing them with training in rehearsal should increase their memory spans. On the other hand, if, as suggested by the literature, 11-year-olds do engage in spontaneous rehearsal, then providing them with training in rehearsal techniques will be of little or no benefit to them in terms of increasing their memory spans."

Method

Design

A between-subjects design was used with two factors. There were two levels of age, a 5-year-old group and an 11-year-old group, and two levels of condition, a "No Rehearsal Instructions" group (the control condition) in which the children were not given any instructions to rehearse; and an experimental condition "Rehearse Out Loud" group (the experimental condition) in which the children were instructed to rehearse out loud as they heard the words. The number of words correctly recalled was the dependent variable or measure. The 5-year-olds were given lists containing between 4 and 8 words, and the 11-year-olds were given lists containing between 5 and 10 words. The different ranges reflect differences in memory spans between the two age groups.

Participants

An opportunity sample of 64 schoolchildren were tested, with 32 children in each age group. The 5-year-old group (15 boys, 17 girls) had a mean age of 5 years, 2 months (age range 4.9 to 6.00 years); and the 11-year-old group (19 boys, 13 girls) had a mean age of 11 years, 3 months (age range 10.2 to 11.6 years). Participants were randomly allocated to either the control or experimental group. Thus, there were 16 children per age group, per condition. These children were selected from one junior and one senior school in the Greater Manchester area and were all volunteers.

Materials

The words were chosen randomly from the following list of monosyllabic words (cat, ear, top, key, pig, bus, boy, time, spoon, oil, leaf, ball, rug, kite, book, pen, nose, hand, bag, and dog) with no repetition of a word in a given list.

Procedure

Each child was tested separately and the time taken was approximately 5–12 minutes. To make sure the words were familiar to each participant, each child was told the full list and asked to repeat each word on the list. The words were spoken to the participant by the experimenter and item presentation was set at a rate of 1 item every 2 seconds. The participant was required to recall the list of words in the same order as they were spoken by the experimenter, with the child saying "pass" for each word she or he could not remember in the list. In the "No Rehearsal Instructions" control condition the following instructions were used:

1. I will say a series of words to you. I want you to try and remember the words in the same order that I read them. Do you understand?
2. Once I have read all the words to you I will raise my hand [the experimenter demonstrates by raising one hand]. Once I raise my hand I want you to say all the words back to me, in the same order that I have read them. Do you understand?
3. If you forget one or more of the words, then say "pass" for each word you have forgotten. Do you understand?

If necessary, these instructions were repeated and simplified for the child. Instructions and procedure for the "Rehearse Out Loud" experimental condition were the same except that each child was instructed to repeat the words out loud as each word was spoken to her or him. The 5-year-old group began by being given a list of 4 words and these were increased until the child began failing on at least 50% of the list (i.e., could not recall more than half the words on the list), the number of words immediately below this was seen as that child's "memory span". The same procedure was used for the 11-year-old group. Each list presentation and recall time took between 20 and 60 seconds, depending on the number of words per list. After testing, each child was thanked and any questions were answered.

Results

Recall was scored as the number of items recalled in their correct position in the list. Table 6.A consists of the means and standard deviations for the 5-year old group and 11-year-old group across conditions. A series of independent t-tests were applied to the data as inferential tests.

	TABLE 6.A		
	Means and standard deviations from Example 2: A practical write-up		
Age	*Control condition*		*Experimental condition*
11 years	Mean	4.40	4.60
	SD	(0.69)	(0.78)
5 years	Mean	3.00	4.00
	SD	(0.81)	(0.88)

As can be seen from Table 6.A, for the younger children more words were recalled in the experimental "Rehearse Out Loud" condition (4.00, SD 0.88), than in the control "No Rehearsal Instructions" condition (3.00, SD 0.81) and this difference was significant ($t(30) = 4.5$, $p < 0.05$). For the older children, recall was higher in the experimental "Rehearse Out Loud" condition (4.60, SD 0.78) than in the control "No Rehearsal Instructions" condition" (4.40, SD 0.69) but this difference was not significant ($t(30) = 0.80$, p = n.s.). These trends can be seen in Figures 6.A and 6.B. The standard deviations do not deviate significantly across conditions for each age group, according to the Levene's test for equal variance ($p = .519$ for the 5-year-old group, and $p = .30$ for the 11-year-old group). In addition, overall recall is higher in the older children than in the younger children. A third independent t-test was applied to compare all the data from the 5-year-old group with all the data for the 11-year-old group and revealed significantly more words recalled by the older children ($t(62) = 8.5$, $p < .05$).

Discussion

The results for the 5-year-olds supported Hypothesis 1 set out in the Introduction: Providing young children with instructions to rehearse did lead to an increase in the amount of words they could recall. The results from the 11-year-olds were consistent with Hypothesis 2 set out in the Introduction: There was no difference in recall between conditions. In addition, overall recall was higher for the older children than for the younger children.

These results can be explained in terms of the literature cited in the introductory section of this report. These results fit in with earlier findings suggesting that very young children, in this case 5-year-olds, do not appear to use rehearsal as a means of enhancing their short-term memory capabilities (e.g., Flavell et al., 1966; Kail, 1990). However, it was shown here that when young children are encouraged to use rehearsal, as they were in the experimental condition, then this rehearsal improves their short-term memory, leading to better recall. The findings from the 11-year-olds are also consistent with earlier literature on the subject. Because they already use rehearsal, requiring them to rehearse aloud, as in the experimental condition here, had no beneficial effect on their short-term memory capabilities (Kail, 1990).

In the wider sense, the findings support the notion of a short-term memory system that is used by children to encode, store, and recall information, in this case spoken words (Baddeley, 1997, 1999; Eysenck & Keane, 2000). Within this system, processes, such as rehearsal, develop with age. It would appear from the findings of the present study that although young children do have the ability to improve their memory by using rehearsal, they not do so naturally, perhaps they do not realise its benefits. One can assume that this mechanism develops alongside other cognitive processes, such as reading, arithmetic, etc., and acts to subserve these later developments (see, e.g., Gleitman et al., 2003).

The experiment did have its drawbacks and there are ways of taking this research forward.

Figure 6.A

Bar chart for 5-year-olds from Example 2: A practical write-up.

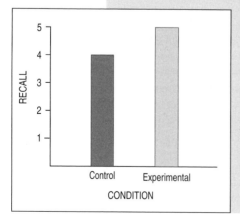

Figure 6.B

Bar chart for 11-year-olds from Example 2: A practical write-up.

For example, much of what was found here is replicating what has been found before. Future experiments should take this further, possibly by looking at a range of age groups between these two extreme ages (e.g., 7-, 8-, and 9-year-olds) to pinpoint the exact age at which rehearsal is used voluntarily. Second, although young children do not appear to use rehearsal by choice, these results do not explain why this is the case. It could be that they do not realise the potential of using such strategies (Flavell et al., 2002) or some other reason. Perhaps a future experiment could look at this from a qualitative viewpoint (e.g., ask the children questions about this). Future research might also wish to study the relationship between possible impairments in memory at an early age, and the onset of later developmental disorders, such as dyslexia (see, e.g., Groome, Dewart, Esgate, Gurney, & Kemp, 1999).

In conclusion, this study looked at whether instructions to rehearse improved memory recall in young and older children. The findings revealed that young children do benefit from rehearsal, in terms of it improving recall in this group, whereas in older children there was no benefit. The findings support the role of strategy use in short-term memory. The findings also show that young children are capable of rehearsing in such a way as to improve their short-term recall, but may not choose to do so spontaneously. Older children appear more than capable of rehearsing. This confirms previous findings in this area and suggests rehearsal can be used to improve memory, which could have applications.

References

Atkinson, R.C., & Shiffrin, R.M. (1968). Human memory: A proposed system and its control processes. In K.W. Spence & J.T. Spence (Eds.), *The psychology of learning and motivation, Vol. 2*. London: Academic Press.

Baddeley, A.D. (1997). *Human memory: Theory and practice*. Hove, UK: Psychology Press.

Baddeley, A.D. (1999). *Essentials of human memory*. Hove, UK: Psychology Press.

Craik, F.I.M., & Lockhart, R.S. (1972). Levels of processing: A framework for memory research. *Journal of Verbal Learning and Verbal Behaviour, 11*, 671–684.

Eysenck, M.W., & Keane, M.T. (2000). *Cognitive psychology: A student's handbook* (4th ed.). Hove, UK: Psychology Press.

Flavell, J.H., Beach, D.R., & Chinsky, J.M. (1966). Spontaneous verbal rehearsal in a memory task as a function of age. *Child Development, 37*, 283–299.

Flavell, J.H., Miller, P.H., & Miller, S. (2002). *Cognitive development* (4th ed.). New York: Prentice-Hall.

Gleitman, H., Fridlund, A.J., & Reisberg, D. (2003). *Psychology* (6th ed.). New York: Norton.

Groome, D., Dewart, H., Esgate, A., Gurney, K., Kemp, R., & Towell, N. (1999). *An introduction to cognitive psychology: Processes and disorders.* Hove, UK: Psychology Press.

Kail, R. (1990). *The development of memory in children* (3rd ed.). New York: Freeman.

Ornstein, P.A., Naus, M.J., & Liberty, C. (1975). Rehearsal and organizational processes in children's memory. *Child Development, 26,* 818–830.

Smith, E.E., Nolen-Hoeksema, S., Fredrickson, B., & Loftus, G.R. (2003). *Atkinson and Hilgard's Introduction to psychology* (14th ed.). New York: Wadsworth.

Appendices

All the raw data, computer printouts and additional materials should be placed in a set of appendices for your own report. Each appendix should be numbered, labelled, and an explanation of its contents given.

Critical evaluation

This practical represents a good first-year practical write-up. However, it could have been improved. There are a number of strengths and weaknesses in the practical write-up that have, taken in combination, resulted in the mark awarded.

Strengths

- It follows the correct structure for a write-up of this kind.
- It has a good Title Page and Abstract, which contain all the relevant details needed to convey the information in these sections.
- It has a good Introduction that:
  (a) goes from the broad base to the specific focus of the practical
  (b) is clear on the main focus of the experiment
  (c) contains primary and secondary sources, which are theory and research based, well supported in terms of references
  (d) has coverage of the theoretical framework adopted
  (e) has a clear set of hypotheses that are to be tested.
- It has a clear Method section containing all the relevant components.
- It has a good Results section which covers the relevant descriptive and inferential statistics required to test the data, as well as a written interpretation of the statistics.

- It has a good Discussion section which:
  - (a) briefly reiterates the main findings
  - (b) relates these findings to the introductory material
  - (c) has good suggestions for improvements
  - (d) has some useful suggestions for future experimentation
  - (e) has a good conclusion section
  - (f) shows some evidence of independent thinking.
- It has a complete Reference section.

Weaknesses

- The main weaknesses in the Introduction are:
  - (a) could have clearly stated the aim of experiment at some point
  - (b) needs more consideration of classic theory/research (e.g., the "multi-store" model of memory)
  - (c) could have shown a little more reading beyond the main references in this area.
- The Method and Results are good – no major weaknesses to cite.
- The Discussion section:
  - (a) should have given more consideration to weaknesses in the conception and design of the experiment (e.g., the fact that it is predominantly a replication of previous research)
  - (b) could have included additional relevant literature
  - (c) could have been stronger in its conclusions (e.g., what do the findings tell us about early and current theories of short-term memory?).

Please note: By improving on these weaknesses, the final mark/grade could have been improved significantly.

Additional guidelines for second-year practicals

The format of an empirical practical report write-up in the second year of a psychology course is essentially the same as that described for a first-year practical write-up. However, there are a number of additional elements that one looks for in the second year of a course, and therefore in a second-year practical write-up, and these are included in the following list. Precise guidelines and criteria should be provided on the second-year research methods part of the psychology course. Second-year practicals and their write-ups tend to:

- incorporate a more advanced type of design, typically incorporating two factors or variables into the design
- incorporate a more thorough search of the literature than would be expected in the first year
- show more evidence of breadth of reading on the particular topic under consideration, with greater evidence of primary source material (i.e., journal articles) than might be found in the first-year practical course (i.e., a stronger literature base)
- show greater evidence of critical evaluation and discussion than is typically found in the first year
- show evidence of working independently (e.g., carry out your own literature search)
- be longer in length, often resulting in a report between 3000 and 4000 words in length
- be presented in a scientific style.

Additional guidelines for the third-year practical

Your final-year dissertation project is an individual piece of work undertaken by you over two semesters. It is designed to develop and test you on a range of knowledge, skills, and abilities. These include:

- literature searching and information gathering
- the ability to carry out a piece of independent research
- data (quantitative or qualitative) handling and analysis
- originality
- problem solving
- analytic reasoning
- critical thinking
- work scheduling and self-directed study
- self-motivation and initiative
- written and oral communication skills.

The final-year honours project is seen by some as the culmination of the student's honours-level work. It is a substantial piece of work that can be a triple or even quadruple unit on the psychology course. (It is also seen by some as an important indicator of your research potential and thus can be "flagged up" in your CV.) The project generally progresses through a number of stages, for example:

1. Submission of a research proposal by the student to a member of staff (usually a project co-ordinator); guidelines are normally provided by the member of staff.
2. Assessment of the research proposal by a staff committee, assessed in terms of its feasibility, resource implications, and ethics.
3. The allocation of an appropriate supervisor to the student (normally attempting to allocate the student to someone who has experience within that research field).
4. The development, execution, and writing up of the project itself (over a period of two semesters).

Check the precise stages used at your own institute.

Again, the overall format of the practical report write-up in the final year of a psychology course is essentially the same as the format found at the previous two levels of study. However, there are a number of key focus points one should bear in mind (and discuss with one's supervisor) when writing up the honours dissertation project. The final-year project should:

1. constitute a substantial piece of psychological study
2. attempt to incorporate some novel element into the research (try to avoid merely replicating a study)
3. demonstrate a thorough search of the literature (the student is encouraged to use a computer-based literature search (e.g., PsycLit, BIDS, Web of Science) to access current literature, such as journal articles, on the chosen topic)
4. include an introduction that incorporates: (a) the aims of the study and a general overview of the major theoretical issues and approaches relevant to the topic; (b) specific background research relevant to the topic (ensure that important issues and concepts are explained clearly); and (c) present concise and clear hypotheses(is) or research question(s) that follow logically from the aims and background literature
5. ensure the design is adequate for the number of variables/factors and aims of the study
6. present results using the appropriate descriptive format, with illustrations, and information regarding the statistical analysis applied to the data; present the results so that they provide a clear account of what happened in the study and how these findings relate to the hypotheses/research questions set out in the introductory section

7. interpret and evaluate the results in a discussion section, in relation to the knowledge base presented in the introduction; any flaws, improvements, or suggestions for future research should also be considered in the discussion
8. follow the guidelines set out in Chapter 6 for references and appendices
9. avoid racist and sexist language
10. adhere to the recommended or imposed word length, this can vary enormously between institutes (e.g., from 6000 to 10,000 words in some instances)
11. avoid plagiarism – it is dealt with seriously.

In addition, make sure that the project subheadings each begin on a new page, that it is typed up and double spaced, that adequate margins are formatted (particularly on the left-hand side to allow for binding), that each page is numbered, that each copy is bound (following advice given by project co-ordinator), and that you submit sufficient numbers of copies to the relevant co-ordinator (on or before the hand-in date). Remember, some projects can be sent off to a conference and may be subsequently published.

When using an observational method

You may need to refer to the following guidelines (in addition to the structure summarised at the end of this section) if you are carrying out and writing a report for a study using the observational method.

Coding (or categorising)

Data should be coded in some way in order to carry out relevant analysis of that data. For example, if you have collected video-taped observations of students interacting with one another on campus (see also Chapter 5 on ethics), you may need to code this in order to analyse the data and reach some conclusions about student interactions. The video footage would be the material from which you extract your data. (The same would apply to handwritten material.) First, you would need to describe the source of the data (e.g., video footage of students interacting around the campus). Second, you need to describe how the material was coded. How you code the data needs to be thought through and carried out in a systematic way. You may use an existing coding scheme taken from previous literature (in which case you must cite the source). In some cases you might need to construct your own coding scheme, using operational definitions of the different codes used and with examples of which behaviour is reflected in which code. You may also wish to provide examples of problematic cases, where particular behaviour did not fall into a particular code category, and describe how you handled such data.

Observer reliability

In this section, you need to include an assessment of the reliability of the coding scheme. You need to describe how the particular coding scheme could be reliably used by another person observing a similar scenario. Typically, you might measure the reliability between two or more independent observers (known as inter-observer reliability), or you could use the same observer across different periods of time (known as intra-observer reliability). In either event, you need to express the result of the observer reliability in a numerical fashion.

Data reduction

In this section you need to describe what changes there have been to the data as a result of the coding phase and the data analysis phase. This is necessary in order to make a sensible interpretation of the data. For example, originally there may have been three categories of behaviour observed by you – "high", "medium'; and "low" – but you may not have observed enough instances of the "low" category in order to draw any meaningful interpretation from this data,. Thus, you might wish to combine the "low" category with the "medium" category, and produce two new categories – a "high" category versus a "not high" category. You would need to describe this process here. Thus, you would have described the problem encountered and how it was addressed within this study.

Summary of format for an observational report: Title, Abstract, Introduction, Method: participants, materials, procedure, coding, observer reliability, and data reduction, Results, Discussion, References, Appendices.

Writing a qualitative report

When writing up qualitative reports, it is necessary to bear in mind that the subsections may differ from the previously given report format in terms of some of the focus points within the subsections of the report. The Title will be a similar format as described for previous types of report. What follows are some key focus points to consider when writing up a qualitative report.

Abstract

The general format should be similar to that identified for empirical reports. With qualitative reports it is imperative that you clearly identify the type of observation and analysis used in the study (e.g., naturalistic observation, discourse analysis, etc.).

Introduction

Overall, the general format will be similar to that outlined for the empirical report. A summary of your literature search on the topic should be presented here. For qualitative reports one should present a description of the methods adopted and a full justification for adopting a particular methodology. Perhaps compare the method chosen with other available techniques and consider why the method you have adopted was the most appropriate for the particular research question under consideration. Provide reasons as to why you have rejected certain methods of study. Another key aspect here is the fact that a specific hypothesis(es) may not be stated. Instead, a research question or aim could be stated. By the end of this section the reader should understand why you have chosen to study the phenomenon in this particular way.

Method

Again, as with quantitative reports, this section should provide relevant details of the design, methods of study, participant information and what procedure was followed. Any preliminary pilot study should be reported in full (e.g., perhaps testing the validity of the techniques in a pilot study). Demographic and other social data, as well as details of where the study was carried out and when it was carried out (e.g., was it in a naturalistic environment?), should be included here. Again, it is important to provide justification for the precise method adopted here and why other alternatives were ruled out. Provide details of what type of information was recorded and what mechanism was used to record these responses. Details of permission given (where appropriate) and what ethical considerations were involved also need to be outlined here. See main Method section earlier for specific format for qualitative studies.

Analysis

Because the type of analysis in qualitative research relies heavily upon the selection and interpretation of material by the researcher, she/he needs to present the results in such a way as to achieve maximum transparency so that the reader can see how and why the analysis proceeded in the way that it did. The best way to achieve this is to follow explicit methods of analysis already described in the literature and to use specific techniques (such as tables/diagrams) to display the data. These methods of analysis and data display will be dictated by the particular qualitative methodology implemented by the researcher, but follow fairly similar lines to those used in observational research (see for example, Mason, 2002).

Discussion

Begin with a summary of the aim or research question under study, and a summary of the findings from the study. Discuss these findings in relation to the background literature and the methods used in the study. Focus on any differences between what you have found in the study and what was found in previous research – perhaps focus on differences such as methodology, measurement tools, type of setting, and so on. Remember to interpret the findings rather than merely reporting them – discuss the findings and their implications for the area under study, as well as what generalisations can be made from the data. On some occasions this section might be combined with the analysis section (an Analysis and Discussion section). It is important here to have a section that looks critically at the overall research you have undertaken. This section should retrospectively consider the methods used, the role of the participant as part of the research experience, potential participant and researcher biases, any design flaws, and what might be improved or changed in future research paradigms.

References

The Reference section should follow the format outlined earlier in this chapter and detailed in Chapter 3.

Appendices

As for empirical reports, the Appendices should be used to include details that are important but which might interrupt the flow of information included in the other relevant subsections. Raw material, transcripts from interviews, details of a pilot study, or other key information should be presented here in a clear, labelled, and ordered format.

Summary of format for a qualitative report: Title, Abstract, Introduction, Method: participants, source of data, transcription of data, Results & Discussion, References, Appendices.

Presenting research at a conference

At some point during your undergraduate studies, usually in the final year, you may be encouraged to present a summary of your work at one of the conferences which take place each year around the country. It could be that you are invited to present at an *undergraduate conference* – which is usually organised by a group of universities within a given area and held at one particular university, or you might wish to present at one of the general or specialist conferences run by the British Psychological Society, or the APA in America (e.g., their annual conference). Typically, you will be asked to present a summary of your final-year research project or dissertation.

The advantages of presenting your work at such a forum are that it can provide you with good experience in presenting your work (e.g., a summary of your final-year project) to a large audience. Presenting at a conference also provides the opportunity for you to meet with and form associations with others in the field and, of course, it enables you to have your work published in the Conference Abstracts or Proceedings. All of this, of course, looks good on your curriculum vitae or job application form. What follows are guidelines on presenting your work at a conference.

Submitting a research article

Before being accepted for presentation at a conference you will normally be required to *submit an abstract* (about 100–150 words) and, in some cases, *an extended version of the paper* (e.g., a 1500-word write-up). The specific guidelines and requirements are normally sent to you after your application for the conference has been received.

Your submission should take *the same format as that of a journal article*. The research article submitted for a conference is typically shorter than a journal article, the former being in the region of 1500 words. The research article should, ideally, be an original investigation (or have some novel aspect to it) that is undertaken to gain knowledge and understanding within the field of psychology. Once submitted, the manuscript will be reviewed by a panel of researchers and its scientific worth will be assessed, in order to determine whether it warrants inclusion in the conference and subsequent publications. An example of a research article submission can be found in Example 6.2.

Example 6.2: A research article

Here is an example of a 1500-word (not including references) research article. This article is in the format one might use as a submission for an extended conference paper, or could be developed further for a journal submission. Indeed the BPS typically require a written manuscript of this type for each submission you make to one of their major conferences (oral or poster presentation). The example of the study shown here focused on measures of exercise dependence in aerobic exercisers.

Exercise Dependence in Aerobic Exercisers: The Impact of Length of Exercise and Gender

F. Harvey* and T. Heffernan**

*Independent Researcher
**Northumbria University, Newcastle-upon-Tyne

Abstract

Exercise dependence is a maladaptive dependency upon excessive exercise, resulting in negative physical, cognitive, and social symptoms (cf., Pierce, 1994). The present study used a non-experimental format to measure levels of exercise dependence in a group of long-term and a group of short-term aerobic exercisers. Gender was also included to observe whether this had any impact on dependency measures. Overall, long-term aerobic exercisers scored higher on the exercise dependency measure than did short-term aerobic exercisers, $F(1,39) = 14.2$, $p < .05$. Gender had no impact ($F < 1$), nor was there any interaction between length of exercise and gender ($F < 1$). These findings are discussed in relation to previous literature on exercise dependency.

Introduction

The physical and psychological benefits that come from taking regular exercise are well documented (e.g., Berger & McInman, 1993; Berger & Owen, 1988; Glasser, 1976; Morgan, 1985). Recent work has led researchers to believe that in extreme forms, obsessive, high-intensity, regular exercise can be detrimental both in physical terms and in psychological terms (Adams & Kirkby, 1997, 1998; Fry, Morton, & Keast, 1991; Pierce, 1994). This has led to the notion that people can actually become atypically dependent upon exercise, a condition often referred to as "exercise dependence" (cf., Pierce, 1994). The characteristics of exercise dependence include: physiological symptoms (such as changes in endorphin levels in the brain), cognitive symptoms (such as psychological compulsion to train, increased levels of depressive mood), and behavioural symptoms (such as the narrowing of the behavioural repertoire to "fit" around the individual's training programme, and a disruption in social activities) (see e.g., Szabo, 1995, 1998).

Research has typically focused on using exercise dependence scales to identify individuals who might be "addicted" to exercise (Dua & Hargreaves, 1992), or to study links between exercise dependence and other psychological states, such as anxiety (Anshel, 1995; Morgan, 1979), mood (Grove, 1995; Plante & Rodin, 1990), and compulsiveness (Kagan & Squires, 1985). The notion of exercise dependence remains a somewhat controversial area, with problems including a need for further refinement of scales that measure the phenomenon; it is a growing area of research in sports psychology and there is a need for more research to be carried out in this area (Hausenblas & Downs, 2002; Pierce, 1994).

One such need is for research that widens the types of exercise groups studied, with previous work focusing on narrow bands of exercise groups, such as long-distance runners (Pierce, 1994). Some recent research has extended this to other groups of athletes, such as competitive power lifters (Pierce & Morris, 1998). Also, little research has been conducted on the impact endogenous factors might have upon exercise dependence, such as personality traits or sex or gender differences (Hausenblas & Downs, 2002).

Research on sex differences in sports performance has produced mixed results (see, e.g., Eagley, 1987; Hyde & Linn, 1986; Maccoby & Jacklin, 1974). For example, Maccoby and Jacklin's classic survey on the literature on sex differences concluded that although the evidence did support the existence on some psychological sex differences in sport's performance (e.g., visual-spatial differences, aggressive behaviour), few conclusions could be drawn from the diverse literature on the subject. One of the main problems with research on sex differences in sports performance is the presumption of an underlying biologically driven model of sex differences, rather than focusing on gender differences (Oglesby & Hill, 1993). Some recent evidence has suggested that women might be more prone to exercise dependency than men (Hausenblas & Downs, 2002; Pierce, Rohaly, & Fritchley, 1997).

The present study explores potential links between characteristics of exercise dependence (in non-clinical samples) in a sample of participants made up of aerobic exercisers. Length of exercise, in terms of time spent exercising, was studied in order to observe any potential interaction between this and measures of exercise dependence. Gender was also observed, as it was felt that further research was needed in order to elucidate this area (McDonald & Hodgdon, 1995).

Method

Design

The design was non-experimental. Length of exercise and gender constituted the independent measures. Two groups were studied; a short-term exercise group ($N = 20$) made up of individuals who engaged in aerobic exercise on average twice a week and who had been exercising for between 2 and 4 weeks, and a long-term exercise group ($N = 20$) who engaged in at least three sessions per week and had been doing so for at least 3 months. Aerobic exercise was defined as aerobics, circuit training, or running. There were equal numbers of males and females per group. Scores on the exercise dependence measure was the dependent measure.

Participants

An opportunity sample of 40 undergraduate university students volunteered for the study (age range 19–23 years; mean age 21 years). There were equal numbers of males and females.

Measures/procedure

Exercise dependence was measured using a psychometric scale developed from 12 items identified as symptoms of exercise dependence derived from the literature. These items reflect ratings of physiological, cognitive, and behavioural manifestations associated with exercise dependence (see, e.g., Pierce, 1994). Each item on the scale required a subjective self-assessment rating of how much the description related to that person, which was quantified. The range of scores for each item was from 1 (which would have the lowest weighting indicative of exercise dependence) to 6 (which would have the highest weighting indicative of exercise dependence). For example, in response to the question: "I give priority over other activities to maintaining my pattern of exercise", a person could score low (e.g., 1 = not applicable to me), to high (e.g., 6 =

very much like me). The total scoring range for the scale was from 12 to 72. The scale was shown to have good internal validity (0.71) and test–re-test reliability (0.58). A total score was calculated for each person. Following their participation in the study, each participant was thanked and offered a debriefing session.

Results

The results from the exercise dependence measure revealed the following. Long-term aerobic exercisers (mean = 45.1, SD = 11.2) scored higher on the scale than did short-term aerobic exercisers (mean = 29.3, SD = 14.9), and this difference was significant, $F(1, 39) = 14.2$, $p < .05$. Males (mean = 35.2, SD = 10.4) and females (mean = 39.2, SD = 15.7) did not differ significantly ($F < 1$). There was no interaction between length of exercise and gender (long-term male exercisers, mean = 42.8, SD = 8.6; long-term female exercisers, mean = 47.4, SD = 13.8; short-term male exercisers, mean = 27.6, SD = 12.2; short-term female exercisers, mean = 31, SD = 12.5), ($F < 1$). In summary, there was a main effect of length of exercise (long-term vs short-term), no main effect of gender, and no interaction between length of exercise and gender.

Discussion

The results here show that measures of physiological, cognitive, and behavioural correlates of exercise dependence are empirically related to the degree of exercise taken by individuals. Gender had no impact on the measures of exercise dependence taken here. Nor did gender interact with length of exercise in determining levels of exercise dependency.

The results lend further support to a number of issues related to exercise dependence and sports. First, the finding that the long-term aerobic exercisers scored higher on the exercise dependence scale used in this study weighs in favour of previous findings that have found a relationship between dependency and long-term exercisers (see, e.g., Dua & Hargreaves, 1992; Hausenblas & Downs, 2002; Pierce, 1994). It should be noted that in this study, long-term exercise was defined as three or more sessions for a minimum of a number of months, whereas other studies have focused on groups who engage in exercise for much longer periods of time (Morgan, 1979), making direct comparisons difficult. However, since the items used in the exercise dependence scale in this study are all taken from the symptom profile for exercise dependency syndrome, significant increases on the exercise dependence measure in the long-term exercisers is taken as being indicative of a link between lengthy periods of exercise and dependency.

Second, the lack of any gender differences on exercise dependency, or any interaction between gender and length of exercise on the measure, weighs in favour of previous literature that have found no sex differences in relation to exercise and psychological outcomes (McDonald & Hodgdon, 1995; Oglesby & Hill, 1993).

Third, the fact that this study has focused on groups of non-professional aerobic exercisers is a welcome shift away from the traditional focus (Adams & Kirkby, 1998; Pierce, 1994), which has typically looked at a narrow band of exercisers (e.g., long-distance runners).

The interpretation of these findings are qualified to some extent by potential limitations of the study. First, it might be argued that using a 12-item scale to measure exercise dependence leads to a restricted number of affective responses being considered. Other measures could be coupled with the scale to provide a fuller account of the impact of long-term exercising on the person's physical and psychological state, e.g., stress measures, mood scales. Second, there is clearly a need to extend the range of exercise groups beyond those studied here. Finally, although the selection of participants was random, one cannot rule out the possibility of pre-morbid factors impacting upon individuals' responses, e.g., personality variables. This could be assessed in a longer term study in which individuals are monitored before they begin exercising.

In conclusion, the results of the present study have revealed that high levels of exercise dependence are found in long-term aerobic exercisers, a finding that is consistent with the general literature (e.g., Hausenblas & Downs, 2002; Pierce, 1994). Gender has no impact on levels of exercise dependence. The results of this study help extend the focus of exercise dependence to non-professional, aerobic exerciser groups.

References

Adams, S., & Kirkby, R. (1997). Exercise dependence: a problem for sports physiotherapists. *Australian Journal of Physiotherapy, 43,* 53–58.

Adams, S., & Kirkby, R. (1998). Exercise dependence: A review of its manifestation, theory and measurement. *Sports Medicine Training, 8,* 265–279.

Anshel, M.H. (1995). Anxiety. In T. Morris & J. Summers (Eds.), *Sport psychology: Theory, applications the issues.* Milton, Australia: Wiley.

Berger, B.G., & McInman, A. (1993). Exercise and the quality of life. In R.N.

Singer, M. Murphey, & L.K. Tennant (Eds.), *Handbook of research on sport psychology* (pp. 729–760). New York: Macmillan.

Berger, B.G., & Owen, D.R. (1988). Stress reduction and mood enhancement in four exercise modes: Swimming, body conditioning, hatha yoga, and fencing. *Research Quarterly for Exercise and Sport, 59,* 148–159.

Dua, J., & Hargreaves, L. (1992). Effect of aerobic exercise on negative affect, negative affect, stress, and depression. *Perceptual and Motor Skills, 75,* 355–361.

Eagley, A.H. (1987). *Sex differences in social behaviour: A social-role interpretation.* Hillsdale, NJ: Lawrence Erlbaum Associates.

Fry, R.W., Morton, A.R., & Keast, D. (1991). Overtraining in athletes. *Sports Medicine, 12*(1), 32–65.

Glasser, W. (1976). *Positive addiction.* New York: Harper-Row.

Grove, J.R. (1995). Issues in sport psychology. In T. Morris & J. Summers (Eds.), *Sport psychology: Theory, applications, the issues.* Brisbane, Australia: Wiley.

Hausenblas, H.A., & Downs, D.S. (2002). Exercise dependence: a systematic review. *Psychology of Sport and Exercise, 3,* 89–123.

Hyde, J.S., & Linn, M.C. (Eds.). (1986). The psychology of gender: *Advances through meta-analysis.* Baltimore: Johns Hopkins University Press.

Kagan, D.M., & Squires, R.L. (1985). Addictive aspects of physical exercise. *Journal of Sports Medicine, 25,* 227–237.

Maccoby, E., & Jacklin, C. (1974). *The psychology of sex differences.* Stanford, CA: Stanford University Press.

McDonald, D.G., & Hodgdon, J.A. (1995). Psychological effects of aerobic fitness training: Research and theory. In S.J.H. Pierce (Ed.), *European perspectives on exercise and sport psychology.* Champaign, IL: Human Kinetics Publishers. (Original work published 1991).

Morgan, W.P. (1979). Negative addiction in runners. *Physician Sports-med, 7,* 57–70.

Morgan, W.P. (1985). Affective beneficence of vigorous physical activity. *Medicine and Science in Sports and Exercise, 17,* 94–100.

Oglesby, C., & Hill, K. (1993). Gender and sport. In R. Singer (Ed.), *Handbook of research on sport psychology* (pp. 718–728). New York: Macmillan.

Pierce, E.F. (1994). Exercise dependence syndrome in runners. *Sports Medicine, 18*(3), 149–155.

Pierce, E.F., & Morris, J.T. (1998). Exercise dependence among competitive power lifters. *Perceptual and Motor Skills, 86*(3), 1097–1098.

Pierce, E.F., Rohaly, K.A., & Fritchley, B. (1997). Sex differences on exercise dependence for men and women in a marathon race. *Perceptual and Motor Skills, 84*(3), 991–994.

Plante, T.G., & Rodin, J. (1990). Physical fitness and enhanced psychological health. *Current Psychology: Research and Reviews, 9,* 3–24.

Szabo, A. (1995). The impact of exercise deprivation on well-being of habitual exercisers. *The Australian Journal of Science and Medicine in Sport, 27,* 68–75.

Poster presentations

Poster presentations are normally displayed for long periods of time at a conference, to allow for a greater number of psychologists attending the event to view your work. Often, these will be in the form of interactive posters – which is where you are asked to present a 5-minute verbal summary along with the poster itself, with a few minutes for questions. A good poster should be self-explanatory. What this means is that *it should be sufficiently detailed and clear to allow the person viewing the poster to understand the aims, method, and major findings after scanning the poster*. Inadequate posters can lead to awkward, difficult discussions due to lack of clarity of the poster material – where you spend time having to explain things that should have been evident in the visual presentation (e.g., what was that research about?). *A poster should be prepared so that it can fit into an area of about 1 m in height and about 1.5 m in width, and should be readable from a distance of about 1 m* – so make sure that the letter size is sufficiently large. It is most important to stress that the information contained in the poster must be presented in brief form – perhaps in bullet form with short, clear sentences.

Arrange the poster in columns, so that it flows better when being viewed. Try not to use too many panels (3 rows of 3, or 3 rows of 4, A4 size, plus a header, is typical). And do not put too much information into the panels. Some people number each of the major subsections to improve this flow. One of the tutors at your institute should be able to provide good advice and feedback on compiling a poster, and you may find examples of previous posters around your department. Many presenters prepare their posters using packages such as Microsoft PowerPoint or Microsoft Publisher. Check what is available in your own department. What follows are guidelines on what should be included in the poster:

1. *Header*. This should be placed at the top of the poster and convey information about: the title of the project (keep it relatively short); each author's name; the name of the institution; and the city and country of origin.
2. *Abstract*. This should provide an overview of the study, including: the aim(s) and the hypothesis(es) (if applicable); a brief description about what method was used; the overall findings; and what conclusions were reached.
3. *Introduction*. This section should present: the aim(s) of the study; very brief information about key background theory/research

related to the study; and any hypothesis(es) or research question tested in the study. Lengthy passages about the background literature will probably be skimmed over or ignored by the viewer.

4. *Methods*. This should provide brief details about: the participant sample used in the study; the techniques used for data collection; brief design details (perhaps in a schematic format); and brief details of procedures used. Again, lengthy passages about procedures will take up too much room and may be ignored by the viewer.

5. *Results*. The results should be restricted to presenting the main descriptive data (means, standard deviations) perhaps in the form of a table and/or graph, a brief account of the trends in the data, and a summary of the findings from the inferential statistics (e.g., the *t*-test revealed a significant difference between the experimental and control conditions, $t(40) = 5.6$, $p < .05$). DO NOT overload this section with information. Subheadings (e.g., Descriptive Data; Trends; Inferential Statistics) can help with viewing this section. Illustrations (tables, figures) should be presented concisely, clearly, with a brief title, and the labels for the table or for the axes of the figure should be clear.

6. *Conclusions*. This section should be confined to a handful of statements highlighting the main findings and contributions of the study to the area. Further discussion of the area can be facilitated by the viewer asking questions.

You may wish to prepare an accompanying handout with the detail of the presentation included on this handout, and possibly more detail, along with key references that provide further reading for the attendees.

Please note: If you wish to keep your poster you must remove it before a certain time has elapsed – otherwise it may well be consigned to the dustbin by the officials at the conference.

Oral presentations

An oral presentation is where you stand up in front of an audience made up of fellow psychologists and talk about a piece of research or a study for about 12 minutes, leaving around 5 minutes for questions. This can be quite a daunting task to anyone who has never presented before at a conference. Speaking in public is an essential skill which you should be given the opportunity to develop at university.

Although your presentation skills will improve with practice, that nervy feeling may not go away – I have seen experienced lecturers/ researchers showing clear signs of nervousness despite their many years of doing the job. Organising yourself well and taking your time can help overcome some of these nerves. Again, *the key to a good presentation is to include the main details of the research* – preparing well and avoiding long rambling regurgitation of the literature. Try to avoid just reading out loud from a wad of notes. *Prepare yourself.* Spend some time thinking about the material that you wish to cover, possibly brainstorming the things that you want to get across in the presentation. Perhaps rank them in terms of which topics you want to include, which would be good to cover if you have the time, and what other information might be needed if you get any questions asked about the area. The following guidelines cover what should be included in an oral presentation:

1. *Introduction*. The aims of your study should be identified relative to previous work in the area. Only talk about essential information relating to the study (e.g., key theory and details of key research previously carried out in the area). Follow this by stating clearly what hypothesis(es) or research question(s) were addressed in the study.
2. *Method*. Include here information about the participant sample and the main techniques used for testing. Brief details about the design and procedure should also be outlined.
3. *Results*. Present the main findings of your study – the descriptive data, a table and/or graph, briefly identify what trends emerged from the data, and key details about inferential analyses.
4. *Conclusions*. Talk about how the main findings of the study relate to the background presented in the Introduction. Be brief when identifying what contributions your study has made to the area under consideration.

Most presenters will use *slides* or *overhead projections* to accompany their talk. This is a very good idea and can act to aid the structure and flow of the talk (as well as direct the attention of the audience away from you). *When giving an oral presentation (or a summary of the poster) talk clearly and pace yourself.* When asked a question by a member of the viewing or listening audience, give yourself thinking time and remember that you probably know more about the work than most people in that audience – so be confident. Do not mumble or gabble, use short words and simple sentences wherever possible, use gestures to emphasise points in your presentation, and if you are worried about "drying up" then have a set of short notes handy to refer to if necessary. If you feel that you cannot answer a question, or you do not understand the question, then be honest and say so.

Checklist for poster or oral presentation

1. Check that the Introduction provides sufficient background information for understanding the main purpose of the study, and that this detail is restricted to essential information needed to identify the purpose of the study.
2. Check that the Method provides sufficient detail about the participant sample, provides the essential design and procedural features of the study, and indicates apparatus/tests used for measurement.
3. Check that the Results are not overloaded by too many results, and that there is enough detail about the main findings derived from the study.
4. Check that the Conclusions are sufficiently clear for the observer/listener to understand the main findings and their implications.
5. Check that the illustrations used are sufficiently large so that they can be seen clearly (i.e., any tables and graphs) and are free from extraneous information or "clutter".
6. Check that you can complete the presentation within the time limit set (e.g., approximately 12 minutes for an oral presentation).
7. For an oral presentation, make sure you have rehearsed your presentation and that you are happy that you understand what you wish to get across to the audience.
8. Finally, make sure you have sufficient handouts (e.g., a summary paper of the study) for distribution to interested parties, a sign-up sheet for those attending the conference who request more information about the study.

A guide to preparing for examinations 7

This chapter presents guidelines on preparing and revising for an impending examination, and provides some useful tips for taking the examination itself. In addition, guidelines on categories typically assigned to written work are also included here. First- and second-year examination essays can be found in Examples 7.1 and 7.2.

An examination is an event during which the student is required to answer questions (usually set by the course tutor) under conditions which have a strict time limit imposed and during which the student is not normally allowed to refer to any external information source (i.e., books, journal articles, notebooks). There are some exceptions to this. One is where you might be allowed to use a calculator and/or a statistics book in an exam that involves statistical analyses. A second is where you have what is known as an *open book exam*. An open book exam is where the student is allowed to take lecture/revision notes relevant to that topic (say Developmental Psychology) into the exam room, and sometimes the student can take in related literature (e.g., books). However, with an open book exam, the student will not normally be allowed to see the examination paper beforehand and their work will be marked using more stringent criteria than for an unseen exam. Where courses run open book exams, the module/course tutor will provide specific guidelines on how such an assessment is implemented.

Some examinations are *seen*, which means that the student has previous knowledge of the exam questions, whereas the majority of exams on psychology undergraduate courses are *unseen*, which means the student does not have access to the questions on the set exam paper. The marking scheme for a seen exam will be different from that for an unseen exam, the former being marked using more stringent criteria than the latter. There is one other type of exam that students may come across, where a multiple-choice questionnaire is used. A *multiple-choice exam paper* usually consists of a series of short questions (e.g., 50 to 100 questions) with each question having four or five possible answers. The aim is to choose the correct answer for each question. Wrong answers can be penalised by deduction of a fraction of a mark (say, a quarter of a mark) for each incorrect answer. The precise format and rules governing multiple-choice question papers should be available on request from your course tutor.

The majority of exam papers conform to the type wherein a series of questions are posed and the student is required to select two or three to answer within a set period of time (typically either two or three hours). The answers are usually in the form of short essays. The keywords likely to appear in examination questions are the same as those outlined in Chapter 3.

Examinations

Why do most psychology courses have an examination component? Exams are seen as *a way of testing what you have learned* over several months on a particular course. You have to prepare revision material, retain the information, and, finally, use that information to answer questions in the examination. Indeed, many employers are impressed by exams and will ask you to list your exam grades on a job application form or curriculum vitae (CV).

Exams are seen by many as being a *fair comparison of different people's abilities*. This is because an exam reflects what you can produce on your own, under strictly supervised conditions, and working to a time limit. Indeed, some students appear to be strong at exams and weak at coursework, and some students vice versa, so having exams is seen by many tutors as a fair way of treating students. Another good reason for using exams as a form of assessment is that it *reduces the possibility of plagiarism* compared with, say, a coursework essay. Whatever your views on how fair, comparable, or useful exams are as a learning tool, it appears that they are here to stay.

The examination period should be seen in a positive light. It can be rewarding and fruitful; a time that marks the finish to a particular course or module, a time where things seem to "come together" on the course. It is a time when the student puts to the test the skills that she or he has been developing throughout the course of study. It can, of course, be a time when anxiety levels reach an all-time high on the course. Try not to become enmeshed in the pre-exam panic that often occurs when an examination period is approaching.

Remember the following things:

1. The techniques and processes required to pass an exam, just like essay writing and compiling an empirical report, are things you can be taught about and that can be practised.
2. Exam revision should become an active process; one in which the student draws upon existing skills and knowledge and uses them to write critically about the topics covered on the course.
3. With experience of having taken some exams, the whole process becomes familiar and one can build upon weaknesses the next time round (remember, series of exams come about periodically).
4. Revision tutorials and advice sessions should enable students to work with one another, sharing information and skills, which can only improve technique and confidence.

What you will find is that if you are well prepared for an exam it provides you with some sense of comfort and helps to reduce the anticipatory anxiety associated with exams (at least that's the theory!). So, what preparation can be done for an exam?

Revising for the examination

Revision session given by the tutor

Most tutors are more than willing to give students some form of revision session (or advice about revision) leading up to the examination. This may be built into the course timetable itself, with (ideally) at least 1 week being allocated to self-directed revision on the part of the student. Please note that some institutes or individual tutors may have a different approach to revision than that outlined here. A formal revision session might involve the student being given:

- an overview of main areas covered
- an exposition of the format the exam will take (e.g., Is it a multiple-choice exam or essay-type questions? What time limit has been set for the exam?)
- either a copy of a past exam paper or instructions on where to find the past exam papers (usually located in the library)

- advice on how best to handle the revision process (some tutors may refuse to give advice on this, in the belief that it is your responsibility)
- answers to any questions the students might have about revision, the forthcoming examination, and so on.

The amount of guidance given by a tutor about revision will obviously vary from tutor to tutor. You must be prepared to go to the tutor and (politely) request further advice about what to expect (and even how best to revise) for a particular exam if you feel unsure about the whole process. This advice can be essential if you are not used to sitting exams (as is the case, for example, with some mature students just returning to education). Remember, it is no good complaining about the lack of advice after the event.

Revision carried out by the student

Having suggested the potential role of the tutor in the preparation process, it is necessary to consider the role of the student – who must ultimately take responsibility for preparing for impending exams.

Things you must do when preparing for examinations

1. Attend all revision sessions and take note of what the tutor says.
2. Clarify any points (or areas to cover) if you are unclear.
3. Look at past exam papers and see what the format is likely to be.
4. Put together a set of revision notes, with brief supporting references (e.g., Freud, 1936; Seligman, 1992) in relevant parts of the text. Remember, you are not expected to provide a full reference section in an exam.
5. Leave sufficient time for revising your notes (e.g., 3–4 days).

Organising material for revision

The key to successful revision is to *organise* your revision material.

1. Set aside several hours during which you are going to organise all of your revision notes
2. Sort the information for a particular course into a hierarchy. If possible start to organise the material for a particular course as soon as possible. Indeed, many tutors would advise starting to organise the material derived from lectures from the start of the lecture programme. Organising course material into a hierarchical

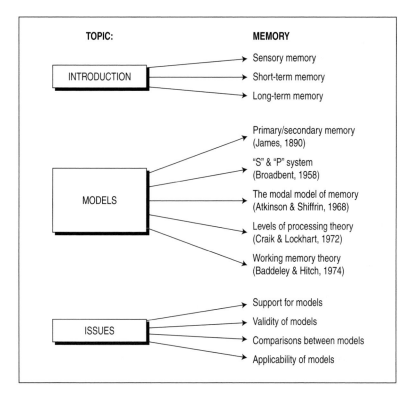

Figure 7.1

A simple plan for organising the material for revision. You can begin by organising the course material into overall headings (in bold) and subheadings.

form can provide a powerful cue for recall at a later stage. An example of how a set of course material can be organised in this way is shown in Figure 7.1.

Such a strategy is flexible enough to allow for most questions on this particular topic to be addressed (e.g., "Describe working memory", "Compare and contrast models of memory and . . .", "Discuss how useful the modal model of memory is . . .", "How have models of memory been applied?", and so on). When organising material for revision, look for relationships between the subsets of material. Organising the material at the encoding stage should improve the subsequent retrieval of that material (see, e.g., Smith et al., 2003).

It is important to note that if you do decide to adopt this approach to revision, it may well take you most (if not all) of your first year before you can implement it effectively. However, if you practise using such techniques during your first year, you should see the benefits during the two final years of the course. (Remember, for most undergraduate degree courses in psychology it is the two final years that determine your degree classification.) Another possible strategy is to sort the information into some kind of "story" with a beginning, middle and end. Whatever specific strategy you use, it is always best if it is you who selects the strategy and organises the material according to that strategy.

Facilitating memory of the material

When revising the material, many people find that reciting the material over and over again helps to consolidate it (i.e., transferring it to long-term memory). However, as pointed out in Chapter 2, actively learning the material can provide a powerful framework and strong memory trace. When revising try to do the following:

1. Organise the material into some overall framework, based around the major issues and/or debates raised on the course itself, possibly using some organisation similar to that shown in Figure 7.1.
2. Use techniques that enable you to condense the material into manageable forms.
3. Critically analyse the material and pose questions about it that you believe are important to the area covered.
4. Consider how the material compares with, or relates to, other issues/areas covered on the course.
5. Think about the strengths and weaknesses of the literature.
6. Think about what method(s) you can use to facilitate the active retrieval of the material. For example, schematic representations (e.g., a "mind map"), lists of main topics and subtopics, along with key references and critical points, or some form of mnemonic technique (see the following sections).

Again, the advice here would be to start organising the material early on in the module/unit, in advance of the exam itself. Your study skills tutor or module/unit tutor at your college or university should be able to provide advice on techniques for improving your revision strategy.

Mnemonics

Mnemonic devices or mnemonics is an umbrella term that refers to techniques used to commit information to memory – to make material more memorable. We have all used a mnemonic device at some point in our lives; e.g., noting something down on a calendar or our hand, keeping a diary (external memory aids), or using some type of internal memory aid such as rehearsing a list of items in our head.

Indeed, mnemonics based on visual imagery have been used by humans at least since 500BC, with verbal mnemonic techniques probably appearing later in our history (Baddeley, 1999).

Visual imagery mnemonics basically involve creating mental images which can be used to form associations between items (e.g., keywords). For example, *peg systems* are where the to-be-remembered items are attached to easily memorised items, known as "pegs". One widely used example of a simple peg system is the rhyme "One is a bun, two is a shoe, three is a tree, four is a door", and so on, which can be used to remember a simple numeric sequence (1, 2, 3, 4). If you use a more elaborate system you might learn to associate to-be-remembered items with salient images. For example, the *method of loci* can be employed as a powerful mnemonic. With this system you might, for example, take an imaginary walk through a familiar location (such as your home) and deposit an image of each of the to-be-remembered items (or sets of items) at each location (e.g., one in the hall, one in the front room, one in the kitchen, and so on). Then, you learn to associate each item (or set of items) with each location. Thus, when you take a mental stroll through the different locations in your home, this should act as a retrieval cue for the full set of to-be-remembered items. The series of to-be-remembered items can be replaced with other items after the original set has served its purpose. This form of visual mnemonics can provide a powerful method for learning, but is subject to some interference effects (see, e.g., Baddeley, 1999).

Verbal mnemonics can range from simple *rote rehearsal* (the repetition of material using verbal memory), to more elaborate *rhyming systems*, whereby items (e.g., names and dates) are remembered by placing them in short sentences that make up small rhymes. Organising the material along the lines of story can also act as a powerful mnemonic. You can also break down a series of items into an *acronym*. An acronym is where you form a pronounceable abbreviation of the series of to-be-remembered words by taking the first letter from each word and learning the sequence of key letters. For example, you could easily abbreviate Maslow's hierarchy of needs (see Chapter 1) into the following acronym: S (self-actualisation) E (esteem) L (love and belonging) S (safety) P (physiological needs) – this could be abbreviated to SELSP. Once the association between each letter and the level in the hierarchy has been learned, all you would need to do in, say an exam setting, would be to jot down the acronym (or series of acronyms for different aspects of the topic) and this should act as a trigger for recall.

Mnemonics work because they impose a structure and organisation on the material you are learning. Upon retrieval, a plan can then be executed which enables you to search systematically for the material you have learned. It effectively acts as a framework for retrieval. Story lines and visual images can act as effective mnemonics, perhaps because people have learned to associate strong imagery with stories and, of course, visual imagery of material (e.g., words) can provide dual coding. Both of these methods are likely to lead to deep and elaborate processing of the material (Gellatly, 1986).

Using index cards can be of use because they force you to summarise the information into fewer and fewer words. Writing key points about the theory/research under revision allows you to focus your attention on the main concepts/facts and you can take these summaries with you wherever you go – on the bus, sitting on a beach watching the sea roll in, or just killing time waiting for a friend to turn up. This is seen as an active method of learning, but may not be as effective as "mind mapping".

Mind maps

Mind maps are basically ways of summarising and organising information and ideas, so that the material can be easily recalled from memory at some future point in time (e.g., during an examination). These techniques have been popularised by authors such as Tony Buzan (see e.g., Buzan & Buzan, 2000). To form a mind map one needs to organise the material around a *central theme* – what Buzan calls a *key memory image*, which summarises the central theme. Around this central theme one can then organise *connecting themes* leading from that key image on to connections with sub-areas and sub-themes related to the topic under revision. For example, if one were to organise, say, Sigmund Freud's theory of personality into a mind map, the following structure could be used. The central theme or key memory image would be the structure and psychosexual development of personality according to Freud's theory. The connections could be organised into key sub-areas of consideration: the tri-partite system of personality, stages of psychosexual development, examples of how the theory can explain human behaviour (e.g., neurosis), issues of validity, conclusions. Within each of these sub-areas one can list the main points to remember, key terms, and supporting references. This can provide a powerful visual "map" of the key areas and how they relate to a central theme/image as well as a written representation of the material under revision.

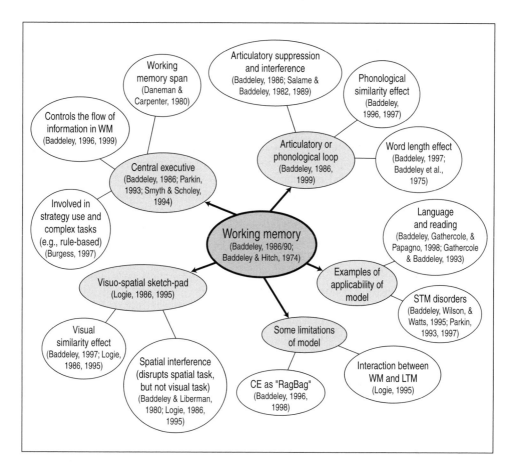

The exact format a mind map takes will depend upon the individual. Some people might be content with a simple hierarchical plan, such as that shown in Figure 7.1. Others might prefer more complex drawings that have sub-components (sub-areas and sub-themes) flowing from one central point (the *key theme* or *key memory image*).

Figure 7.2 is an example of a "mind map" – a visual way of summarising and organising material so that it can be more easily recalled. This map is a way of mind mapping the working memory model. It progresses from a central theme (working memory), on to the main sub-themes (the sub-slave systems), and on to the components and processes making up these systems (e.g., the word length effect). The diagram also contains applications of the model (e.g., language learning, reading), as well as some of its major limitations.

Figure 7.2

Mind mapping the working memory model.

Key references are presented at the relevant locations. This map could be extended to include more information, e.g., practical applications of model, its link to long-term memory, and so on.

The best advice regarding which method to use is to try a few alternatives (simple plan/complex diagram) and settle for the one you feel most happy with. By organising the material in such a way, one can work through the "map" and revise it until you become very familiar with that format. This can act as a powerful trigger of information in the examination itself. Revision notes (e.g., from lectures, tutorials, and revision sessions), as well as past examination papers, can all be used to practise these techniques. Make sure your diagram incorporates key words or phrases that encapsulate ideas for you. When these key words or phrases are recalled in the examination, the connecting information about the concept, theory, etc. should be retrieved in greater detail.

The advantages of using such a technique are clear. If one can form a strong visual image of a collection of information, and use this alongside other techniques (e.g., rehearsal, reading revision material), then these two forms of coding can act to form strong memory traces that will withstand the test of time – decay. Remembering information in a "dual code" format is a key concept in memory and cognition, and enables the person to make good use of visual as well as verbal parts of the brain. Mind mapping is generally seen as an effective and active learning strategy because it frees up one's thinking – it creates 'shortcuts' to the more substantial body of information under study.

Context can also have an effect on remembering. Revising in the same room where you will subsequently take the test can be useful – the "cues" in the study setting can act as "memory triggers" that can facilitate remembering. Some researchers go so far as to suggest that chewing the same flavoured gum in the exam that you have used during revision, can act as a memory aid (Quinn, 1995) – but I don't recommend this as your main revision strategy.

Revising the material

Revise in short bursts rather than one long session. Stagger your revision sessions (e.g., do a 1 to 2-hour revision session, then take a break, and repeat the process once or twice more during the day). Testing and retesting yourself on the material you are revising can also be of help (e.g., going over a particular point or reference can aid consolidation). Some people revise using a whole range of senses. Thus, some people form mental images of the information or, as mentioned earlier, put the whole argument into some story form. Again, if you think it might help, "read it, write it, say it, sing it, and imagine it" (Lengefield, 1996).

Finally, make sure you have covered enough topics in your revision of the area to pass the exam. Aim to revise at least one more topic than is minimally required (e.g., revise four areas instead of the three needed to cover the number of questions likely to appear on the exam paper). Question spotting and restricting your revision to the bare minimum number of areas is not recommended as a strategy. See also Acres (1987) and Lengefield (1996) for good general advice on study skills strategies and exams.

Carrying out a "mock" examination

A very useful strategy for testing how well you have learned the material would be to have a "mock exam" during which you try to answer a number of questions from a past paper within the time limit set for the exam. This is a highly recommended strategy, which will be the closest you are likely to come to the real thing. Of course, preparing revision notes can be made easier if you work as part of a small group. This can alleviate some of the boredom brought about by many long hours of revision. Getting together with a few fellow students and going through a "mock exam" is also a very good idea because not only should it alleviate some of the tedium of working alone (although it is acknowledged here that some people like to work alone), but also you can look at each other's work and provide feedback. If you do decide to work as part of a group, make sure the work (for example, collating revision notes) is allocated on an even basis and that your fellow students are turning up at the agreed times. Also make sure that your final revision notes, examples of answers, etc. are your own individual interpretations of the literature.

Things to avoid when preparing for examinations

1. Do not leave your revision until the last minute (e.g., the day before).
2. Do not just rely on past papers, hoping the questions will be the same.
3. Do not rely on the hearsay of other students. If you want to know something, ask your tutor (the worst she or he can say is "no").

4. Do not go on a drinking session the night before an exam: as alcohol can act to dull your memory.

5. Avoid drugs in general. These often have short- and long-term consequences that can damage your health and interfere with your progress in terms of learning, revision and exam performance.

6. Try not to eat a heavy meal before an exam; it can make you feel drowsy and lethargic.

7. Try to get a regular sleep pattern in place – sleep deprivation/ disruption can have a negative impact upon your cognitive processes, including memory.

8. Try not to get involved in any group hysteria immediately before going into the exam (at that stage it's impossible to change things).

Taking the examination

Having considered what exams are and how one might prepare for them, it is logical to think about what strategy one can adopt during the exam itself. People can behave quite erratically when under stress. Having a plan of action might help to overcome the panic and related erratic behaviour that some people experience in the exam room. What follows are some guidelines on how to take the exam itself. Again, it is stressed that you may well choose to adopt a modified approach to the one proposed here. When you are seated in the exam, make sure you have all the necessary things with you at the desk. Check that you have the right examination paper in front of you (some exams have several subjects sitting at the same time). The invigilator will announce the start of the examination and any other relevant details (such as the rules of conduct). Remember, if you need to gain the attention of the invigilator, raise your hand as a signal and one of the invigilators will attend to you.

Once the exam has started, the first 10 minutes or so are crucial. In this time you can organise yourself so that the remainder of the time can be spent concentrating on getting your arguments (with supporting references) down on paper. So, what should be done within this first 10 minutes or so?

- Take a few minutes reading through all the questions on offer. Make sure you are aware of any specific requirements on the

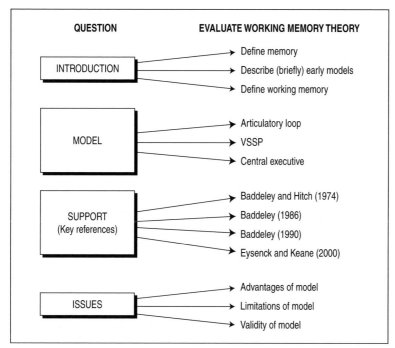

Figure 7.3

Constructing an essay plan: This simple essay plan could help when organising material for a particular topic (e.g., working memory theory).

paper. For example, some papers have a compulsory question in Part A and a choice from those questions in Part B; or require you to answer so many questions from each section on the paper.

- Make sure you know how many questions you need to answer.
- Ensure that you allocate an equal amount of time per question (unless the exam paper states otherwise).
- Decide which questions you are going to answer (perhaps base your choice on how familiar you are with the background literature for that particular topic).
- Perhaps draw up a plan for each question. This might include jotting down the main points and references for each topic; for some, this might offer a structure around which an essay can be organised. It is acknowledged here that some people don't use plans. In fact, research shows that producing essay plans in exams does not lead to higher grades (Norton & Hartley, 1986). If you do choose to use plans in the examination context, each plan could be a modified version of the hierarchy used in the revision stage (e.g., in Figure 7.1). For example, see Figure 7.3.

- Keep a check on the time – you'll be surprised how quickly it goes.
- Make sure each answer has a coherent structure to it; that it *actually answers the question set*; and reaches some conclusion(s).

What are the main components of a good answer likely to be?

A general format for a good exam answer is one that:

- has an opening paragraph explaining what the question is asking and how (put briefly) you are going to answer it
- defines any important terms contained within the question
- attempts to answer the question posed in the title
- presents and interprets relevant theory and research in support of the relevant concept(s), but also presents literature that is critical of that concept. Try to include up-to-date literature in addition to relevant historical theory and/or research, which will, of course, depend on the nature of the question set; that is, whether you are asked to describe, discuss, evaluate, etc. (see list of keywords in Chapter 3)
- has a good structure, with each new section flowing from the previous one
- shows interpretation and critical awareness of the literature wherever possible
- draws the essay to a close by stating what conclusion(s) (if any) can be drawn from the discussion/evaluation of the literature.

Please note: If you think your tutor has a preference for a format that may differ from this checklist, check with her or him beforehand.

If you run out of time on a particular essay, indicate this on your script (and perhaps make some brief notes with reference to the points/literature you would have discussed). Only by doing this will your tutor realise that you have run out of time, and may show some leniency when marking the script.

Finally, if you find yourself drawing a complete "blank" in an exam situation, then remain calm and attempt to access the information (which is there somewhere in your mind). This might be done, for example, by jotting down whatever information comes into your head about the topic – this may act as a "trigger" to the revised material. If it helps, think about a key figure in the area (e.g., if it were short-term memory one might select Alan Baddeley), or, as possibly a last resort, think of the lecturer who taught you the material in the hope that even this (potentially traumatic) vision might unlock your memory blockage.

Examples 7.1 and 7.2 are two completed examples of essays written under "mock" examination conditions. The first is an example of what one might expect at the first-year (level 1) stage, and the second comes from a second-year (level 2) piece of work. It is thought that by having both examples the reader can gain some insights into what is expected both at first-year level and beyond.

Example 7.1: A first-year examination essay

This sample essay is of an upper second-class standard, being awarded a mark of 64 per cent. It represents a good first-year unseen examination answer.

Area: Personality
Level: Year 1: Level 1
Status: (Unseen) Exam (part of a 2-hour paper, in which the student must answer 2 questions), following revision. Handwritten answer. Under invigilation.

Essay Paper   (Time taken: 1 hour)
Students must answer 1 question from this section.

1. Evaluate Freudian theory, with particular reference to the psycho-sexual stages of development.
2. Compare and contrast psychoanalysis and psychotherapy.
3. Are personality traits fixed?

Question 1. Evaluate Freudian theory, with particular reference to the psychosexual stages of development.

Essay plan

1. Outline of Freud's theory of personality.
2. Outline of psychosexual stages of development.
3. Advantages of theory.
4. Criticisms of theory.

Essay answer

In order to evaluate Freudian theory, and in particular, Freud's notion of the psychosexual stages of development of personality, it is first necessary to outline the theory and stages themselves, before going on to consider some of the pros and cons of Freudian theory.

Sigmund Freud developed his theory of the personality over many years, and formalised it around the early-mid part of this century. Freud was interested in how one's personality was constructed and what forces shaped our adult personality. Personality generally refers to those characteristics that make us different from others (e.g., our idiosyncratic behaviours, feelings, and so on). Freud believed that a personality has three parts – the id, the ego, and the superego. The id is seen by Freud as the "seat of all our instinctual drives" – such as sex, hunger, aggression. The second part is the ego, which acts to regulate the urges of the id and transform these into a socially acceptable form – to reality. Finally, Freud suggested that we develop a superego, which he said was like a conscience mechanism, which acted together with the ego to keep the forces of the id in check. This tri-partite system of the personality is well documented (e.g., Carver & Scheier, 2004; Freud, 1940/1970; Smith et al., 2003).

Having outlined the three-part personality, it is now necessary to consider the psychosexual stages of personality development and their importance. These are called psychosexual because they are developmental stages that are affected by sexual experience of one sort or another. These stages are outlined later (see, e.g., Sternberg, 1998, for more details on these stages):

The oral stage (from 0 to 1 year): At this stage the child gains pleasure from sucking and biting. The usual focus points at this stage are things such as the breast, "pacifiers", etc.

The anal stage (from 1 to 3 years): At this stage the child gains pleasure from retaining or expelling its waste products. It is an important stage because it is at this stage that many parents "potty train" their child. This will be returned to later.

The third stage is the phallic stage (about 5 to 6 years). It is at this stage that the child begins to gain stimulation from its genital region and it is at this point that, according to Freud, the child develops a strong sexual desire for the parent of the opposite sex (the Oedipus complex in boys, and the Electra complex in girls). Since the child cannot possess their parent, he or she learns to internalise these urges and control them. This stage is important because it is at this point that the superego develops and helps to control the id impulses.

The final two stages are called the genital and latency stages (from about 6 years onwards) and it is during these stages that the child learns to focus on acceptable forms of external stimulation (e.g., opposite sex peers) and develops "normal" sexual relationships with others.

If the child progresses through these stages and resolves things at each stage, he or she will develop a "healthy" adult personality. If not, the child will become "fixated" at a stage and this will have a bad effect of their later personality – that person will develop maladaptive traits (Gleitman et al., 2003; Hayes, 1994). For example a fixation at the oral stage can lead to a reliance on cigarettes; a fixation at the anal stage can lead to a very disorganised behaviour pattern later in life; and if the phallic stage is not negotiated with success, then this can lead to a weak (or lack of a) conscience mechanism (Fransella, 1981; Mischel, 1999).

So these stages are crucial in the forming of the adult personality – according to Freudian theory. Although the theory is interesting and has led to a number of current therapies for treating things like neurosis, the whole area does have its problems. For example, Freud's concentration on the sexual aspects of development led some to detach themselves from his work – people like Carl Jung and Alfred Adler (both around the same time as Freud). Most damaging to the theory is the fact that it cannot really be tested for validity – since Freud and his followers did not produce much in the way of "data" that could be tested (Smith et al., 2003). So, to conclude, Freud's ideas were useful in generating future work on personality and linking this with development, but they have been heavily criticised over the years.

Critical assessment

This essay answer was given a mark of 64%. This is a good mark and reflects the incorporation of a number of those characteristics that make up a good essay – as outlined in Chapter 3. Although the essay achieved a good mark, it is necessary to point out its strengths (which enabled it to achieve the mark it did), as well as its weaknesses (which prevented it from achieving a higher mark).

Strengths

- It identifies the structure of the essay.
- The structure of the essay is adhered to.
- There is a beginning, middle, and end to the essay.

- It addresses the topic well.
- It provides a selection of supporting references.
- It shows critical evaluation.
- It has a conclusion section to finish the essay.

Weaknesses

- It needs more support for the claims made in the essay, more primary source material (research articles), rather than textbook references.
- It could have been made clear that Freud's theory is not the only theory about the personality.
- It spends too much time on description, when more time could have been spent on evaluation of the main focus of the essay.
- The conclusion section is weak.

Please note: Improving these weaknesses would have improved the final mark/grade for this examination essay.

Example 7.2: A second-year examination essay

This sample essay is of a lower second-class standard, being awarded a mark of 57%. It represents a second-year unseen examination answer.

Area: Cognitive Psychology: Memory
Level: Year 2: Level 2
Status: (Unseen) Exam (part of a 2-hour paper, in which the student must answer 2 questions), following revision. Handwritten answer. Under invigilation.

Essay Paper   (Time taken: 1 Hour)
Students must answer 1 question from this section.

1. How valid is Baddeley and Hitch's working memory model?
2. Working memory has a number of applications. Discuss.
3. Critically evaluate the working memory model.

Question 1. How valid is Baddeley and Hitch's working memory model?

Essay plan

1. Working memory defined/Baddeley and Hitch (1974).
2. Central executive.

3. Articulatory loop.
4. Visuo-spatial sketch pad.
5. Validity – pros & cons, subsequent studies.

Essay answer

Baddeley and Hitch's (1974) working memory model consists of three components: (1) Central Executive – which has a limited capacity and is the most important component; and is used for most demanding cognitive tasks; uses the other two components as "slave systems" for specific purposes. (2) Articulatory Loop – stores information phonologically, i.e., speech based, uses rehearsal, and preserves word order. (3) Visuo-spatial Sketch Pad – stores visual and/or spatial information (Baddeley, 1997, 1999).

Articulatory loop validity

Baddeley, Thomson, and Buchanan (1975) found serial recall was better for short words than long words. Further studies by Baddeley et al. (1975) show that participants' serial recall when reading out loud was approximate to 2 seconds each word, implying that the articulatory loop has a temporal duration, much like a "tape loop". Baddeley et al. (1975) found that this "word length" was eliminated with articulatory suppression – where participants were given words visually while repeating the numbers 1–8. This also showed that "inner speech" or subvocal speech was involved. This contrasts with Miller's (1956) and Simon's (1974) chunking of units of information, as Baddeley et al. (1975) suggests that rate of rehearsal is important. Zhang and Simon (1985) studied three Chinese materials: characters, words, and radicals. If chunking was in force all three should have the same memory span. However, recall was greatest for characters (1-syllable words) and worst for radicals (which were unpronounceable) – which supports Baddeley et al. (1975).

Although word length effects are eliminated by articulatory suppression, they weren't by visual. Therefore, Baddeley (1986, 1997) revised the articulatory loop into a phonological loop consisting of (a) a passive phonological store concerned with speech production and (b) an articulatory process concerned with speech perception, and having access to the phonological store. Where auditory word presentation gains direct access into the phonological store, this can then gain access to the articulatory processes (e.g., rehearsal); which then feeds back into the phonological store. Visual presentation gains indirect access to the phonological store through verbal labelling (Baddeley, 1997). So, we process visual and auditory differently. The phonological loop aids in written comprehension, i.e., learning to read and understand what is written.

Visuo-spatial sketch pad (VSSP) validity

Baddeley (1986, p. 109) describes it as a "system well adapted to the storage of spatial information much as a pad of paper might be used by someone drawing, for example, to work out a geometric puzzle". Eysenck and Eysenck (1980) found visualisable imagery was disrupted by spatial tasks, implying that visual imagery was encoded spatially. Logie (1986) argued visual coding was important in the VSSP as disruptive line drawings needed visual as well as spatial coding. Spatial tasks are important in geographic orientation.

Central executive validity

Baddeley (1986) likened this to Shallice's (1982) supervisory attentional system with its limited capacity. It takes over demanding cognitive tasks "troubleshooting" for less adequate systems with tasks such as problem solving. Baddeley (1986) argued that damage to frontal lobes hindered the central executive and may account for short-term memory deficits in patients where no long-term learning deficit occurred. Parkin (1993) had a patient with frontal lobe damage who had problems making complex decisions – seemingly supporting Baddeley's frontal lobe theory. The central executive may not be unitary, but may be made up of two or more components (Smyth & Scholey, 1994).

The amount of research generated by Baddeley and Hitch's (1974) working memory model – the applications to learning to read; cognitive tasks; how we encode visually and spatially; how learning can be interrupted; applying it for a better understanding of possible effects of brain damage – all go to make it a valid theory (see, for example, Parkin, 2000). The central executive has not been fully explained by Baddeley and Hitch's (1974) working memory theory and its processes are not yet fully understood (Baddeley, 1998; 1999). However, this alone, is not enough to make the working memory theory invalid.

Critical assessment

This essay answer was given a mark of 57%. The student reported that this represented an increase in performance from the previous year (and follows her having sought advice on revision from her course tutor). It should be noted that the adoption of a particular revision strategy does not guarantee a significant improvement in grades. Performance in a particular examination can involve other factors in addition to revision, e.g., motivation, interest in a particular subject matter, how good your memory is, etc. Although this essay achieved a good mark, it is necessary to point out its strengths (which enabled it to achieve the mark it did), as well as its weaknesses (which prevented it from achieving a higher mark).

Strengths

- It identifies the structure of the essay.
- The structure of the essay is adhered to.
- It outlines the memory model under consideration.
- It assesses each component of the model and provides support.
- It has a selection of secondary and primary sources (i.e., book and journal article references), which are integrated into the structure.
- The essay has a flow to it, from the opening structure to components of model to consideration of the validity of the model, to the conclusion section.
- It attempts to answer the question set out in the title.
- It does not contain much of the (sometimes exhaustive) waffle found in some examination essays.
- It concludes something about the topic under consideration.

Weaknesses

- It lacks originality in its writing – it adheres to a fairly standard approach to the topic and uses a fairly standard set of references.
- It could have had an opening paragraph, defining terms such as "memory" and suggesting how the question would be addressed.
- It is lacking in detail of the sources cited, particularly the primary source material (i.e., research articles).
- It lacks in current material (e.g., research articles), such as Logie's (1999) review of working memory published in *The Psychologist*; also, Baddeley's (2003) review of working memory and language.
- The flow of the essay could be improved by having "link" sentences, such as: "Having now considered the articulatory

loop, it is necessary to consider the other 'slave-system' known as the visuo-spatial . . .".

- More could have been written about the applications of the model – which might have bolstered the argument for its validity.
- Some limitations of the model should have been considered.
- The conclusion section could have been strengthened.

Please note: Improving these weaknesses would have improved the final mark/ grade for this examination essay.

Please note: Although the second-year example appears to have more coverage of the literature, more supporting primary and secondary references, and a stronger basis for its argument than the first-year example, it actually received a lower mark. This is because a student is expected to show a progression going into his or her second (and third) year. Thus, for the second-year essay to achieve the same (or greater) mark than the first-year essay, the former would have had to show a greater depth of knowledge, provide more support, more critical evaluation/ discussion, and so on. Therefore, a student's marks in Year 2 can be quite different from those achieved in Year 1.

After the examination

After taking the exam, try to avoid the usual post-mortem that always seems to follow immediately after such an event. There is no point in going through what you did or did not do during the exam – you cannot change things at this stage. If you do start to compare your experience in the exam with another student's experience, you will probably start having doubts (often unfounded) about your own performance, which will only interfere with any further revision you have to do.

Failing an examination

The majority of students (provided they have revised well) will pass their exams the first time round. However, if you fail an exam, most courses allow you to resit. If this happens, you will be asked to resit at a later date and you should seek further advice from your tutor. Explain to the tutor what you did in that first exam and try to establish where improvements can be made. (The tutor will not tell you what to write about, but can provide some general advice on how to improve your technique.) If you do find yourself in the position of having failed a resit, then seek advice from your tutor about what procedures are in place at your institute to deal with this.

How essays are marked

The final section of this chapter provides guidelines as to what constitutes an answer in a particular class or range of marks (for example, a first-class answer). These guidelines apply to coursework and examination essays.

Although academic institutes will differ to some extent about what constitutes a particular mark/class assigned to an essay, the following typical guidelines will more or less be adhered to in most institutes. Check the precise percentage range for each category used in your own department/section, as there are variations in these across institutes. In addition to these components, marks may be gained or lost depending on how legible, neat, and comprehensible your essay appears to the marker.

A first-class mark (usually 70% upwards)

A first-class essay is one that:

- clearly and fully addresses topic/essay question
- states the structure at the beginning and adheres to that structure
- shows integration of a range of materials
- flows from one argument to another
- provides theoretical and/or empirical support where relevant
- shows critical evaluation of relevant theory/research
- demonstrates originality in the writing
- comes to a close with some good conclusion(s) about the topic.

As you move through the years (from first year, to second year, and so on) you will be expected to show evidence of having read more primary source material, e.g., journal articles. (See Chapter 3 for further details on the distinction between primary and secondary sources.) The more of these components you have in your essay, the higher your mark will be within the first-class category.

An upper second-class mark (usually 60–69%)

A typical upper second-class answer will:

- make a clear attempt to address/answer the essay question or topic set out in the title
- have a fairly well-organised structure that is adhered to throughout most of the essay
- flow from one statement to the next, from one argument to the next
- provide theoretical and/or empirical support where relevant, but less coverage of primary sources than found in a first-class answer
- show some critical evaluation of relevant theory/research
- draw some conclusion(s) from the literature presented.

A lower second-class (usually 50–59%)

A typical lower second-class answer will :

- present material relevant to the topic, and attempt to answer the essay question or address the topic well
- have elements of a structure to it, but this structure is loose and does not flow from statement to statement, or from argument to argument
- have a weak line of argument; many arguments will be based on little supporting evidence
- cite sources (mainly book references) that come from the main reading list provided in lectures or from the course outline
- show little (if any) evaluation of the material
- make many unsupported claims
- reach weak (if any) conclusion(s).

A third-class mark (usually 40–49%)

A typical third-class answer will:

- make some attempt to answer the question/address the topic
- have no clear structure to the essay
- make unfounded assertions
- present no clear relationship between lines of argument
- have many obvious omissions
- have some, but very little, supporting evidence for claims made
- fail to reach any conclusion(s).

Pass grade

Some institutes have a pass grade to indicate work that has narrowly missed the fail category (e.g., 39%). The pass grade essay could:

- loosely attempt to answer question, but have many errors/omissions
- include some related psychological content, but without paying enough attention to detail
- have little structure and be badly organised
- have no coherent flow of arguments, or theme running through essay
- provide little (if any) support
- provides no sensible conclusion(s).

Fail

An essay given a fail mark is likely to:

- fail to answer question set or address topic
- have no detectable structure or framework
- comprise a set of statements that do not relate to each other
- lack any line of argument
- fail to support claims made with any sources
- have no conclusion(s).

After the degree: Opportunities for a psychology graduate 8

The overall aim of this final chapter is to encourage students to think beyond their course of study in psychology and to consider what opportunities are available after their completion of the degree. The chapter considers what it means to have graduate status, provides details on postgraduate study and applied areas of psychology, as well as other applications. The final section also provides advice on writing a curriculum vitae (CV) and cover letter.

Having completed an undergraduate degree in psychology, the next step is to decide what to do afterwards. Some psychology students go on to do further training in psychology or a related area. Some go on to carry out psychological research, whereas others will do other things (e.g., teach on psychology courses, apply psychology to "real-world" problems). However, many students use their graduate status to obtain jobs in fields far removed from the formal topics covered on their psychology courses. For example, one student might apply for a job in personnel work, another might apply for a managerial role, whilst another still might enter onto a conversion course and completely change their focus (conversion courses to other fields such as law are not uncommon). In addition, a number of graduates decide to work or engage in further study abroad.

Prospects.co.uk produced statistics on first destinations of psychology graduates. These statistics change each year and are included here merely to give you some idea of what psychology graduates do after graduation. They reveal the following:

- 62.9% of psychology graduates obtained permanent employment in the UK
- 1.8% obtained overseas employment
- 11% went on to further academic study for a higher degree in the UK

- 5% went on to further study for a diploma, certificate or professional qualification (including PGCE) in the UK
- 4.6% went on to some other form of training in the UK
- 0.2% undertaking further study or training overseas
- 7.9% were not available for employment, study or training
- 5.6% were believed to be unemployed
- 1% were seeking employment, study or training, but not registered unemployed

Source: Prospects.ac.uk (2003). What graduates do? http://www.prospects.ac.uk/

For some useful guidance on working or studying abroad as well as contact addresses, see, for example, the booklets titled; *Careers: Work and Study Abroad,* and *Postgraduate Study and Research*, produced by the Association of Graduate Careers Advisory Service (AGCAS). The latest versions of these booklets should be available from your Careers Service on campus. You can visit the AGCAS website (www.agcas.org.uk). Whatever you decide to do as a graduate, a number of things are clear:

1. Being a graduate increases your chances of finding employment (seek advice from your Careers Advisory Service).
2. Because psychology is a subject that entails so many topics which can relate to everyday life (e.g., group dynamics, assessing people, attempting to understand human motivation, etc.), it will have something in common with the majority of careers that graduates are likely to pursue.
3. The types of skills developed on a degree course are attractive to potential employers.

Therefore, having a degree in psychology is likely to be seen in a positive light by a potential employer. The aim of this chapter is to provide advice on some of the opportunities open to a graduate of psychology. These opportunities should be considered sooner (early in your final year) rather than later. The Careers Services within your institute can provide good guidance about future potential careers for graduates. In addition, many institutes run "career days", and employers hold "careers fairs" at which many companies advertise their potential career routes to graduates.

There are a number of sources of information providing generic and specific graduate careers advice. *The Times Higher Education Supplement* and the *Guardian Education Supplement* are two potential sources for graduate employment, both of which are normally subscribed to by universities. The internet provides a rich source of potential graduate employment agencies. For example, http://www.prospects.ac.uk/ is a site that contains graduate careers advice, job vacancies and information on further study. Your own university or college careers service should be able to provide information and websites for a number of similar agencies.

Graduate status

Attaining a Bachelor's degree in psychology means that the recipient has gained a good, *general* grounding in psychology. These can be BA (Bachelor of Arts) or BSc (Bachelor of Science) degrees. The major difference between the two types is the amount of scientific content included on the course (such as research methods, statistics, biological emphases, etc.). Most psychology degree courses are of the BSc type. Obtaining a Bachelor's degree in psychology means that you have gained an all-round but basic knowledge of psychology (which is why you study so many topics on a psychology course). This is important, because it means that to *specialise* in an area of psychology you must undergo further training in an applied area, or take some form of postgraduate course (for example, an MSc in Occupational Psychology). You can specialise in psychology via a number of routes, such as postgraduate training or research, or applied psychology courses – both routes are considered here.

Postgraduate training and research

Postgraduate degree courses fall mainly into two categories (there are exceptions to this, e.g., postgraduate certificates or diplomas), a *Master's* degree and a *Doctorate* (or PhD). So, what's the difference? Traditionally, a Master's degree meant that on completion of the degree you were qualified to practise in a particular area of psychology. Currently, the possession of a Master's degree indicates that you have advanced knowledge in a specialist area of psychology. This is still true today – many institutes run MScs in Counselling Psychology, Educational Psychology, Occupational Psychology, and so on. However, with most specialisms in psychology, experience in a related aspect is required in addition to the relevant undergraduate and postgraduate qualifications. For example, to become an educational psychologist in England a person must attain a good undergraduate degree qualification, a relevant teacher training postgraduate qualification, as well as teaching experience and the postgraduate qualification in Educational Psychology itself. Historically, being in possession of a PhD meant that you were qualified to teach at a university. Currently, the completion of a PhD indicates that the recipient has a full specialist knowledge of a particular area of the discipline and that this knowledge of the subject extends right up to the boundaries of current theory and research (Phillips & Pugh, 2000). The PhD is the highest degree awarded by a university. It means that the holder is an authority on a particular area (e.g., schizophrenia), and that she or he is a fully professional researcher within that field; i.e., that she or he has developed advanced researching skills related to the subject specialism. In this sense the PhD is seen as training or an "apprenticeship" in research: a period where one "learns the trade" of becoming a researcher and gains recognition by one's peers.

Progress through a PhD

Initial registration for a PhD is typically for an MPhil (Master of Philosophy), with a transfer onto PhD status after the successful completion of a transfer exercise and transfer report after about 18 months (full time). This depends upon whether the person registering for the PhD has a Master's Degree or not. If they have, they may be able to avoid the MPhil transfer route. The transfer typically involves a formal procedure: a detailed submission (a literature review, a write-up of the work completed to present the aims and schedule for the rest of the study period through to writing up the thesis). A specialist in the field, acting in a neutral role, normally assesses this transfer document. The feedback received from this person is included with other information (e.g., a supervisor's report) to determine whether the student should be allowed to progress to the PhD level of study. You can obtain a copy of the document entitled "So you want to do a PhD: Guidelines for prospective psychology research students" from the Scientific Affairs Board and Psychology Post-Graduate Affairs Group of the BPS (1999).

It should be noted that the regulations governing the process outlined here may differ somewhat between institutions and when studying overseas, so you must check with the particular institute before embarking on this course of study.

Funding issues

Funding for Master's and PhD courses is normally secured by the university or institute advertising such places. For example, a university might receive funding from one of the major research funding bodies, such as the Economic and Social Research Council, the Medical Research Council, or some other source. Normally a student on one of these courses will have all their university fees and costs paid, and usually receive some form of maintenance grant. The size of the grant may vary, but is typically in the region of £4000 or £5000 per year, and could be more if it is a studentship that requires the student to teach as part of their contract (e.g., as a practical demonstrator; running seminar classes, etc.). A good place to start looking for information about funding issues is to obtain a copy of the Association of Graduate Careers Advisory Services (AGCAS) booklet entitled: *Post-graduate Study and Research in the UK*, which should be available from your Careers Advice Centre on campus.

In addition, students can earn extra cash by taking on some academic duties at the university itself (such as marking scripts). Normally, the funding for a PhD will include some (limited) funds for travelling to conferences both at home and abroad, where you can present some of your research findings. In addition to this, many people undertake Master's and PhD degree courses on a part-time basis, and in many cases operate on a self-funding basis. Anyone interested in either of these two modes of study should contact the relevant university/institute to find out more about the costs/procedures involved. See: Research Opportunities, *The Times Higher Education Supplement*, published around late February each year, for a list of universities and names of people to contact for further information on postgraduate research opportunities.

Undertaking a Master's or PhD course of study requires a great deal of commitment and hard work on the part of the individual. In many cases, studying for a PhD will involve you pursuing a particular line of research – unlike an undergraduate course, where you are taught as part of a large class. For some people this can be a daunting task. However, being awarded a higher degree like a PhD can bring with it a feeling of individual achievement quite unlike that experienced at any other level of study. Attaining PhD status also brings with it recognition and academic credibility within your discipline (see, e.g., Graves & Varma, 1997 or Phillips & Pugh, 2000 for some excellent insights into the whole process of PhD study). For further information on postgraduate studies (taught and research based), a list of the institutes which run these courses, the facilities available, and funding aspects, see for example, Hobsons (2003) *Postgrad: The Magazine* – an up-to-date copy should be available from the Careers Services on your campus. See also *The Psychologist* – "How employers see psychologists" (1991); "Student special issue"

(1994); and "A day in the life of a PhD student" (1995) – for some useful insights into careers in psychology, postgraduate study, researching, funding aspects, and what it's like to be a PhD student.

British Psychological Society

The British Psychological Society (BPS), founded in 1901, is a body that exists to promote the advancement of the study of psychology and applications of psychology. In addition, it acts to maintain high standards of education and conduct within the psychology profession. The BPS produces a range of materials: its own journal, *The Psychologist*, within which articles and information are published on a monthly basis; books and a range of journals published under the BPS publishing label. It also provides accreditation for many undergraduate and postgraduate courses throughout Britain. The British Psychological Society has set up an information package on the Internet (home page http://www.bps.org.uk/), which can be used to access invaluable information about a range of facilities offered by the BPS.

In order to become eligible for postgraduate training in psychology in the UK (e.g., to train to become a clinical psychologist, or an educational psychologist) you must be eligible for the *Graduate Basis for Registration* (or GBR). In order to be eligible for GBR you must have a relevant qualification in psychology from a UK institute that has been Society-accredited to confer GBR status: a point that is worth checking with your own institute as soon as possible. If you are not eligible for GBR then you can take a qualifying exam (contact the BPS for details on this). *It is important that your course has been Society-accredited for GBR if you are thinking of going on to specialise in psychology* (e.g., if you wish to become a clinical psychologist). In order to gain full professional status, those who decide to pursue a professional career in psychology:

- must have BPS GBR status (or have undergone the appropriate qualifying exam)
- must have completed an appropriate period of postgraduate training in the relevant area of applied psychology (which may include the appropriate period of supervised practice)
- must be eligible for entry onto the BPS register of chartered psychologists.

The major specialisms in psychology are briefly considered here. These include: Clinical Psychology, Educational Psychology,

Occupational or Organisational Psychology, Criminological or Forensic Psychology, Health Psychology, and Counselling Psychology; and,
more recent in terms of their development, Neuropsychology, Psychotherapy and Sports Psychology. See your Careers Service on
campus for information and for a compendium of taught and research
courses in the UK and Ireland. This information should contain a full
list of postgraduate courses, details of facilities at particular institutes,
and details on financial support. Clearly, the specialist courses
available and potential salary levels will differ from country to
country. Those students outside the UK must check with their own
governing body (e.g., the APS in America) and access information
about such courses and salaries. Also, write to the British Psychological Society, St Andrew's House, 48 Princess Road East, Leicester
LE1 7DR, UK for further details on particular specialisms in psychology (website: www.bps.org.uk/). The BPS can also supply you
with lists of accredited postgraduate courses and a copy of their
Careers in Psychology booklet. See also the BPS booklet entitled *Studying
Psychology*, which has further information about careers and courses of
study in psychology. Your campus library should also have sections
dedicated to literature on the various specialisms in psychology. You
can write to the BPS for details on registration qualifications and
further training, pay scales, and prospects and conditions for each of
these specialisms. The APA in the USA should supply similar information about membership, training, and careers in psychology.

The American Psychological Society (APA) was founded in 1988
by a group of scientifically oriented psychologists who were interested in advancing scientific psychology and its representation at a
national level. Their mission statement is to promote, protect, and
advance the interests of psychology as a science. The society pro-
motes research, application and teaching of psychology. Like the BPS,
the APS has information on research, journals and books, subsections,
and jobs in psychology. The contact address is 1010 Vermont Avenue,
NW, Suite 1100, Washington, DC 20005–4907, USA (website http://
www.psychologicalscience.org/). You could also contact the American Psychological Association (APA) for information on similar
topics. The address is 750 First Street, NE, Washington, DC 20002–
4242 (website http://www.apa.org/).

Applied psychology

Applied psychology refers to the application of theoretical and
methodological advancements made in psychology to the study of

practical aspects and problems experienced in everyday life. Over the years a number of applied areas have developed into distinct sub-divisions, or specialisms, within psychology. These specialisms are accredited by the British Psychological Society and it is therefore appropriate to elaborate on three different kinds of status within the society before going on to consider these specialisms in greater detail. (Similar procedures and information about specialisms may also apply to the USA.)

Clinical psychology

In general, clinical psychology is the application of psychological theory and methods to problems in health and illness. A clinical psychologist interviews and provides therapeutic intervention to those people who suffer from a range of physical impairments and psychological disturbances. These disturbances can include clients who suffer from irrational fears, depression, schizophrenia, etc., or people suffering from severe learning difficulties. In addition, a clinical psychologist can be actively engaged in the general health field practising a variety of techniques, such as relaxation therapy, working with the elderly, and so on. They usually work either on a one-to-one basis with a client, or with groups of clients. They can operate from any of a number of places, such as a hospital, a health centre, or may visit a client at home. More often than not, the clinical psychologist will form part of a wider clinical team working together for the benefit of the patient; for example, with a psychiatrist, hospital staff, social workers, etc. The majority of psychologists in this field in Britain operate within the National Health Service, but some go on to private practice. Many are engaged in research in addition to their other duties.

Training to become a clinical psychologist involves postgraduate training at PhD level (Doctoral programme) – referred to as a Doctorate in Clinical Psychology, also known as DClin courses. These are mostly full-time courses that take 3 years to complete (full time). They recruit each year and normally require a first-class or upper second-class psychology undergraduate degree as a minimum entry requirement. Your undergraduate degree must be accredited by the British Psychological Society (BPS). Competition for places on a postgraduate clinical psychology course is quite high – so getting the best possible degree classification is essential. Typically, some type of related work experience is desirable before applying, such as working as an assistant psychologist/research assistant in a relevant area. The specific aim of such a course is to provide essential knowledge and training in the following areas: assessment, treatment/intervention, research, professional conduct, management and teaching, related to clinical psychology.

Typically, each course will have several funded places and sometimes a few self-funded places (where the applicant is responsible for arranging their own financial support, payment of course fees, etc.). Applications for clinical psychology courses are processed via the clearing house scheme. Application packs and handbooks are normally available from September to December for courses commencing in September/October of the following year. This information is available from the Clearing House for Postgraduate Courses in Clinical Psychology, University of Leeds, 15 Hyde Terrace, Leeds LS2 9LT (website: www.leeds.ac.uk/chpccp). There is a small charge for the application. A specific timetable of deadlines is in the handbook. The BPS can supply information about accredited courses at universities around the country.

PERSONAL CHARACTERISTICS (PCs). The types of PCs looked for in applicants generally include: a genuine desire to become practically involved in helping others to solve their health and illness problems, very good interpersonal skills, the ability to work as part of a team, good evidence of intellectual ability, the ability to apply a scientific (and psychological) approach to the study of human behaviour, good analytic skills, and a positive nature from which you can learn to overcome setbacks experienced in the profession (and life).

Once you have completed the relevant postgraduate clinical psychology course, you are then eligible to practise as a professional clinical psychologist, either within the health service, in a community service setting, or as a private practitioner. At present, availability of posts for trained clinical psychologists is high and fairly high salaries can be earned soon after qualification and experience is gained to senior level. Salaries start at Grade A, at around £17,000 for newly qualified psychologists, and in the region of £27,000–£36,000 for more experienced psychologists. Grade B applies to senior experienced clinical psychologists managing departments or large specialist sections, with salaries ranging from £37,000 to £60,000. Some trained clinical psychologists will go on to private practice where the salary level can vary greatly, or go into other fields, such as Forensic Psychology. Many applicants who are unsuccessful on their first application go on to gain experience in the clinical field by securing a (paid) post as a psychology technician, or as an assistant psychologist. This will involve working as part of a team (perhaps based in a hospital, a special unit, or some other institute) whose role is to monitor patients suffering from psychological disturbances, as well as to implement intervention strategies, normally working under the supervision of a clinical psychologist.

In addition, many graduates go on to study a particular aspect or aspects of clinical psychology within a Master's or PhD programme. This will take the same form as any other postgraduate research project (see the section on postgraduate training/research) but does not constitute a licence to practise as a professional clinical psychologist.

Further reading: See, for example, Beck (1992), Blackburn (2001), Gale and Chapman (1984), and Van Hasselt and Hersen (2000) for useful insights into clinical psychology and related issues.

Educational psychology

An educational psychologist is someone who uses psychological theory and application within a range of educational settings, including schools, colleges, nurseries, special units, or even in the person's home. The educational psychologist tackles problems encountered by young people in education, and will spend most of her or his time assessing children's progress, their academic needs, their emotional needs, and providing help and/or advice on a range of issues, e.g., applying techniques to improve the reading skills or writing skills of a child who has impairments in these processes. If a particular child is experiencing such difficulties, then the psychologist might advise teachers on how best to structure their teaching with the aim of enhancing the child's performance. Some educational psychologists work specifically with adults in the educational setting, for example, helping students who experience educational difficulties. In addition, some advise on learning methods and processes, curriculum development, and other aspects of the educational setting, e.g., intervention when the child is engaging in behaviour that has an adverse effect on her or his learning (as in truancy, for example).

Most of the psychologists working in this field in Britain will be employed by local education authorities, working in schools, nurseries and special units, but some run private practices or act as independent consultants, and many will be engaged in research. As with many specialisms in psychology, to qualify as an educational psychologist one has to undergo postgraduate training, usually in the form of a 1- or 2-year Master's course in Educational Psychology – referred to as an MSc or MEd in educational psychology. On such a course, theoretical and practical elements are incorporated in order to equip the student with the necessary knowledge and skills to practise as an Educational Psychologist. A good first degree in psychology is required (with an upper second-class grade or more often required), which is BPS accredited. To practise in England, Wales, and Northern Ireland, you also need a teaching qualification (e.g., a Post-graduate Certificate in Education, PGCE), up to 2 years teaching experience with children or young adults up to the age of 19 years, as well as the training at Master's level itself. This is the typical route through which people become educational psychologists. In Scotland, teaching experience is not required. Usually, following training, the educational psychologist will be required to practise under supervision for up to 1 year.

Important note: the route to becoming an educational psychologist in England, Wales, and Northern Ireland may be changing within the next 2 to 3 years. The new route is likely to become a 3-year full-time taught training course (possibly called a Doctorate in Educational Psychology). This is to include taught and placement elements within the degree, reducing the need for teacher training (PGCE) and teaching experience, although this has yet to be ratified (contact BPS for updated information). Applications for England and Wales should be made through the Clearing House for Postgraduate Courses in Educational Psychology, Local Government Management Board, Layden House, 76–86 Turnmill Street, London EC1M 5QU. Applications for study in Scotland or Northern Ireland or Eire should be made directly to the relevant institution. The BPS can supply information about accredited courses. For further information about educational psychology you can contact the BPS on their website (www.bps. org.uk/ed, or for Scotland www.bps.org.uk/scoted) or contact the Association of Educational Psychologists website (www.aep.org.uk).

PERSONAL CHARACTERISTICs (PCs). The types of PCs looked for in applicants generally include: have very good (if not excellent) communication skills, be sensitive to the client's needs, be tactful and diplomatic, be assertive and possess good negotiating skills, possess good time-management skills, be a good administrator, possess an inquiring mind (how and why things occur).

Again, once qualified and experienced, the salary level can be fairly high. For assistant educational psychologists pay is in the region of £21,000 to £24,000; Scale A from £26,000 to £35,000; at Scale B Senior or Principal from £34,000 to £46,000. See *The Psychologist*, "Education Section", 1992, for some useful discussion points on psychology and education. In addition, many graduates go on to study a particular aspect or aspects of educational psychology within a Master's or a PhD. This can take the same form as any other postgraduate research project (see the section on postgraduate training/research), but does not necessarily constitute a licence to practise as a professional educational psychologist.

Further reading: See, for example, Gale and Chapman (1984), Sprinthall, Sprinthall, and Oja (1997), and Woolfolk (1998), for some useful insights into educational psychology and related topics.

Occupational/organisational psychology

An occupational or organisational psychologist uses specific psychological knowledge and applications within a work or business setting. This specialism is also referred to as Ergonomics, Applied Psychology, Industrial Psychology, Management Consultancy – to name but a few titles. The types of work setting an occupational psychologist might be in will vary, such as companies (in the private and public sectors), hospitals, prisons, government and public services. The main role of the psychologist in this specialism is devising selection procedures for new staff – devising and carrying out tasks designed to look for particular characteristics (such as numeracy, attitudes, skills, personality) that will best suit the job. The psychologist will also be involved in monitoring existing staff performance; devising ways of improving the work setting; and addressing particular problems that arise in relation to work (for example, advising on stress in the workplace). Some psychologists work with industry to improve designs for particular work settings (for example, on aircraft design) or engage in research within the occupational setting. Many occupational psychologists will operate in several work settings throughout their working week and work as part of a team – often working alongside managers, training officers, trade union representatives, etc. A number of the psychologists working in this field will be engaged in consultancy and/or research.

Training as an occupational or organisational psychologist involves a first degree in psychology (first class or upper second class) which is BPS accredited; a 1-year full-time (2-year part-time) postgraduate Master's degree (MSc) in Occupational Psychology, followed by a 2-year placement, working under supervision, or 3 years supervised practice and completion of the Society's Post-graduate Certificate in Occupational Psychology. Competition for places on such courses is also high. Once qualified, psychologists working in this specialism can command salaries in the following range: in the region of £17,000 to £22,000 at graduate trainee psychologist level; £19,000 to £26,000 at higher psychologist level; £24,000–£34,000+ at senior psychologist level, and in excess of this at principal psychologist level. Individuals can go on to become consultants in their field (salaries in the private sector or industry can vary from £15,000 to £100,000). See also *The Psychologist*, "Testing in the workplace" (1994), for some useful insights into issues regarding occupational psychology. The BPS can supply information about accredited courses.

Again, many graduates go on to study a particular aspect or aspects of occupational psychology within a Master's or PhD (e.g., stress in the workplace). This will take the same form as any other postgraduate research project (see the section on post-graduate training/research), but again does not necessarily constitute a licence to practise as a professional occupational psychologist.

Further reading: Beck (1992), Gale and Chapman (1984), Miner (1992), and Robbins (2002) for some useful insights into occupational/organisational psychology and related topics.

Criminological/forensic psychology

This specialism is also sometimes referred to as Legal Psychology. Criminological Psychology generally refers to the work of those psychologists who become involved in applying psychological theory and methods to the study of many aspects of crime. A forensic psychologist is a term that refers to a psychologist who works within a legal framework. For example, an experimental psychologist might carry out research on theoretical explanations of crime, looking at the role of eyewitness testimony in the legal process, evaluating the legal processes in court, or advising the police on training procedures. Over the last two decades, research has flourished in areas such as: crime detection, police selection and training, courtroom dynamics, rules of law, etc.

Further reading: See, for example, Ainsworth (2000), Blackburn (2001), Colman (1995a), Feldman (1993), Hall-Williams (1984), and Stephenson (1993) for good coverage of many of these aspects.

Forensic (meaning related to court) psychology specifically relates to those psychologists acting as experts who offer psychological evidence in criminal cases (as well as being involved in civil cases). The majority of forensic psychologists work in custodial, rehabilitation and treatment/intervention contexts, such as within a young offenders institute, in a prison setting, or within secure and special hospitals. The main role of a forensic psychologist is to gather information in relation to the trial of a suspect, the collection of evidence for appeal boards, parole boards, or tribunal hearings (Blackburn, 2001). In this respect, the role of a forensic psychologist is a specialist function. In addition, she or he can be involved in researching criminal behaviour, as well as with the assessment and treatment of offenders. Thus, the forensic psychologist is a much more specialised, focused individual whose main role is, as the term suggests, to act as an expert adviser within a legal forum. One example of the role played by a forensic psychologist comes from their involvement in the prediction of future criminal behaviour of convicted offenders (recidivism). This is particularly important where you have a very violent offender (such as a rapist). The main aim of so-called "predictions research" is to provide advice within a legal setting (such as a tribunal considering the early release of a prisoner). At such a hearing the forensic psychologist will give a professional opinion as to whether the prisoner is likely to reoffend and therefore pose a threat to the public (see, for example, Blackburn, 2001).

Psychologists working in these specialist fields in Britain often work in the penal system or in the National Health Service. Traditionally, many of those working as forensic psychologists came mainly from other specialisms (such as clinical psychology and psychiatry). However, there are a number of postgraduate courses springing up across the UK (and USA). These courses are specifically designed to train graduates in areas such as Criminological Psychology and Forensic Psychology, or they embed psychology within the study of the criminal justice system. Such courses can be at Diploma level (1–2 years of study), or at Master's level (2–3 years of study), and can be either on a full-time or part-time basis. Funding for such courses is varied, with some courses providing accompanying grants, whereas others may be self-funded. There are a number of BPS accredited courses now in existence, for example, in Birmingham, Kent, Leicester, Liverpool and Surrey, and more recently at Manchester Metropolitan University. The BPS can supply information about accredited courses.

Graduates wishing to specialise in this field should have a good first degree (preferably upper second class or above) which is accredited by the BPS, an accredited postgraduate course in Forensic Psychology (1 year full-time) and the completion of the BPS's Stage 2 of the Diploma in Forensic Psychology. A period of supervised practice – under the supervision of a registered chartered forensic psychologist – is normally involved. Once these criteria have been met, you become eligible for status as a chartered forensic psychologist. There are a number of other possibilities for developing a career in forensic psychology (e.g., undertake a PhD in Forensic Psychology, then obtain a post where you receive supervised training), so you are advised to look into possible routes with your relevant body (the BPS in Britain or APA in America). The largest single employer of forensic psychologists in the UK is HM Prison Service, and there may be a route through which one can train to become a forensic psychologist within the service (please contact them directly); their website is: www.hmprisonservice.gov.uk/corporate. However, forensic psychologists can be employed in the health service and the social services.

PERSONAL CHARACTERISTICS (PCs). The types of PCs looked for in applicants generally include: good relationship-building skills, i.e., with the client group; have an intellectual understanding of, and interest in, people and their behaviour; be non-judgemental in your work; be able to cope with a potential element of personal risk in your work.

There is a selection procedure run by the Civil Service for Basic Grade Psychologist posts for those wishing to become a prison psychologist. Psychologists working in the prison service are employed as civil servants and are subject to pay and conditions similar to other civil servants. Those employed in a secure unit or a special hospital are employed under NHS conditions and subject to their pay and employment conditions. Academic forensic psychologists (such as those researching and teaching in a university) are subject to the appropriate lecturers' pay and conditions. Others will be commissioned to fulfil particular roles, such as consultancy work, private research, or various forms of casework, and will negotiate pay and conditions with their employer. Salaries will vary greatly, but pay rates for newly appointed forensic psychologists (outside of academia) start at around £15,500 up to £60,000+ for senior psychologists.

Since Criminological Psychology/Forensic Psychology is at present a fast-growing area, the number of such courses is on the increase. In addition, many graduates go on to study a particular aspect or aspects of psychology and crime within a Master's or PhD (e.g., on offender profiling). Again, such projects take the same form as other postgraduate research projects (see the section on postgraduate training/research).

Further reading: For additional reading on the relationship between psychology and crime, see Ainsworth (2000), Bartol (2002), Blackburn (2001), Cooke, Baldwin, and Howison (1993), Faulk (1994), Hollin (1995), and Howitt (2002). See also *The Psychologist*, "Criminological and legal psychology" (1991) for some useful insights into criminological and legal psychology.

Health psychology

Health psychology is a relatively new field of applied psychology, and is the interface between psychology and medicine. More specifically, it refers to the contributions that psychology makes (in terms of theory, research and application) to the study of a range of issues pertaining to health. Some examples include: health promotion or maintenance, psychological aspects of illness, health risks, prevention of illness/recurrence of illness, processes involved in health care delivery, and treatment issues. A health psychologist, then, is a specialist who works on a one-to-one basis with a client, or with groups of clients, on a number of medical issues.

In addition, a health psychologist might also be involved in policy decisions related to health issues, and engage in research. Many current health psychologists are derived from the field of clinical psychology (or other health-related areas). However, specialist postgraduate courses in health psychology have developed recently. Such courses include training in the theoretical foundations/current knowledge of health psychology, research methodology, risk factors/vulnerability factors, behaviour change, health promotion, health policy, and so on, as well as having a research project component. Since 2001 graduates are required to undertake either an accredited MSc (Master's course) or Stage 1 of the BPS's qualifications in Health Psychology, followed by Stage 2. These courses can be either full time or part time, and can take the form of self-funded or grant-funded courses. Often, people taking these courses are trained nursing staff or other health professionals. Pay and employment conditions vary according to the employer and the nature of the contract (for further information, visit www.bps.org.uk/health).

Health psychologists may not necessarily remain with one type of employer (e.g., working within a hospital under an NHS authority), and may change between settings, for example, moving from a hospital contract to working within a health service unit. There is, at present, no clear career structure and pay scales, although it is expected (for example, by the BPS) that accredited health psychology training courses and a route for registration will be developed in the near future. Indeed, there is a new route being planned by the BPS called "Chartered Health Psychologist", that will consist a three-pronged training approach, which will contain academic, research and supervised practice components. The BPS can supply information about accredited courses.

As suggested earlier, on a health psychology course theoretical, methodological and treatment/intervention issues are addressed. A study of the health care system and policy, health-related behaviour and behaviour change, life stress, chronic illness, health promotion and intervention, may all be addressed at some point during the study of health psychology.

Further reading: For good insights into the topics covered in health psychology see, for example, Gatchel, Baum, and Krantz (1997), Kaplan, Sallis, and Patterson (1993), Niven (1994), Sarafino (2001), and Taylor (2002).

As with other areas, particular aspects of health psychology can be studied at postgraduate Master's or PhD level (e.g., the study of socio-economic status and smoking behaviour as a PhD thesis). Again, this does not necessarily constitute a licence to practise as a health psychologist. The route to such courses of study, as well as issues of funding, etc., are similar to other specialisms.

PERSONAL CHARACTERISTICS (PCs). The types of PCs looked for in applicants would generally include: demonstrate a high level of interpersonal skill, skills in negotiation and a high level of persuasiveness, having an intellectual understanding of and interest in people and their behaviour, being able to work as part of a team and having good "networking" skills, have an inquiring mind and a questioning approach, have good communication skills, an ability to see things from a "real-world" perspective.

Further reading: See also the following issues of *The Psychologist*: "Health" (1994) for discussion of some issues in health psychology; "A day in the life of a health psychologist" (1993) for some useful insights into the role of a health psychologist; and "Quality health care and psychologists" (1998) for insights into opportunities for graduates and health care managers in the health care system.

Counselling psychology

Counselling psychology involves counselling individuals or groups of people who experience academic, occupational, and/or psychological disturbance that is not intensive enough to warrant a serious mental disorder. In many ways, some of the duties of a therapist will overlap with that of a clinical psychologist. Psychologists working in this field can find themselves based in any one of a number of situations, ranging from primary health care agencies (e.g., GP surgeries), to counselling clinics, academic settings, or business organisations.

Usually, to become a counselling psychologist, you have to complete an BPS accredited MSc/Diploma/Doctorate in Counselling Psychology equivalent to the BPS's Part 1 and Part 2 Society Diploma, which is 3 years full-time or equivalent part-time. You should contact the BPS (or APA) for details of these courses. Postgraduate training is most likely to be self-financed, costing in total (including fees) approximately £2500 per year, but you are advised to discuss methods of funding with the particular institute involved (e.g., there are sometimes trust funds, foundations and companies who may provide financial assistance). Salary levels range from about £16,000 to £60,000, depending upon age, experience, and the nature of your post. You can contact the BPS (website: www.bps.org.uk/counselling) or the British Association for Counselling Psychologists (www.bacp.co.uk).

Further reading: For a useful discussion on a range of issues relating to counselling in Britain, see the special issue of *The Psychologist*, "Counselling psychology" (1990). See also Connor (1994) and Sanders (1996) for good insights into psychological counselling.

Research and teaching

Research psychologists

A research psychologist applies her or his knowledge and research skills to carry out a specific research project, the focus of which can be any one of a number of specialist areas/research focuses in psychology. The research psychologist can either devote her or his time to one particular area (for example, a research project into brain damage and memory loss), or carry out experimental research into a number of areas. Usually, such research posts are advertised through national journals or newspapers and specific details about the post can be obtained from the institute advertising the post. Such contracts are normally for a fixed term (for example, 1, 2, or 3 years) and are supported by a salary. Gaining research experience in this way can provide the graduate with invaluable experience in literature searching, and carrying out research, as well as in writing reports and journal articles. It can also lead to other opportunities. For example, if you were working at a university and another post arose (e.g., a lecturing position), you could apply for that post knowing that you have good research experience and experience of the institute itself. Research psychologists work in a variety of areas, other than an academic setting: these include working for government agencies and for private companies. Salaries for researchers vary so contact the institution.

Teaching psychology

Teaching psychology can take any one of a number of forms. A graduate might take up a full- or part-time post teaching psychology. This could be in the further education sector, for example, teaching at a college on GCSE and A-Level psychology courses, or on an Access course. Or it could be in the higher education sector for example, within a university or institute of higher education teaching on a psychology undergraduate degree course, or a diploma course. In the university sector, there is growing pressure on those wishing to become full-time psychology lecturers to have completed (or be in the process of completing) a postgraduate course of study in psychology. Often those who apply for a post at a university will have a PhD in psychology (or some related subject), or will obtain one in the near future.

In 1991 a Diploma in the Applied Psychology of Teaching was introduced so that graduates of BPS-approved psychology degree courses could gain a BPS-accredited qualification for teaching psychology in Britain. For example, the BPS Diploma in the Applied Psychology of Teaching is a 2-year full-time qualification (it can also be completed part time) for those who have already gained some teaching experience, and permits you to gain chartered psychologist status within the BPS. Contact the BPS for full details of this course. University lecturers will teach specific areas of psychology, contribute to research within the psychology department/section, as well as carry out related administrative duties. Areas of teaching may vary, but often include those areas studied at postgraduate level (e.g., if your PhD was in cognitive psychology, then you might be expected to teach specific topics within cognitive psychology, such as memory, perception, and so on). Some lecturing staff will be qualified in one of the areas of applied psychology outlined earlier, and may return to lecturing to teach applied psychology and to conduct research.

Salary levels vary, but broadly fall within the range £17,000–38,000, depending upon your age, qualifications and experience, and the level at which you are appointed. A lecturer in further education and higher education may be paid between £17,000 and £25,000; a senior lecturer is paid between £24,000 and £31,500; and a principal lecturer (where appropriate) is paid between £30,000 and £34,000. Some universities work from the following pay scale: Lecturer A may be paid between £20,000 and £24,000, Lecturer B may be paid between £25,500 and £32,500, and senior lecturer paid between £34,000 and £38,000. These pay scales are updated each year. This may be extended beyond this level if you become a deputy head, a head, or professor. A lecturer who is deemed "active" in research will contribute to the overall research profile of the psychology department or section, as well as being encouraged to apply for external grants (e.g., from the Medical Research Council) to fund research projects. Further income can be made through private teaching, examining at other institutes, various types of consultancy fees (with the permission of your institute), publishing, etc.

Further reading: See Brody and Hayes (1995) for some useful insights into teaching psychology.

Other areas (non-accredited)

In addition to postgraduate research, such as Master's and Doctoral (PhD) programmes, and applied psychology, many psychologists use their knowledge/skills in other related areas. These include *neuropsychology*, *psychotherapy*, and *sports psychologists*.

Neuropsychology

Neuropsychology is the study of the brain and its neuropsychological function. It involves applying our knowledge and methods gained within psychology and its related disciplines (e.g., neuroscience) to the study of brain-damaged patients. Neuropsychologists are responsible for the assessment and rehabilitation of patients with brain injury or other neurological diseases. They work with people of all ages who have neurological problems caused by a range of conditions, such as brain injury, stroke, tumours, neurodegenerative disease, and so on. A neuropsychologist can be a practitioner, a researcher, or an academic who teaches neuropsychology, or can be a combination of these. He/she may be employed in acute settings – working with other professionals (e.g., neurosurgeons) within a regional neurosciences centre, in rehabilitation centres, within a community services facility, or, if an academic, within a university department. Neuropsychologists are often employed by the NHS and salaries are in the range of those given for clinical psychologists (for more information visit the website: www.bps.org.uk/neuro).

Psychotherapy

Psychotherapy covers the psychological intervention or treatment of a range of mental and physical difficulties using a range of different perspectives and methods. A psychotherapist may take one predominant approach, e.g., psychoanalytic, or may be somewhat more "eclectic" in their approach. This can be done with groups of clients or on an individual basis, and can involve adults or children. These approaches can vary from intimate discussions over a period of years, or can be for just one or two sessions. Group treatment can involve acting out scenarios or the group encouragement of releasing inhibited feelings that are thought to be at the root of the "problem".

This type of application is typically seen as a post-qualification specialism, that is, an area in which one specialises gaining a primary postgraduate qualification in, say, clinical psychology. It is possible to gain a psychotherapy qualification that is not recognised by the BPS or APA. For those wishing to gain further information they can contact the Royal College of Psychiatrists (website: www.rcpsych. ac.uk).

Sports psychology

Historically, the role of psychology in sports was one in which a sports coach might approach a psychologist for advice on particular psychological phenomena that might have an impact on their athletes' performance. Currently, the new sub-specialism of sports psychology represents an applied, flourishing area in which theory, research and application are combined to address many aspects of sports and athletics. Sports psychology, then, refers to the application of psychological theory and techniques in the sports setting, usually specifically related to athlete's performance. Indeed, much of what psychology is about – such as the study of perception, memory, imagery, motivation, personality, behaviour change, stress, group dynamics, etc. – are all of direct relevance to the sports setting. In addition to this, the sports setting offers a very good opportunity to carry out real-life research in that it provides the setting to look at psychological phenomena in the natural environment. This does not exempt the researcher from carrying out controlled, laboratory-based experimentation into sports-related psychological phenomena.

A sports psychologist can be involved in a number of roles: for example, to monitor the performance of athletes, to implement psychological techniques to improve athletes' performance; as well as carrying out research in the area. It is not uncommon to find a sports psychologist attached to any one of a range of sporting groups, such as a football club, or athletics association. A sports psychologist can be heavily involved in research, perhaps gathering data on sports-related phenomena, such as the effects of psychological stress on athletes; exercise dependence syndrome, etc. A sports psychologist will be involved in applied aspects, such as improving motivation or mental training in sports, or focusing on other psychological characteristics, such as stress, drug dependence, burnout, etc. The salary level for a sports psychologist will vary greatly, depending upon the level of qualification obtained and the nature of the contract of employment.

Further reading: For good insights into theoretical concepts and applications in sports psychology, see Bakker, Whiting, and van der Brug (1993), Biddle (1995), Bull (1991), Grant (1988), Moran, M. (2003), Morris and Summers (1995), and Williams (1993). See also *The Psychologist*, "Sport: Special issue" (1991) and *The Psychologist*, "Psychology in Sport: trends, analysis, conclusion" (1997) for some useful insights into research in sports psychology.

In the UK, the British Association of Sport and Exercise Science (BASES) runs an accreditation scheme for sports psychologists. The University of Exeter offers an MSc in Exercise and Sport Psychology (the first in England). It is anticipated that further courses will develop. In the USA there are over 100 academic courses related to sports psychology (for more information you can visit the BASES website: www.bases.org.uk).

Of course, individuals can study clinical, educational, occupational, forensic, health, counselling, neuropsychological, psychotherapeutic, or sports-psychological phenomena at Master's or PhD level, typically within a university setting. What such a line of study may lead to in terms of job, salary level, etc. will vary, and it may be a good idea to look into this before embarking upon a 2- or 3-year postgraduate line of study. You should contact individual institutes for lists of such courses of study.

Other specialisms

In addition, some psychologists go on to work in the following areas: *consumer psychology* – which covers a range of posts in marketing and market research, and which is particularly popular in the USA; *environmental psychology* – the application of psychology to problems concerning one's physical surroundings (e.g., the interaction between people and their environment, such as noise pollution, natural disasters, etc.). Environmental psychology often forms part of an undergraduate degree course, with few postgraduate courses in existence (e.g., the University of Surrey runs an MSc); and pet psychology – a comparatively new area in which psychology is applied to problems with regard to pets, such as "pet behaviour counselling" in which a pet's behaviour is monitored and behaviour modification is implemented (where appropriate). There is no recognised route for pet psychology, with few courses in the area (with the exception of an MSc/Diploma route in Companion Animal Behaviour Counselling being run at the University of Southampton).

Further reading: See also Anastasi (1979), Beck (1992), Gale and Chapman (1984), Grasha (1995), and Hartley and Branthwaite (1999) for further reading on applied areas of psychology.

In addition to the specialisms outlined here, many psychology graduates go on to work in a whole host of other fields. Indeed, there are good employment prospects for psychology graduates in areas such as market research, advertising, nursing, social work, sales, management posts, and so on. A degree in psychology is also seen as a good basis for future careers where further training is necessary, such as the police, the armed forces, private companies, to name but a few: see the BPS leaflet *Careers in Psychology: A guide to courses and opportunities in psychology* (BPS).

Preparing your curriculum vitae (CV)

What is a curriculum vitae (CV)?

A CV should focus on particular aspects of you and your relevant life experience. The term curriculum vitae is Latin and means (approximately) "the story of your life" – but again, it is stressed that only those details pertinent to your future career should be included. There would be little point in including a long narrative of your life.

Corfield (2003) identifies six major categories that make up a CV. These comprise: personal details, details of your education, details of your employment, your interests, an additional information section, and details of two or three people who are willing to act as referees on your behalf. A summary of each category follows.

1. *Personal details*:
   - forename and surname
   - full address and postcode
   - telephone number (plus any extension number)
   - date of birth
   - marital status, health (optional)
   - nationality (stating if a work permit has been granted if applicable).
2. *Details of education*:
   - starting from secondary school onwards
   - in chronological order
   - include name of the institute, dates attended, and qualifications attained (including subjects taken and grades achieved).
3. *Details of employment*:
   - summary of jobs/work experience
   - in reverse chronological order (i.e., most recent or current to first job)
   - include dates, names of employers, duties involved.
4. *Interests*:
   - include physical and other activities (e.g., football, music)
   - indicate your interests outside the work setting (briefly list these as a separate section, or include in the following section).
5. *Additional information*:
   - include (briefly) other information relevant to the application
   - include activities engaged in where gaps appear in your work record (e.g., travelling across America)
   - brief details of final-year project/dissertation (a 150–200-word summary can be useful)
   - any computing and word-processing skills
   - membership of recognised association(s) (such as the British Psychological Society).
6. *References:*
   - provide details of two or three people acting as referees
   - provide name, title, address, telephone number, and position of employment (e.g., head of department)
   - make one an academic referee who knows your work.

> **Please note**: The Additional Information section should be altered, depending upon what career/job it is you are applying for – so change this part of the CV whenever you feel that it is appropriate. Clinical psychology (used here in the sample CV) is only one of a number of specialisms that is popular with students.

Corfield's (2003) book *Preparing Your Own CV* provides good guidelines on putting together your own CV. It also includes several examples of completed CVs. What follows is a fictional example of a graduate version of a CV.

Example of a graduate version of a CV

Curriculum Vitae

Name: Thomas Smith

Address: 30 Docklands Road, Childwall, Liverpool L12 8AP

Telephone: 0171 000 000

Date of birth: 29.07.1962

Education: St. Peter & Paul's, Burgess Road, Childwall, Liverpool. 1973–1980. 5 O Levels in: Maths, English, Biology, Politics, Sociology. 2 A Levels in: Psychology (B) and Sociology (A). University of Teesside, Borough Road, Middlesbrough, Cleveland. 1993–1996. BSc (Hons) Degree in Psychology (Upper second).

Employment: Bloggs' Biscuit Factory, Docklands Wharf, Childwall, Liverpool. 1985–1993. Duties included plant worker; plant supervisor. Smith's Construction, Harrow Lane, Childwall, Liverpool.1980–1985. Duties included running family building firm. Construction work.

Additional Information: In addition to studying psychology, my course has helped me to develop a range of skills, including good listening, oral and written communication skills, time-management and organisational skills, critical thinking, individual and team work, numeracy and literacy. I am keen to develop a career in Clinical Psychology. I have recently gained some experience working as a volunteer in a hostel for schizophrenic patients.

My final-year project focused on vividness and memory involved with traumatic events and received a first-class mark (75%). In the project I interviewed a number of volunteers (students). Half of the volunteers were asked to recall a traumatic event (e.g., losing a loved one, being the victim of an attack) and half of them recalled a non-traumatic event (e.g., attending a social function, carrying out a chore). They were also asked to rate these events on a vividness rating scale. Overall, the findings revealed that the recall of traumatic events was accompanied by higher ratings on the vividness scale than the recall of non-traumatic events, and this difference was significant. It was concluded that levels of vividness in remembering and the emotional content attached to certain memories interact when recalling past memories, particularly traumatic ones. These findings were discussed in relation to relevant theory and research in this area.

I am punctual, hardworking, friendly, and able to mix well with others. I am familiar with a number of computer software packages, including Microsoft Word, SPSS for Windows, and using the Internet. I am a student subscriber of the British Psychological Society. I have a full, clean driving licence.

Interests: Reading, sports, and music.

Referees:
1. Dr. David Paynton, Principal Lecturer in Psychology, Department of Psychology, University of Teesside, Middlesbrough, Cleveland. Phone: 01642 000 000 ext. 0000.
2. Mr Tony Biggs, Teacher, 4 Drake Avenue, Childwall, Liverpool. Phone: 0171 000 000.

Some important points about the CV

1. Keep it brief: about two–three sides of A4 paper.
2. Make sure all the essential details are included in it – *including the transferable skills you have developed.*
3. Make sure it is typed and adheres to a clear, coherent structure.
4. Ensure that your referees have a copy of the CV (otherwise they will be providing a reference based on little knowledge about you).
5. Make sure your referees are "live" (i.e., they are still willing to act as referees for you and still at the addresses stated in the CV).
6. Always inform your referees of an application you make.

7. Send a copy of your CV along with the application form.
8. If you have published work or have relevant consultancy work, type this out clearly on an additional page and attach it to the CV.
9. Update the CV periodically.
10. Send a covering letter with the CV and/or application form, which highlights why you have applied for the post and your suitability.

An example of the main text of a *cover letter* follows. You will need to provide details of your name and address and the name and address of the person to whom you are sending the whole application, and sign the letter personally.

Example of main text of a cover letter

I would like to apply for a place on the Doctorate in Clinical Psychology course run at your institute, for the forthcoming academic year. Please find enclosed an application form and a copy of my curriculum vitae. I am very keen to enter into Clinical Psychology as a profession and feel that I would be well suited to studying for a career as a Clinical Psychologist. [You may wish to expand this section by elaborating upon any life experience(s) you think might be appropriate to this career.]

You will note from my curriculum vitae that I have achieved an upper second-class BSc (Hons) Degree in Psychology, with my final-year dissertation project gaining a first-class mark. I have studied several areas relating to clinical psychology on the course, including modules on Brain and Behaviour, Cognitive Neuropsychology, Abnormal Psychology, and of course, my final-year dissertation which focused on memory and traumatic events. I have also studied research methods, statistics, and research writing on the course. Studying for my degree has enabled me to develop a number of key skills, including good listening, oral and written communication skills, time-management and organisational abilities, numeracy and literacy, group and individual work, as well as report-writing skills.

In addition, I have gained experience as a voluntary worker in a schizophrenic hostel, where I was responsible for interacting with schizophrenic patients who were being assessed for their capability of living in the community. During this time I gained experience in the nature of the disorder, interacting with the team of workers responsible for the patients (e.g., Health Workers, Clinical Psychologists, and Psychiatrists), as well as interacting with the patients themselves. I feel that this has provided me with invaluable experience. In addition, I am organised, punctual, and am used to working to strict deadlines.

It is my strong feeling that if I am successful in my application, I would make a good student, be successful in my postgraduate study, and eventually progress to become a hard-working professional Clinical Psychologist.

Yours faithfully,

Remember that your CV and cover letter represent the first point of contact you will probably have with a prospective employer (apart from your application form, where applicable), so sending a "sloppy", incomplete or incoherent CV may result in your being turned down at the first stage. See also McKee (1995) for guidance on preparing a CV. Once you have submitted your CV (and accompanying application form) to a potential employer/academic institute, it is a matter of waiting to hear whether or not you have been shortlisted and will be interviewed. If you are asked to attend an interview, it is up to you to sell yourself to the interviewer(s).

Further reading: For good insights into the interview process and guidance on how to improve your interview technique, see, for example, Breakwell (1990), Brown and Breakwell (1990), and Hague (1993).

A final note from the author

Studying psychology can be both challenging and satisfying. The challenges include all those aspects involved in studying on a psychology course. The satisfaction comes from the knowledge gained in psychology and the ability to use that knowledge to solve problems about human behaviour.

An undergraduate degree course in psychology sets the basis for future work in the area. It provides a good grounding in psychology so that, if she or he wishes to, a student can go on to specialise in a particular part of psychology. A psychology degree can, of course, be useful when competing in the general graduate careers market. This is because, in addition to the knowledge gained on a psychology degree, the degree itself equips you with transferable skills that are welcomed by most employers. As stated earlier in the book, these will include good listening, oral and written communication skills, numeracy and literacy, critical and creative thinking skills, problem-solving and decision-making abilities, individual and team work skills, organisation and self-discipline, as well as being able to judge your own performance. The more of these skills one can develop during their study (and beyond), the better.

Finally, for those who are about to graduate, good luck with your future careers – whether they be inside or outside the field of psychology.

References

Acres, D. (1995). *How to pass exams without anxiety* (3rd ed.). Plymouth, UK: Northcote House.

Adams, S., & Kirkby, R. (1997). Exercise dependence: A problem for sports physiotherapists. *Australian Journal of Physiotherapy, 43,* 53–58.

Adams, S., & Kirkby, R. (1998). Exercise dependence: A review of its manifestation, theory and measurement. *Australian Sports Medicine Training, 8,* 265–279.

Agras, S., Sylvester, D., & Oliveau, D. (1969). The epidemiology of common fears and phobias. *Comprehensive Psychiatry, 10,* 151–156.

Ainsworth, P.B. (2000). *Psychology and Crime: Myths and reality.* Harlow, UK: Longman.

Alloy, L.B., Acocella, J., & Bootzin, R.R. (1998). *Abnormal psychology: Current perspectives* (8th ed.). New York: McGraw-Hill.

American Psychiatric Association. (2000). *Diagnostic and statistical manual for mental disorders* [DSM-IVR] (4th ed. revised) Washington, DC: American Psychiatric Association.

American Psychological Association. (2003). *Research ethics and research regulations.* [Internet]. U.S.A. http://www.apa.org/science/research.html [Accessed December, 2003].

Anastasi, A. (1979). *Fields of applied psychology* (2nd ed.). New York: McGraw-Hill.

Anshel, M.H. (1995). Anxiety. In T. Morris & J. Summers (Eds.), *Sport psychology: Theory, applications and issues.* Brisbane: Wiley.

Aronson, E. (2003). *The social animal* (9th ed.). New York: Freeman.

Aronson, E., Ellsworth, P.C., Carlsmith, J.M., & Gonzales, M.H. (1995). *Methods of research in social psychology* (3rd ed.). New York: McGraw-Hill.

Atkinson, R.C., & Shiffrin, R.M. (1968). Human memory: Proposed system and its control processes. In K.W. Spence & J.T. Spence (Eds.), *The psychology of learning and motivation* (Vol. 2). London: Academic Press.

Baddeley, A.D. (1966). Short-term memory for word sequences as a function of acoustic, semantic and formal similarity. *Quarterly Journal of Experimental Psychology, 18,* 262–265.

Baddeley, A.D. (1983a). Working memory. *Philosophical Transactions of the Royal Society of London, Series B, 89,* 708–729.

Baddeley, A.D. (1983b). *Your memory: A user's guide.* Harmondsworth, UK: Penguin.

Baddeley, A.D. (1986). *Working memory.* Oxford: Oxford University Press.

Baddeley, A.D. (1990). *Working memory.* Oxford: Clarendon Press.

Baddeley, A.D. (1996). The fractionation of working memory. In *Proceedings of the National Academy of Sciences,* USA, 93, 13468–13472.

Baddeley, A.D. (1997). *Human memory:*

Theory and practice (Rev. ed.). Hove, UK: Psychology Press.

Baddeley, A.D. (1998). Recent developments in working memory. *Current Opinion in Neurobiology, 8,* 234–238.

Baddeley, A.D. (1999). *Essentials of human memory.* Hove, UK: Psychology Press.

Baddeley, A.D. (2003). Working memory and language: An overview. *Journal of Communication Disorders, 36(3),* 189–208.

Baddeley, A.D., & Hitch, G.J. (1974). Working memory. In G. Bower (Ed.), *Recent advances in learning and motivation* (Vol. 8). New York: Academic Press.

Baddeley, A.D., Thomson, N., & Buchanan, M. (1975). Word length and the structure of short-term memory. *Journal of Verbal Learning and Verbal Behaviour, 14,* 575–589.

Baddeley, A.D., & Lieberman, K. (1980). Spatial working memory. In R. Nickerson (Ed.), *Attention and Performance VIII*, 521–539. Hillsdale, NJ: Lawrence Erlbaum Associates Inc.

Baddeley, A.D., Wilson, B.A., & Watts, F.N. (1995). *Handbook of memory disorders.* Chichester, UK: Wiley.

Baddeley, A.D., Gathercole, S.E., & Papagno, C. (1998). The phonological loop as a language learning device. *Psychological Review, 105(1),* 158–173.

Bakker, F.C., Whiting, H.T.A., & van der Brug, H. (1993). *Sport psychology: Concepts and applications.* Chichester, UK: Wiley.

Bandura, A. (1973). *Aggression: A social learning analysis.* Englewood Cliffs, NJ: Prentice-Hall.

Bandura, A. (1977). *Social learning theory.* Englewood Cliffs, NJ: Prentice-Hall.

Bandura, A., Adams, N.E., & Beyer, J. (1977). Cognitive processes mediating behavioural change. *Journal of Personality and Social Psychology, 35,* 125–139.

Bandura, A., Ross, D., & Ross, S. (1961). Transmission of aggression through imitation of aggressive models. *Journal of Abnormal and Social Psychology, 63,* 575–582.

Bandura, A., Ross, D., & Ross, S. (1963). Imitation of field-mediated aggressive models. *Journal of Abnormal and Social Psychology, 66,* 3–11.

Barlow, D.H., & Hersen, M. (1987). *Single case experimental design* (2nd ed.). London: Pergamon Press.

Barnes, R. (1995). *Successful study for degrees* (2nd ed.). London: Routledge.

Baron, R.A., & Byrne, D. (2004). *Social psychology: Understanding human interaction* (10th ed.). Boston: Allyn & Bacon.

Bartol, C.R. (2002). *Criminal behaviour: A psychosocial approach* (6th ed.). Englewood Cliffs, NJ: Prentice-Hall.

Bausell, R.B. (1986). *A practical guide to conducting empirical research.* New York: Harper & Row.

Beck, A.T. (1967). *Depression: Causes and treatments.* Philadelphia, PA: University of Pennsylvania Press.

Beck, A.T. (1983). Cognitive therapy of depression: New perspectives. In P. Clayton & J. Barrett (Eds.), *Treatment of depression: Old controversies and new approaches* (pp. 265–290). New York: Raven.

Beck, R.C. (1992). *Applying psychology: Critical and creative thinking* (3rd ed.). Englewood Cliffs, NJ: Prentice-Hall.

Becker, H.S. (1966). *Social problems: A modern approach.* New York: Wiley.

Berger, B.G., & McInman, A. (1993). Exercise and the quality of life. In R.N. Singer, M. Murphey, & L.K. Tennant (Eds.), *Handbook of research on sport psychology* (pp. 729–760). New York: Macmillan.

Berger, B.G., & Owen, D.R. (1988). Stress reduction and mood enhancement in four exercise modes: Swimming, body conditioning, hatha yoga, and fencing. *Research Quarterly for Exercise and Sport, 59,* 148–159.

Berkowitz, L. (1993). *Aggression: Its causes, consequences, and control*. New York: McGraw-Hill.

Best, J.B. (1995). *Cognitive psychology* (4th ed.). St. Paul, MN: West.

Biddle, J.H. (Ed.). (1995). *European perspectives on exercise and sport psychology*. Leeds, UK: Human Kinetics.

Blackburn, R. (2001). *The psychology of criminal conduct: Theory, research and practice*. Chichester, UK: Wiley.

Breakwell, G.M. (1990). *Interviewing*. Leicester, UK: British Psychological Society.

Breakwell, G.M., Hammond, S., & Fife-Shaw, C. (2001). *Research methods in psychology* (2nd ed.). London: Sage.

British Psychological Society. (1990). *Guidelines for the use of non-sexist language in report writing*. Leicester, UK: British Psychological Society.

British Psychological Society. (1996). *Careers in psychology: A guide to courses and opportunities in psychology*. Leicester, UK: British Psychological Society.

British Psychological Society. (1997). *Studying psychology*. Leicester, UK: British Psychological Society.

British Psychological Society. (2000). *Code of conduct, ethical principles and guidelines*. Leicester, UK: British Psychological Society.

British Psychological Society. (2001). Evolution and behaviour. *The Psychologist, 14(8)*, 414–430.

British Psychological Society. (2003). In a positive light: Positive psychology special issue. *The Psychologist, 16(3)*, 126–143.

British Psychological Society, Scientific and Affairs Board/Psychology Post-graduate Affairs Group. (1999). *So you want to do a PhD? Guidelines for prospective research students*. Leicester, UK: British Psychological Society.

Broadbent, D. (1958). *Perception and communication*. London: Pergamon Press.

Brody, R., & Hayes, N. (1995). *Teaching introductory psychology*. Hove, UK: Lawrence Erlbaum Associates.

Brown, J.C. (1977). *Freud and the post-Freudians*. Harmondsworth, UK: Penguin.

Brown, M., & Breakwell, G. (1990). *How to interview and be interviewed*. London: Sheldon Press.

Bryant, P., & Bradley, L. (1985). *Children's reading problems*. Oxford: Blackwell.

Bull, S.J. (1991). *Sport psychology: A self-help guide*. Marlborough, UK: Crowood Press.

Burgess, P.W. (1997). Theory and methodology in executive function. In P. Rabbitt (Ed.), *Methodology of frontal and executive function*. Hove, UK: Psychology Press.

Buzan, T., & Buzan, P. (2000). *The mind map book*. London: BBC Books.

Carlson, N.R. (2004). *Physiology of behavior* (8th ed.). Boston: Allyn & Bacon.

Carver, C.S., & Scheier, M.F. (2004). *Perspectives on personality* (5th ed.). Boston: Allyn & Bacon.

Cashdan, A., & Wright, J. (1990). Intervention strategies for backward readers in the primary school classroom. In P. Pumfrey & C. Elliott (Eds.), *Children's difficulties in reading, spelling, and writing*. London: Falmer.

Christenson, L.B. (2004). *Experimental methodology* (9th ed.). Boston: Allyn & Bacon.

Clark-Carter, D. (1997). *Doing quantitative psychological research: From design to report*. Hove, UK: Psychology Press.

Coates, R., Hamilton, C., & Heffernan, T.M. (1997, July). *The development of visuo-spatial working memory: Effects of interference tasks on passive and active VSWM components*. Paper presented at the Spatial Cognition Conference, Rome.

Colman, A.M. (Ed.). (1995a). *Applications of psychology*. New York: Longman.

Colman, A.M. (Ed.). (1995b). *Psychological*

research methods and statistics. New York: Longman.

Connor, M. (1994). *Training the counsellor.* London: Routledge.

Cooke, D.J., Baldwin, P.J., & Howison, J. (1993). *Psychology in prisons* (2nd ed.). London: Routledge.

Coolican, H. (1990). *Research methods and statistics in psychology.* London: Hodder & Stoughton.

Corfield, R. (2003). *Preparing your own CV.* London: Kogan Page.

Costello, T.W., & Costello, J.T. (1992). *Abnormal psychology.* New York: HarperCollins.

Counselling psychology [Special issue]. (1990). *The Psychologist, 3(12).*

Cozby, P.C. (1989). *Methods in behavioral research* (2nd ed.). Mountain View, CA: Mayfield.

Craik, F.I.M., & Lockhart, R.S. (1972). Levels of processing: A framework for memory research. *Journal of Verbal Learning and Verbal Behaviour, 11,* 671–684.

Criminological and legal psychology [Special issue]. (1991). *The Psychologist, 4(9).*

Cronbach, L.J. (1990). *Essentials of psychological testing* (5th ed.). New York: Harper & Row.

Cuba, L. (1993). *A short guide to writing about social science* (2nd ed.). New York: HarperCollins.

Daneman, M., & Carpenter, P.A. (1980). Individual differences in working memory and reading. *Journal of Verbal Learning and Verbal Behaviour, 19,* 450–466.

Daneman, M., & Carpenter, P.A. (1983). Individual differences in integrating information between and within sentences. *Journal of Experimental Psychology: Learning, Memory and Cognition, 9,* 561–584.

Darwin, C. (1859). *The origin of species.* London: Macmillan.

Davison, G.C., Neale, J.M., & Kring, A.

(2003). *Abnormal psychology* (9th ed.). New York: Wiley.

Dickman, S.J. (1990). Functional and dysfunctional impulsivity: Personality and cognitive correlates. *Journal of Personality and Social Psychology, 58,* 95–102.

Doise, W. (1990). On the social development of the intellect. In K. Richardson & S. Sheldon (Eds.), *Cognitive development to adolescence.* Milton Keynes, UK: Open University Press.

Dollard, J., Doob, L.W., Miller, N.E., & Sears, R.R. (1939). *Frustration and aggression.* New Haven, CT: Yale University Press.

Donaldson, M. (1980). *Children's minds.* London: Fontana Press.

Drew, S., & Bingham, R. (1997). *The student skills guide.* Aldershot, UK: Gower.

Dua, J., & Hargreaves, L. (1992). Effect of aerobic exercise on negative affect, stress, and depression. *Perceptual and Motor Skills, 75,* 355–361.

Eagley, A.H. (1987). *Sex differences in social behavior: A social-role interpretation.* Hillsdale, NJ: Lawrence Erlbaum Associates, Inc.

Earl, J. (1993). A day in the life of a health psychologist. *The Psychologist, 6(11),* 505–506.

Education section [Special issue]. (1992). *The Psychologist, 5(3).*

Ellis, A., & Young, A.W. (1996). *Human cognitive neuropsychology.* Hove, UK: Lawrence Erlbaum Associates Ltd.

Elmes, D.G., Kantowitz, B.H., & Roediger, H.L., III. (1995). *Research methods* (5th ed.). St. Paul, MN: West.

Equinox. (1992, February 21). *Born to be gay?* Channel 4.

Eron, L.D. (1982). Parent–child interaction, television violence, and aggression in children. *American Psychologist, 37,* 197–211.

Eysenck, H.J., & Eysenck, S.B.G. (1969).

Personality structure and measurement. London: Routledge.

Eysenck, M.W. (1994). *Perspectives on psychology.* Hove, UK: Lawrence Erlbaum Associates Ltd.

Eysenck, M.W. (Ed.). (1998). *Psychology: An integrated approach.* Harlow, UK: Addison Wesley Longman.

Eysenck, M.W. (2002). *Simply psychology* (2nd ed.). Hove, UK: Psychology Press.

Eysenck, M.W., & Eysenck, M.C. (1980). Effects of processing depth, distinctiveness, and word frequency on retention. *British Journal of Psychology, 71*, 263–274.

Eysenck, M.W., & Keane, M.T. (2000). *Cognitive psychology: A student's handbook* (4th ed.). Hove, UK: Psychology Press.

Faulk, M. (1994). *Basic forensic psychiatry* (2nd ed.). Oxford: Blackwell Science.

Feldman, P. (1993). *The psychology of crime.* New York: Cambridge.

Ferguson, G.A., & Takane, Y. (1990). *Statistical analysis in psychology and education* (6th ed.). Maidenhead: McGraw-Hill.

Fisher, S., & Greenberg, R.P. (1977). *The scientific credibility of Freud's theories and therapy.* Hemel Hempstead, UK: Harvester Wheatsheaf.

Flavell, J.H., Beach, D.R., & Chinsky, J.M. (1966). Spontaneous verbal rehearsal in a memory task as a function of age. *Child Development, 37*, 283–299.

Flavell, J.H., Miller, P.H., & Miller, S. (2002). *Cognitive development* (4th ed.). New York: Prentice-Hall.

Fransella, F. (Ed.). (1981). *Personality: Theory, measurement and research.* New York: Methuen.

Freedman, J.L. (1984). Effects of television violence on aggressiveness. *Psychological Bulletin, 96*, 227–246.

French, C.C., & Colman, A.M. (1995). *Cognitive psychology.* London: Longman.

Freud, A. (1936). *The ego and the mechanisms of defence.* New York: International Press.

Freud, S. (1912). *Totem and taboo.* London: Routledge & Kegan Paul.

Freud, S. (1970). *An outline of psychoanalysis* (J. Strachey, Trans.). New York: Norton. (Original work published 1940.)

Freud, S. (1974). *The ego and the id* (J. Riviere & J. Strachey, Trans.). London: Hogarth Press. (Original work published 1927.)

Freud, S., & Breuer, J. (1955). *Studies on hysteria.* London: Hogarth Press.

Fromm, E. (1979). *To have or to be?* (2nd ed.). London: Sphere.

Fry, R.W., Morton, A.R., & Keast, D. (1991). Overtraining in athletes. *Sports Medicine, 12(1)*, 32–65.

Gale, A., & Chapman, A. (Eds.). (1984). *Psychology and social problems: An introduction to applied psychology.* Chichester, UK: Wiley.

Gardner, H. (1982). *Developmental psychology* (2nd ed.). Boston: Little, Brown.

Gatchel, R.J., Baum, A., & Krantz, D.S. (1997). *An introduction to health psychology* (3rd ed.). New York: McGraw-Hill.

Gathercole, S.E., & Baddeley, A.D. (1993). *Working memory and language.* Hove, UK: Lawrence Erlbaum Associates Ltd.

Gazzaniga, M.S., Ivry, R.B., & Mangun, G.R. (2002). *Cognitive neuroscience: The biology of the mind* (2nd ed.). New York: Norton.

Gellatly, A. (Ed.). (1986). *The skilful mind: An introduction to cognitive psychology.* Milon Keynes, UK: Open University Press.

Glasser, W. (1976). *Positive addiction.* New York: Harper-Row.

Glassman, W.E. (1995). *Approaches to psychology.* Milton Keynes, UK: Open University Press.

Gleitman, H., Fridlund, A.J., & Reisberg, D. (2003). *Psychology* (6th ed.). New York: Norton.

Grant, B.W. (1988). *The psychology of sport: Facing one's true opponent*. London: McFarland.

Grasha, A.F. (1995). *Practical applications of psychology* (4th ed.). Boston: Little, Brown.

Graves, N., & Varma, V. (Eds.). (1997). *Working for a doctorate: A guide for the humanities and social sciences*. New York: Routledge.

Gravetter, F.J., & Wallnau, L.B. (1996). *Statistics for the behavioral sciences* (4th ed.). St. Paul, MN: West.

Gray, A. (1979). *Pavlov*. London: Fontana.

Greene, J., & D'Oliveira, M. (1999). *Learning to use statistical tests in psychology* (3rd ed.). Milton Keynes, UK: Open University Press.

Groome, D., Dewart, H., Esgate, A., Gurney, K., Kemp, R., & Towell, N. (1999). *An introduction to cognitive psychology: Processes and disorders*. Hove, UK: Psychology Press.

Grove, J.R. (1995). Issues in sport psychology. In T. Morris & J. Summers (Eds.), *Sport psychology: Theory, applications, the issues*. Brisbane: Wiley.

Hague, P. (1993). *Interviewing*. London: Kogan Page.

Hall-Williams, J.E. (1984). *Criminology and criminal justice*. London: Butterworth.

Hartley, J., & Branthwaite, A. (Eds.). (1999). *The applied psychologist* (2nd ed.). Milton Keynes, UK: Open University Press.

Hausenblas, H.A., & Downs, D.S. (2002). Exercise dependence: A systematic review. *Psychology of Sport and Exercise, 3*, 89–123.

Haworth, J. (Ed.). (1996). *Psychological research: Innovative methods and strategies*. London: Routledge.

Hayes, N. (1994). *Foundations of psychology*. London: Routledge.

Health [Special issue]. (1994). *The Psychologist, 7(3)*.

Heffernan, T.M. (1996). Task predictability and rehearsal: A developmental perspective. In *Proceedings of the British Psychological Society, Vol. 4(2)*. Brighton, UK.

Heffernan, T., Green, D.W., McManus, I.C., & Muncer, S. (1998). *Comments on network analysis and lay interpretations: Some issues of consensus and representation* by S.J. Muncer & K. Gillen. *British Journal of Social Psychology, 37*, 253–254.

Heffernan, T.M., Moss, M., & Ling, J. (2002). Subjective ratings of prospective memory deficits in chronic heavy alcohol users. *Alcohol and Alcoholism, 37*, 269–271.

Heffernan, T., & Muncer, S. (1999, July). *Applying network analysis to perceived causes of crime: A comparison of offenders and non-offenders*. Paper presented at the VI European Congress of Psychology, Rome.

Heiman, G.W. (2000). *Basic statistics for the behavioral sciences* (4th ed.). Boston: Houghton Mifflin.

Herganhan, B.R. (1992). *An introduction to the history of psychology* (2nd ed.). Belmont, CA: Wadsworth.

Highfield, R. (1994, January 19). Great brains fight for your mind. *Daily Telegraph*, p. 14.

Hinkle, D.E., Wiersma, W., & Jurs, S.G. (1998). *Applied statistics for the behavioral sciences* (4th ed.). Boston: Houghton Mifflin.

Hitch, G.J., Halliday, M.S., Schaafstal, A.M., & Heffernan, T.M. (1991). Speech, "inner speech", and the development of short-term memory: Effects of picture-labeling on recall. *Journal of Experimental Child Psychology, 51*, 220–234.

Hobfoll, S.E., Banerjee, P., & Britton, P. (1994). Stress resistance resources and health: A conceptual analysis. In S. Maes, H. Leventhal, & M. Johnston (Eds.), *International review of health psychology* (Vol. 3). Chichester, UK: Wiley.

Hobsons. (2003). *Postgrad: The magazine* (Vol. 3). Chichester, UK: Hobsons.

Hollin, C.R. (Ed.). (1995). *Working with offenders*. Chichester, UK: Wiley.

Horgan, J. (1994). Can science explain consciousness? *Scientific American, 271*, 72–78.

Hothersall, D. (1995). *History of psychology* (3rd ed.). New York: McGraw-Hill.

How employers see psychologists [Special issue]. (1991). *The Psychologist, 4(10)*.

Howitt, D. (2002). *Forensic and Criminal Psychology*. Harlow, UK: Pearson.

Hughes, F.P., & Noppe, L.D. (1990). *Human development across the life span* (2nd ed.). St. Paul, MN: West.

Hyde, J.S., & Linn, M.C. (Eds.). (1986). *The psychology of gender: Advances through meta-analysis*. Baltimore: Johns Hopkins University Press.

James, W. (1890). *Principles of psychology* (Vol. 1). New York: Holt.

Jones, J.L. (1995). *Understanding psychological science*. New York: HarperCollins.

Kagan, D.M., & Squires, R.L. (1985). Addictive aspects of physical exercise. *Journal of Sports Medicine, 25*, 227–237.

Kail, R. (1990). *The development of memory in children* (3rd ed.). New York: Freeman.

Kantowitz, B.H., Roediger, H.L., III, & Elmes, D.G. (1994). *Experimental psychology*. St. Paul, MN: West.

Kaplan, R.M. (1999). *A child's odyssey* (3rd ed.). St. Paul, MN: West.

Kaplan, R.M., Sallis, J.F., Jr., & Patterson, T.L. (1993). *Health and human behavior*. New York: McGraw-Hill.

Kazdin, A.E. (2003). *Research design in clinical psychology* (4th ed.). Boston: Allyn & Bacon.

Kimble, D., & Colman, A.M. (Eds.). (1994). *Biological aspects of behaviour*. London: Longman.

Kimmel, A.J. (1996). *Ethical issues in behavioural research: A survey*. Oxford: Blackwell.

Kingman, S. (1994, September 17). Quality control for medicine. *New Scientist, 143*, 22–26.

Laughlin, H.P. (1967). *The neuroses*. Washington, DC: Butterworth.

Lengefield, U. (1996). *Study skills strategies: How to learn more in less time*. London: Crisp.

Lewis, S. (1995). A day in the life of a PhD student. *The Psychologist, 8(7)*, 299–300.

Leyens, J.P., Camino, L., Parke, R., & Berkowitz, L. (1975). Effects of movie violence on aggression in a field setting as a function of group dominance and cohesion. *Journal of Personality and Social Psychology, 32(2)*, 346–360.

Logie, R.H. (1986). Visuo-spatial processes in working memory. *Quarterly Journal of Experimental Psychology, 38A*, 229–247.

Logie, R.H. (1995). *Visuo-spatial working memory*. Hove, UK: Lawrence Erlbaum Associates Ltd.

Logie, R.H. (1999). Working memory. *The Psychologist, 12(4)*, 174–178.

Lorenz, K. (1966). *On aggression*. New York: Harcourt, Brace & World.

McCarthy, R.A., & Warrington, E.K. (1990). *Cognitive neuropsychology: A clinical introduction*. Cambridge: Academic Press.

Maccoby, E., & Jacklin, C. (1974). *The psychology of sex differences*. Stanford, CA: Stanford University Press.

McDonald, D.G., & Hodgdon, J.A. (1995). Psychological effects of aerobic fitness training: Research and theory. In S.J.H. Pierce (Ed.), *European perspectives on exercise and sport psychology*. Champaign, IL: Human Kinetics Publishers. (Original work published 1991.)

McKay, M. (1996). The Neale analysis of reading ability revised: Systematically biased? *British Journal of Educational Psychology, 66*, 259–266.

McKee, P. (1995). *How to write a CV that works*. Plymouth, UK: How To Books.

McShane, J. (1991). *Cognitive development:*

An information processing approach. Oxford: Blackwell.

Malim, T., Birch, A., & Wadeley, A. (1996). *Perspectives in psychology* (2nd ed.). Basingstoke, UK: Macmillan.

Marks, I.M. (1969). *Fears and phobias.* New York: Academic Press.

Marshall, L., & Rowland, F. (1998). *A guide to learning independently* (3rd ed.). Milton Keynes, UK: Open University Press.

Mason, J. (2002). *Qualitative researching* (2nd ed). London: Sage.

Miller, G.A. (1956). The magic number seven, plus or minus two: Some limits on our capacity for processing information. *Psychological Review, 63,* 81–93.

Miner, J.B. (1992). *Industrial organizational psychology.* New York: McGraw-Hill.

Mischel, W. (1999). *Introduction to personality* (6th ed.). Orlando, FL: Harcourt Brace.

Moran, M. (2003). *Exploring sport psychology.* London: Routledge.

Morgan, W.P. (1979). Negative addiction in runners. *Physician Sports-med, 7,* 57–70.

Morgan, W.P. (1985). Affective beneficence of vigorous physical activity. *Medicine and Science in Sports and Exercise, 17,* 94–100.

Morris, T., & Summers, J. (1995). *Sport psychology: Theory, applications and issues.* New York: Wiley.

Myers, D.G. (2001). *Social psychology* (7th ed.). New York: McGraw-Hill.

Niven, N. (1994). *Health psychology: An introduction for nurses and other health care professionals.* Edinburgh: Churchill Livingstone.

Northedge, A. (1997). *The sciences good study guide.* Oxford: Oxford University Press.

Norton, L.S. (1990). Essay-writing: What really counts? *Higher Education, 20,* 411–442.

Norton, L.S., & Hartley, J. (1986). What factors contribute to good examination marks? The role of notetaking in subsequent examination performance. *Higher Education, 15,* 355–371.

Oglesby, C., & Hill, K. (1993). Gender and sport. In R. Singer (Ed.), *Handbook of research on sport psychology* (pp. 718–728). New York: Macmillan.

Oppenheim, A.N. (2000). *Questionnaire design, interviewing and attitude measurement* (2nd ed.). London: Pinter.

Ornstein, P.A., Naus, M.J., & Liberty, C. (1975). Rehearsal and organizational processes in children's memory. *Child Development, 26,* 818–830.

Paivio, A. (1979). *Imagery and verbal processes.* Hillsdale, NJ: Lawrence Erlbaum Associates, Inc.

Paivio, A. (1983). *Imagery and verbal processes* (2nd ed.). Hillsdale, NJ: Lawrence Erlbaum Associates, Inc.

Parkin, A.J. (1993). *Memory: Phenomena, experiment, and theory.* Oxford: Blackwell.

Parkin, A.J. (1997). *Memory and amnesia.* Oxford: Blackwell.

Parkin, A.J. (2000). *Essential cognitive psychology.* Hove, UK: Psychology Press.

Payne, D.G., & Wenger, M.J. (1998). *Cognitive psychology.* Abingdon, UK: Houghton Mifflin.

Phillips, E.M., & Pugh, D.S. (2000). *How to get a PhD* (3rd ed.). Milton Keynes, UK: Open University Press.

Piaget, J., & Inhelder, B. (1973). *Memory and intelligence.* London: Routledge & Kegan Paul.

Pierce, E.F. (1994). Exercise dependence syndrome in runners. *Sports Medicine, 18(3),* 149–155.

Pierce, E.F., & Morris, J.T. (1998). Exercise dependence among competitive power lifters. *Perceptual and Motor Skills, 86(3),* 1097–1098.

Pierce, E.F., Rohaly, K.A., & Fritchley, B. (1997). Sex differences on exercise dependence for men and women in a marathon race. *Perceptual and Motor Skills, 84(3),* 991–994.

Pinel, J.P.J. (2003). *Biopsychology* (5th ed.). Boston: Allyn & Bacon.

Plante, T.G., & Rodin, J. (1990). Physical fitness and enhanced psychological health. *Current Psychology: Research and Reviews, 9,* 3–24.

The Psychologist (2001). *Evolution and behaviour Vol. 14 (8).*

The Psychologist (2003). *In a positive light, Vol. 16 (3).*

Psychology in sport. (1997). *The Psychologist, 10(2).*

Quinn, V.N. (1995). *Applying psychology* (3rd ed.). New York: McGraw-Hill.

Rachman, S.J. (1976). Therapeutic modelling. In M. Felman & A. Broadhurst (Eds.), *Theoretical and experimental bases of behaviour therapy.* Chichester, UK: Wiley.

Ramsden, P. (Ed.). (1988). *Improving learning.* London: Kogan Page.

Reyna, V.F. (1985). Figure and fantasy in children's language. In M. Pressley & C.J. Brainerd (Eds.), *Cognitive learning and memory in children: Progress in cognitive development research.* New York: Springer-Verlag.

Robbins, S.P. (2002). *Organizational behavior* (10th ed.). New York: Prentice-Hall.

Robinson-Riegler, G., & Robinson-Riegler, B. (2004). *Cognitive psychology: Applying the science of the mind.* Harlow, UK: Pearson.

Robson, C. (1994). *Experiment, design and statistics in psychology.* Harmondsworth, UK: Penguin.

Robson, C. (2002). *Real world research* (2nd ed.). Oxford: Blackwell.

Roediger, H.L. (1980). Memory metaphors in cognitive psychology. *Memory and Cognition, 8,* 231–246.

Rogers, C. (1990). Motivation in the primary years. In C. Rogers & P. Kutnick (Eds.), *The social psychology of the primary school.* London: Routledge.

Rogers, C. (1995). *A way of being.* Boston: Houghton Mifflin.

Rossano, M.J. (2003). *Evolutionary psychology: The science of human behavior and evolution.* New York: Wiley.

Sabini, J. (1995). *Social psychology* (2nd ed.). New York: Freeman.

Saks, M.J., & Krupat, E. (1988). *Social psychology and its applications.* New York: Harper & Row.

Salame, P., & Baddeley, A.D. (1982). Disruption of short-term memory by unattended speech: Implications for the structure of working memory. *Journal of Verbal Learning and Verbal Behaviour, 21,* 150–164.

Salame, P., & Baddeley, A.D. (1983). Differential effects of noise and speech on short-term memory. In *The Proceedings of the Fourth International Congress on Noise as a Public Health Problem,* Turin, Italy, pp. 751–758. Edizioni Tecniche a cura del Centro Ricerche e Studi Amplifon.

Salame, P., & Baddeley, A.D. (1989). Effects of background music on phonological short-term memory. *Quarterly Journal of Experimental Psychology -A, (1),* 107–122.

Sanders, D. (1996). *Counselling for psychosomatic disorders.* London: Sage.

Sarafino, E.P. (2001). *Health psychology: Biopsychosocial interactions* (4th ed.). New York: Wiley.

Saunders, D. (Ed.). (1994). *The complete student handbook.* Oxford: Blackwell.

Schroeder, B.A. (1992). *Human growth and development.* St. Paul, MN: West.

Seligman, M.E.P. (1992). *Helplessness on development, depression and death.* New York: Freeman.

Seligman, M.E.P. (2002). *Authentic happiness.* New York: Free Press.

Seligman, M.E.P., Walker, E., & Rosenhan, D. (2001). *Abnormal psychology* (4th ed.). New York: Norton.

Serling, R.J. (1986). Curing a fear of flying. *USAIR,* 12–19.

Shallice, T. (1982). Specific impairments in planning. *Philosophical Transactions of the Royal Society London, B, 298,* 199–209.

Shaughnessy, J.J., & Zechmeister, E.B. (2002). *Research methods in psychology* (6th ed.). New York: McGraw-Hill.

Simon, H.A. (1974). How big is a chunk? *Science, 183,* 482–488.

Smith, B., & Brown, S. (Eds.). (1995). *Research, teaching and learning in higher education.* London: RoutledgeFarmer.

Smith, E.E., Nolen-Hoeksema, S., Fredrickson, B., & Loftus, G.R. (2003). *Atkinson & Hilgard's introduction to psychology* (14th ed.). New York: Wadsworth.

Smith, M., & Smith, G. (1990). *A study skills handbook.* Oxford: Oxford University Press.

Smith, R.E. (1993). *Psychology.* St. Paul, MN: West.

Smyth, M.M., & Scholey, K.A. (1994). Characteristics of spatial memory span: Is there an analogy to the word length effect, based on movement time? *Quarterly Journal of Experimental Psychology, 47A,* 91–117.

Solso, R.L., & Maclin, M.K. (2002). *Experimental psychology.* New York: Longman.

Solso, R.L., Johnson, H.H., & Beal, M.K. (2002). *Experimental psychology: A case approach* (7th ed.). New York: Longman.

Sport [Special issue]. (1991). *The Psychologist, 4(4).*

Sprinthall, R., Sprinthall, N., & Oja, S. (1997). *Educational psychology: A developmental approach* (7th ed.). New York: McGraw-Hill.

Spyridakis, J., & Standal, T. (1987). Signals in expository prose: Effects on reading comprehension. *Reading Research Quarterly, 22,* 285–298.

Squid, G.Y. (n.d.). The ethnography of adultery in royal clans. *Monarchy and Monarchs, 13,* 32–48.

Stephenson, G.M. (1993). *The psychology of criminal justice.* Oxford: Blackwell.

Sternberg, R.J. (1998). *Cognitive psychology* (3rd ed.). New York: Harcourt Brace.

Strachey, J. (Ed.). (1958). *The standard edition of the complete psychological works of Sigmund Freud* (Vol. XIII). London: Hogarth Press.

Student [Special issue]. (1994). *The Psychologist, 7(10).*

Sue, D., Sue, D., & Sue, S. (2002). *Understanding abnormal behavior* (7th ed.). Boston: Houghton Mifflin.

Szabo, A. (1995). The impact of exercise deprivation on well-being of habitual exercisers. *Australian Journal of Science and Medicine in Sport, 27,* 68–75.

Szabo, A. (1998). Studying the psychological impact of exercise deprivation: are experimental studies hopeless? *Journal of Sport Behaviour, 31(2),* 139–148.

Taylor, S.E. (2002). *Health psychology* (5th ed.). New York: McGraw-Hill.

Taylor, S.E., Peplau, L.A., & Sears, D.O. (1997). *Social psychology* (9th ed.). New York: Prentice-Hall.

Testing in the workplace [Special issue]. (1994). *The Psychologist, 7(1).*

Van Hasselt, V.B., & Hersen, M. (2000). *Advanced abnormal psychology* (2nd ed.). New York: Plenum Press.

Wadeley, H. (1991). *Ethics in psychological research and practice.* Leicester, UK: British Psychological Society.

Watson, P. (1980). *War on the mind.* Harmondsworth, UK: Penguin.

Watson, R.I., & Evans, R.B. (1991). *The great psychologists: A history of psychological thought* (5th ed.). New York: HarperCollins.

Wenar, C. (2000). *Developmental psychopathology* (4th ed.). New York: McGraw-Hill.

Williams, J.M. (Ed.). (1993). *Applied sports psychology: Personal growth to peak performance.* Mountain View, CA: Mayfield.

Wolpe, J. (1973). *The practice of behaviour*

therapy (3rd ed.). Elmsford, NY: Pergamon Press.

Woolfolk, A.E. (1998). *Educational psychology* (7th ed.). New York: Prentice-Hall.

Zhang, G., & Simon, H.A. (1985). STM capacity for Chinese words and idioms: Chunking and acoustical loop hypotheses. *Memory and Cognition, 13,* 193–201.

Author index

Acocella, J. 5
Acres, D. 163
Adams, N.E. 144, 147
Agras, S. 59
Ainsworth, P.B. 191, 194
Alloy, L.B. 5, 16
American Psychiatric Association 67, 107, 142
Anastasi, A. 201
Anshel, M.H. 144
Aronson, E. 15, 18, 19, 88
Association of Graduate Careers Advisory Service 180
Atkinson, R.C. 70, 128, 157

Baddeley, A.D. 16, 17, 39, 43, 71, 74, 97, 128, 132, 157, 161, 170, 171, 172, 173
Bakker, F.C. 200
Baldwin, P.J. 194
Bandura, A. 19
Barlow, D.H. 91
Barnes, R. 27, 31, 37, 53
Baron, R.A. 15, 18, 19, 20
Bartol, C.R. 194
Baum, A. 195
Bausell, R.B. 48
Beach, D.R. 128
Beal, M.K. 91
Beck, A.T. 17, 69
Beck, R.C. 188, 191, 201
Becker, H.S. 72

Berger, B.G. 143
Berkowitz, L. 19
Best, J.B. 10, 17
Biddle, J.H. 200
Bingham, R. 38
Birch, A. 3
Blackburn, R. 14, 15, 188, 191, 192, 194
Bootzin, R.R. 5
Bradley, L. 62
Branthwaite, A. 201
Breakwell, G.M. 53, 82, 88, 92, 97, 105, 106, 206
British Psychological Society 49, 63, 107, 182 see also subject index
Broadbent, D. 16, 17, 157
Brody, R. 198
Brown, J.C. 5
Brown, M. 206
Brown, S. 27
Bryant, P. 62
Bull, S.J. 200
Buzan, T. 160
Byrne, D. 15, 18, 19, 20

Camino, L. 19
Carlsmith, J.M. 88
Carlson, N.R. 7, 21
Carver, C.S. 168
Cashdan, A. 62
Chapman, A. 188, 190, 191, 201
Chinsky, J.M. 128

Christenson, L.B. 88, 106
Clark-Carter, D. 97, 104
Coates, R. 76
Colman, A.M. 7, 17, 106, 191
Connor, M. 196
Cooke, D.J. 194
Coolican, H. 94, 98, 102, 104, 105
Corfield, R. 202, 203
Costello, J.T. 14
Costello, T.W. 14
Cozby, P.C. 51, 53, 82, 85, 86, 90, 97
Craik, F.I.M. 128, 157
Cronbach, L.J. 92, 93
Cuba, L. 43

D'Oliveira, M. 96, 97, 99, 102, 104
Darwin, C. 1, 6, 7
Davison, G.C. 6, 7, 8, 12
Dewart, H. 16, 133
Dickman, S.J. 77
Doise, W. 42
Dollard, J. 19
Donaldson, M. 10
Doob, L.W. 19
Downs, D.S. 144, 146
Drew, S. 38
Dua, J. 144, 146

Eagley, A.H. 144
Ebbinghaus, H. 1

Ellis, A. 17
Ellsworth, P.C. 88
Elmes, D.G. 53, 68, 69, 88, 92, 97, 102, 106
Equinox. 77
Eron, L.D. 19
Esgate, A. 16, 133
Evans, R.B. 3
Eysenck, H.J. 77
Eysenck, M.W. 5, 6, 7, 14, 16, 17, 22, 79, 91, 128, 132
Eysenck, S.B.G. 77

Faulk, M. 15, 194
Feldman, P. 191
Ferguson, G.A. 104
Fife-Shaw, C. 81
Fisher, S. 5
Flavell, J.H. 128, 132
Fransella, F. 5, 11, 12, 68, 169
Fredrickson, B. 128
Freedman, J.L. 19, 42, 43
French, C.C. 17
Freud, S. 1, 3, 4, 19, 38, 63, 68, 70, 160, 168
Fridlund, A.J. 5
Fritchley, B. 144
Fry, R.W. 144

Gale, A. 188, 190, 191, 201
Galton, F. 1
Gardner, H. 9, 10
Gatchel, R.J. 195
Gazzaniga, M.S. 21
Glasser, W. 143
Glassman, W.E. 65
Gleitman, H. 5, 6, 9, 11, 14, 22, 69, 132, 169
Gonzales, M.H. 88
Grant, B.W. 200
Graves, N. 183
Gravetter, F.J. 104
Gray, A. 14
Green, D.W. 73
Greenberg, R.P. 5

Greene, J. 96, 97, 99, 102, 104
Groome, D. 16, 17, 133
Grove, J.R. 144
Gurney, K. 16, 133

Hague, P. 206
Hall-Williams, J.E. 191
Halliday, M.S. 8, 74
Hamilton, C. 76
Hammond, S. 81
Hargreaves, L. 144, 146
Hartley, J. 165, 201
Harvey, F. 143
Hausenblas, H.A. 144, 146
Haworth, J. 106
Hayes, N. 5, 12, 14, 22, 169, 198
Heffernan, T.M. 8, 73, 74, 76, 143
Heiman, G.W. 104
Herganhan, B.R. 3, 13, 15
Hersen, M. 10, 91, 188
Highfield, R. 77
Hill, K. 144, 147
Hinkle, D.E. 104
Hitch, G.J. 8, 39, 41, 74, 157, 170, 171, 172
Hobfoll, S.E. 73
Hobsons. 183
Hodgdon, J.A. 145, 147
Hollin, C.R. 194
Horgan, J. 76
Hothersall, D. 3
Howison, J. 194
Hughes, F.P. 9, 10
Hyde, J.S. 144

Inhelder, B. 64
Ivry, R.B. 21

Jacklin, C. 144
Johnson, H.H. 91
Jones, J.L. 106
Jurs, S.G. 104

Kagan, D.M. 144
Kail, R. 9, 128, 132

Kantowitz, B.H. 68, 88
Kaplan, R.M. 9, 10, 195
Kazdin, A.E. 91
Keane, M.T. 128, 132
Keast, D. 144
Kemp, R. 16, 133
Kimble, D. 7
Kimmel, A.J. 111
Kingman, S. 76
Kirkby, R. 144, 147
Koffka, K. 2
Kohler, W. 2
Krantz, D.S. 195
Kring, A. 6
Krupat, E. 20

Lengefield, U. 163
Leyens, J.P. 19
Liberty, C. 128
Ling, J. 73
Lockhart, R.S. 128, 157
Loftus, G.R. 128
Logie, R.H. 39, 161
Lorenz, K. 19

Maccoby, E. 144
McCarthy, R.A. 17
McDonald, D.G. 145, 147
McInman, A. 143
Maclin, M.K. 2
McManus, I.C. 73
McShane, J. 10
Malim, T. 3
Mangun, G.R. 21
Marks, I.M. 8
Marshall, L. 31, 37, 53
Maslow, A. 2, 10, 11, 13
Mason, J. 106
Mischel, W. 169
Miller, G.A. 171
Miller, N.E. 19
Miller, P.H. 128
Miller, S. 128
Miner, J.B. 191
Moran, M. 200
Morgan, W.P. 143, 144, 148
Morris, J.T. 144

Morris, T. 200
Moss, M. 73
Muncer, S. 73, 76
Myers, D.G. 18

Naus, M.J. 128
Neale, J.M. 6
Niven, N. 195
Nolen-Hoeksema, S. 128
Noppe, L.D. 9, 10
Northedge, A. 46
Norton, L.S. 53, 61, 62, 64, 66, 74, 165

Oglesby, C. 144, 147
Oja, S. 190
Oliveau, D. 59
Oppenheim, A.N. 91, 92, 93
Ornstein, P.A. 128
Owen, D.R. 143

Paivio, A. 72
Parke, R. 19
Parkin, A.J. 17, 39, 161, 172
Patterson, T.L. 195
Payne, D.G. 17
Peplau, L.A. 19
Phillips, E.M. 182, 183
Piaget, J. 9, 10, 42, 64
Pierce, E.F. 144, 146, 147
Pinel, J.P.J. 1, 6
Plante, T.G. 144
Pugh, D.S. 182, 183

Quinn, V.N. 14, 162

Reisberg, D. 5
Reyna, V. F. 73
Robbins, S.P. 191
Robinson-Riegler, B. 17
Robinson-Riegler, G. 17
Robson, C. 85, 86, 88, 90, 92, 93, 102, 104, 105, 106

Rodin, J. 144
Roediger, H.L. 68, 74
Rogers, C. 2, 10, 12, 13, 73, 88
Rohaly, K.A. 144
Rosenhan, D.L. 2
Ross, D. 19
Ross, S. 19
Rossano, M.J. 21
Rowland, F. 31, 37, 53

Sabini, J. 19, 20
Saks, M.J. 20
Sallis, J.F., Jr. 195
Sanders, D. 196
Sarafino, E.P. 195
Saunders, D. 31, 37, 53
Schaafstal, A.M. 8, 74
Scheier, M.F. 168
Scholey, K.A. 39, 172
Schroeder, B.A. 9, 10
Sears, D.O. 19
Seligman, M.E.P. 2, 6, 14, 15, 17, 21, 22, 47
Shallice, T. 172
Shaughnessy, J.J. 85, 106, 110, 111
Shiffrin, R.M. 128, 157
Simon, H.A. 171
Smith, E.E. 5, 6, 7, 9, 12, 14, 15, 16, 22, 42, 128, 157, 168, 169
Smith, M. 47
Smith, R.E. 7
Smyth, M.M. 39, 172
Solso, R.L. 2, 91
Sprinthall, N. 190
Sprinthall, R. 190
Spyridakis, J. 63
Squid, G.Y. 74
Squires, R.L. 144
Standal, T. 63
Stephenson, G.M. 191

Sternberg, R.J. 5, 6, 12, 18, 22, 69
Strachey, J. 71
Sue, D. 2, 6, 7, 8, 10, 17, 18, 47
Sue, S. 2, 6, 7, 8, 10, 17, 18, 47
Summers, J. 200
Sylvester, D. 59
Szabo, A. 144

Takane, Y. 104
Taylor, S.E. 19, 20, 195
Towell, N. 16

van der Brug, H. 200
Van Hasselt, V.B. 10, 188
Varma,V. 183
Von Helmholtz, H. 1

Wadeley, A. 3
Wadeley, H. 111
Walker, E. 2
Wallnau, L.B. 104
Warrington, E.K. 17
Watson, J.B. 14
Watson, P. 65
Watson, R.I. 3
Wenar, C. 10, 17
Whiting, H.T.A. 200
Wiersma, W. 104
Williams, J.M. 200
Woolfolk, A.E. 190
Wright, J. 62

Young, A.W. 17

Zechmeister, E.B. 85, 106, 110, 111
Zhang, G. 171

Subject index

Page numbers in **bold type** represent figures/diagrams

Abstracts, Psychological 52–3
abstracts, report writing 115–16, 127–8, 140, 142, 132
active learning 27–9, 37, 158
aggression 19
anal stage 5
analysis, data *see* data analysis; statistical analysis
analysis (psychoanalysis) 5–6
applied psychology 20, 22, 185–6
    journals 50 *see also* occupational psychology
applied social psychology 20
American Psychological Association (APA) 67, 107, 142, 185
assistant psychologists 187
attitude scales 92–4

Bachelors degree 79, 206–7
basic needs 11, 12
Bath ISI Data Service 52
behavioural psychology journals 49

behaviourism/ behaviourist perspective 3, 13–16
behaviour shaping 14, 16
classical conditioning 13–14, 15
conditional reflex 13
conditioned response 13, 14
criticisms of 16
defined 14
development of 2
discrimination 14
discriminative stimulus 15
extinction 14
generalisation 14
objective psychology 13, 14
operant conditioning 15, 16
Pavlov/Pavlovian conditioning 13–14
punishment 15
reinforcement 15
Skinner and 14–15
social learning theory 15
stimulus-response associations 14, 15
Thorndike and 15

unconditioned response/ stimulus 13
Watson and 14
"being" mode 27
between-subjects design 83
bibliographies 67 *see also* referencing
biological perspective 2, 3, 6–8
biomedical model 6, 7
British Psychological Society (BPS) 107, 108, 142, 184–5, 186

causal inference 85–6, 97–8
citations, format of 67–9, 70–1
Citation Index, Social Science 52
clinical psychology 184, 186–8
    assistant psychologists 187
    journals 50
    personal characteristics 187
    psychology technicians 187
    training for 186
coding data 105, 138–9
cognitive-behavioural therapy 17–18

cognitive neuroscience 17, 20–1
cognitive perspective 3, 16–18
  Broadbent's contributions 16, 17
  information processing 17
  journals 50
concrete operational stage 10
conditional reflex 13
conditioned response 13, 14
conditioning: classical 13–14, 15
  operant 15, 16
  Pavlovian 13–14
conference presentations 115, 142–52
  advantages 142
  checklist of contents 143–8
  oral presentations 150–2
  poster presentations 149–50, 152
conference proceedings 75–6
confounding variables 84–5, 119
conscience, mechanism 4
consumer psychology 201
control procedures 84–5
correlational methodology 96–7
counselling 185, 196
  journals 50
  person-centered 12
counterbalancing 84, 85
criminological psychology 185, 187, 191–4
  defined 191–2
  personal characteristics 193
  training 192–4

Curriculum vitae 179, 201–6
  categories within 202
  cover letter 205–6
  defined 201–2
  example 203–4
  key parts 204–5

data 97–104
  causal inference 97–8
  coding 105, 138–9
  conclusions from 105–6
  generating 104–5
  interval 99
  nominal 98–9
  ordinal 99
  ratio 99–100
data analysis: 136
  descriptive 121, 122, 123, 140–1
  inferential 121, 122, 123
  qualitative 105, 140–1
  statistical see statistical analysis
degree, Bachelors 79, 206–7
deep processing 27–9, 37
dependent variables 83, 119
descriptive statistics 100–1, 121, 122, 123
design, experimental 83–4, 118
developmental perspective 2, 8–10
  journals 50, 114
  Piaget's work 9–10
  qualitative/quantitative change 8–9
  stages of development 8, 9, 10
developmental psychopathology 10
discrimination 14
discriminative stimulus 15
displays, poster 149–50, 152
drives/impulses 4

educational psychology 184, 188–90
  training for 188–9
ego 4
environmental psychology 201
ergonomics 185, 190–1
essay writing: concluding section 53, 54
  definition 45
  essay plan 53–4, **165**
  examples 54, 55–61
  final modifications 55
  first draft 54
  first person, use of 63
  indicating your own ideas 64
  introduction 53, 54
  key words 46
  literature searching 47–9, 51–3, 136, 137
  main body of essay 53, 54
  plagiarism 65–6, 138, 154
  precision 62–3
  racist language 63
  reference section 54 (see also referencing)
  second draft 54–5
  sexist language 63
  signalling 63–4
  stages in 45–6
  title 46–7
  understanding, demonstrating 64–5
  writing style 45, 62–5 see also report writing
"et al." (use of) 68–9
ethics 137, 138
  guidelines 107–11
evolutionary psychology 7, 20, 21
exams 153–77
  context 162
  definition 153
  example of exam essay 167–74
  facilitating recall 158–62, 166–7

failing 174–5, 177
first-class answer 175
format of answer 165, 166
hierarchies 156, 165
mock exams 163
multiple choice 153–4
open book 153
pass grade 176–7
preparation 156
rationale behind 154–5
second-class answer 175–6
seen exams 153
technique 164–7
things to avoid 163–4
third-class answer 176
unseen exam 153 *see also* revision
experimental methodology 82–6, 118, 135–8
between-subjects design 83
causal inference 85–6
confounding variables 84–5, 119
control procedure 84–5
counterbalancing 84, 85
dependent variables 83, 119
design 83–4, 118
hypothesis 47–8, 79, 82
independent variables 83, 118, 119
matching 83, 84–5
mixed design 83
randomisation 83, 84, 85
within-subjects design 83–4)
experimental psychology journals 50
extinction, response 14

failing an exam 174–5, 177
fixation 5
forensic work *see* criminological psychology

formal operational stage 10
Freudian theory 1–2, 3–6

generalisation 14
genital stage 5
graduate status 179–181

Harvard system, referencing 67
"having" mode 27
health psychology 185, 194–5
training for 194
humanistic perspective 2, 10–13, 21
basic needs 11, 12
belonging/love 11
criticisms 12–13
definition 10
esteem 11
ideal self 12
Maslow's hierarchy of needs 11, 12
person-centered counselling 12
Rogerian theory/therapy 10, 12
safety 11
self-actualisation 2, 11, 12
hypotheses 47–8, 79, 82
formulation 79, 82, 89

id 4
ideal self 12
impulses/drives 4
independent variables 83, 118, 119
industrial psychology 185, 190–1
inferential data: causal 85–6, 97–8
statistical analysis 100–1, 121, 122, 123
Internet/online: literature searching 51–3
references 75

interviews, research methodology: semi-structured 91–2
structured 91
unstructured 92

job opportunities *see* psychology, applications
jobs, applying for *see* Curriculum vitae
journals 49–51
developmental psychology 50, 114
general psychology 49, 114
references 67, 73–4
report writing for 142, 143–8 *see also* literature searching

latency stage 5
learning, active/passive 27–9, 37
lectures 29–31 *see also* note taking
legal psychology *see* criminological psychology
lifespan psychology (stages of development) 8, 9, 10
Likert scales 93
literature reviews 42–3
see also reference materials
literature searching 47–9, 80, 82, 86, 104, 136–7
Internet/online 51–3 *see also* journals
reference materials

management consultancy 185, 190–1
maps, mind 160–2, **161**
Maslow's hierarchy of needs 11, 12
matching 83, 84–5
memory *see* recall
revision

methods, research *see*
  experimental
  methodology
  research methodology
mind maps 160–2, **161**
mixed design 83
mnemonics 158–60
modelling, social 19
multiple choice
  examinations 153–4

needs, Maslow's hierarchy
  11, 12
negative reinforcement 15
neuropsychology 185,
  198–9
neuroscience, cognitive 17,
  20–1
nominal data 98–9
non-experimental method
  82, 88–97
  attitude scales 92–4
  case studies 90–1
  correlational method
    96–7
  interviews 91–2
  non-participant
    observation 89
  observational method 89,
    138–9
  participant observation
    89–90
  questionnaires 94–6
  research questions 89
  surveys 91–6
nonparametric statistics
  100
note taking 37–41
  linear 39–40
  recording your notes
    39–40
  selectivity 37, 38–9
nuisance variables 84–5,
  119

objective psychology 13,
  14

observational method 89,
  138–9
  participant 89–90
  non-participant 89
occupational psychology
  185, 190–1
online literature searching
  51–3
operant conditioning 15,
  16
oral presentations 150–2
oral stage 5
ordinal 99
organizational psychology
  185, 190–1

parametric statistics 100
passive learning 27–9,
  37
Pavlovian conditioning
  13–14
person-centered
  counselling 12
personality 4, 5
  journals 50
pet psychology 201
phallic stage 5
plagiarism 65–6, 138, 154
pleasure principle 4
positive psychology 20,
  21–2
positive reinforcement 15
poster presentations
  149–50, 152
postgraduate: courses 181
  funding 182–4
  status 183
  research 181–4
  training 181–4
preoperational stage 10
prison psychologists *see*
  criminological
  psychology
processing, deep/surface
  27–9, 37
psyche, unconscious 4
psychoanalysis 5–6
psychoanalytic/

psychodynamic
  perspective 2, 3–6
post-Freudian theory 5
psychosexual stages 4–5,
  167–9
Psychological Abstracts
  52–3
psychology, applications
  see applied psychology;
  clinical psychology;
  cognitive neuroscience;
  consumer psychology;
  counselling;
  criminological
  psychology;
  developmental
  psychopathology;
  educational psychology;
  environmental
  psychology;
  evolutionary
  psychology; health
  psychology;
  neuropsychology;
  occupational
  psychology; pet
  psychology; positive
  psychology;
  psychoanalysis;
  psychotherapy; research
  psychologists; social
  psychology; sports
  psychology; teaching
psychology: definition 1
  degrees 79, 206–7
  journals 49, 114
  perspectives in 2–3
  as scientific study 1, 2,
    12, 13, 14
psychopathology,
  developmental 10
psychotherapy 6, 185,
  199
PsycLit 53
public speaking 150–2
punishment
  (behaviourism) 15

qualitative report writing 139–41
qualitative research methodology 82, 104–6
  analysing data 105
  coding data 105
  conclusions from data 105–6
  generating data 104–5
  literature searching 104
  question formation 104
  write-up 105, 139–41
qualitative/quantitative research, distinction 79–80
quantitative report writing 113–39
quasi-experimental method 18, 82, 86–8, 118
  control series 88
  nonequivalent control group 86–7
  time-series 87–8
questions, formulating research 89, 104 *see also* hypothesis
questionnaires 94–6
quotations 69–7 *see also* plagiarism

random sampling 80–1
randomisation 83, 84, 85
reality principle 4
recall, facilitating 158–62, 166–7
  mind maps 160–2, **161**
  mnemonics 158–60
reference materials:
  empirical reports 41, 117
  review articles 42–3
  summarising reviews 43–4
  theoretical papers 42
referencing 66–77
  bibliographies 67
  book references 67, 71–3
  citing in the text 67–9, 70

citing in reference section 67, 70–1
conference proceedings 75–6
definition 66–7
direct quotations 69–70
"et al." (use of) 68–9
edited books 72–3
essay writing 54
general media 76–7
Harvard system 67
Internet references 75
journal articles 67, 73–4
presenting reference section 70–1
report writing 124–5, 126, 133–4, 141, 147–8
sources, primary/secondary 70
tests/other materials 77
reflexes, conditional 13
reinforcement, negative/positive 15
repeated-measures design 84
report writing
  abstracts 115–16, 127–8, 140, 142, 132
  apparatus 119
  appendices 125, 126, 134, 141
  conference/journal 142, 143–8 (*see also* conference presentation)
  design 118, 129
  discussion 123–4, 126, **132**–3, 141, 146–7
  ethical considerations 137, 138
  example of write-up 126–35
  experimental hypothesis 117, 129
  introduction to experiment 116–18, 124, 128–9, 140, 143–5
  materials 119, 130

  method 118–21, 126, 129–31, 140, 145
  participants 119, 130, 145
  procedure 120–1, 130–1, 145–6
  qualitative report writing 139–41
  quantitative report writing 113–39
  references 124–5, 126, 133–4, 141, 147–8
  results 121–3, 131, 146
  structure of report 114
  title page 114–15 *see also* data analysis
  write-up, research
research methodology:
  data 97–104
  ethical guidelines 107–11
  experimental method 82–6, 118, 135–8
  literature searching 80, 82, 86
  non-experimental method 82, 88–97
  qualitative approach 82, 104–6
  qualitative/quantitative distinction 79–80
  quasi-experimental method 18, 82, 86–8, 118
  sampling procedures 80–2
  statistical analysis 97–104, 121–3
research psychologists 196–7
response: conditioned 13, 14
  extinction 14
  unconditioned 13
review articles 42–3
revision 155–63: example 157, 161
  organising revision 156–8, **157**

Rogerian theory/therapy 10, 12

sampling procedures 80–2
opportunity sampling 81–2
quota sampling 81
random sampling 80–1
scales, Likert scales 93
scientific method 1, 2, 12, 13, 14
Scirus 53
self-actualisation 2, 11, 12
seminars 31–5
definition 31–2
preparation 32–3
things to avoid 34–5
uses 34, 36–7
skills development 23–5
core skills 23, 24
transferable skills 23, 24, 25 see also study skills
social learning theory 15
social psychology 3, 18–20
journals 50
Social Science Citation Index 52
sources, primary/ secondary 70
speaking, public 150–2
sports psychology 185, 199–200
stages: developmental 8, 9, 10
psychosexual 4–5, 167–9

statistical analysis 97–104
descriptive statistics 100–1, 121, 122, 123
flow diagram of statistical tests **103**
inferential statistics 100–1, 121, 122, 123
nonparametric statistics 100
parametric statistics 100
see also data analysis
stimulus: discriminative 15
-response associations 14, 15
unconditioned 13
study skills advice: active revision 27–9, 37, 158
"being" mode 27
deep processing 27–9, 37
"having" mode 27
lectures 30, 31
mind maps 160–2, **161**
mnemonics 158–60
note taking 37–41
passive revision 27–9
surface processing 27–9
see also essay writing
superego 4
surface processing 27–9
surveys 91–6

technicians, psychology 187
teaching psychology 179, 197–9
further education 197
higher education 198
qualifications 198

television viewing, and aggression 19
tests, referencing 77
therapy, cognitive-behavioural 17–18
training: clinical psychology 186
counselling psychology 196
criminological psychology 192–4
educational psychology 188–9
health psychology 194
occupational psychology 190–1
post-graduate 181–4
for teaching 198
tutorials 35–6

unconditioned response 13
unconditioned stimulus 13
unconscious mind 4

violence 19

Web of Knowledge (WOK) 51
within-subjects design 83–4
working in psychology see psychology, applications
write-up, research 105, 139–41 see also essay writing; report writing